Modern Economics

*the text of this book is printed
on 100% recycled paper*

About the Author

Robert D. Leiter (B.S., City College of New York; M.A., Ph.D., Columbia University) was Professor of Economics at the City College of the City University of New York. He taught undergraduate and graduate courses in economics. He served as an economic consultant to the government, business firms, and labor unions. Dr. Leiter published nine books and numerous articles in professional journals.

MODERN ECONOMICS

SECOND EDITION

Robert D. Leiter

BARNES & NOBLE BOOKS

A DIVISION OF HARPER & ROW, PUBLISHERS

New York, Hagerstown, San Francisco, London

To
Joyce

First BARNES & NOBLE BOOKS edition published 1977

LIBRARY OF CONGRESS CATALOG CARD NUMBER:
76-12062

ISBN: 0-06-460138-2
77 78 79 80 5 4 3 2 1

Preface

Since this book was first published in 1968, only minor alterations have occurred in the basic structure of economics as a discipline. As a result of important modifications in societal priorities, there have, however, been significant shifts in the issues that receive the greatest emphasis and most attention in textual discussions. These new developments have been recognized and incorporated in this new edition of *Modern Economics*.

During the past thirty years the study of economics has undergone significant changes. Quantitative measurement and empirical evidence are used much more extensively to explore and develop many aspects of economic activity that previously had been analyzed by economists almost entirely on the basis of logic and deductive reasoning. Public policy proposals are now investigated by procedures comparable to those employed in the physical sciences, and more accurate predictions have therefore been possible. A better understanding of economic interrelationships has enabled governments to exercise greater control over economic events.

This text concentrates on the main issues facing the nation—economic growth, inflation, economic security, and balance of payments. Included are those generally accepted ideas and established facts necessary to an introductory course, as well as relevant areas that have not yet been fully explored and examined by economists and in which considerable uncertainty and controversy still prevail. Essential economic knowledge is presented in a clear, systematic, and compact form, although of course space requirements limit the extent to which precise details are incorporated.

As a systematic study, economics depends upon a theoretical underpinning and upon the various tools developed by economists. Theory and tools are useful to the extent that they help to analyze economic activity and determine or establish reasonable economic policies. In general, the theory included in the text is introduced to provide some requisite insight into economic phenomena and the tools are intended to make economic relationships and problems easier to understand.

This text, written for students who have had no previous training in economics, may be used in a one-semester course or, with supplementary readings, in a one-year course. Although the main purpose of the book is to prepare students to become intelligent and useful citizens and to participate more effectively in society, the contents are such that students who may wish to go on to more advanced work in economics should be well prepared to do so.

The discussion of national income and employment (Part II) precedes the section on the price system (Part III) and distribution (Part IV), but it is possible to rearrange the material so that microeconomics (Parts III and IV), which deals with relationships among different prices and markets in the economy, is studied before macroeconomics (Part II), which deals with broad economic aggregates and averages. It is also feasible to introduce international economics (Part V) earlier in the course, if desirable. Many students will find this text to be of practical help in supplementing required assignments in other texts. They may also profitably use the appended list of books of varying difficulty that examine various phases of the textual material in greater detail.

Over the years, colleagues and students have given me invaluable assistance in developing and formulating my ideas on the relevant subject matter to be included in an introduction to economics and on the manner in which this material should be presented. I have felt free to call upon many of these colleagues and upon the editorial staff of the publisher for advice and guidance while this project was under way. I am grateful for the help and encouragement received, but I assume sole responsibility for any shortcomings of the text.

Table of Contents

1 Economic Concepts and Analysis

Chapter 1
ECONOMIC TERMINOLOGY

Some words that occur in everyday usage have a specialized meaning in economics. This chapter defines and examines some concepts and terms of economics so that the student may understand and put to better use the material that follows. A general survey is made of the contents of economics and the processes of economic activity.

CONTENTS OF ECONOMICS

Knowledge accumulated by mankind has increased as civilization has advanced. The process was slow at first but has quickened in recent times. Although it was once possible for an individual of unusual ability to become familiar with almost all that was known in his day—as was the case of Aristotle in the ancient period and possibly Francis Bacon at the beginning of the modern era—such an accomplishment no longer seems likely. The quantity and diversity of information have become too extensive.

Economics, though only one of the many growing branches of human knowledge, is already subdivided into many parts and has become so complex that very few persons today are fully cognizant of all its various components and ramifications. Nevertheless it is worthwhile for students to examine various facets of economics, to see some of the relationships which exist, and to learn a few of the principles used to explain the occurrence or sequence of economic events.

Economics is a social science and thus studies the behavior of men. Although it overlaps other social sciences to a certain extent, it does concentrate and revolve around a specific area of human endeavor. Economics deals with most of a nation's activities that are intended to satisfy material and cultural needs and desires. It treats the problems of how society determines what goods will be

3

produced with the limited resources available, how they will be produced, and for whom. Such goods may then be consumed or put to further production.

In setting forth the contents of economics, a large number of topics are touched upon in more or less detail. Wealth, income, welfare, business organization, unemployment, poverty, government regulation of business activity, public finance, and social legislation are among the matters that must be considered to understand how the economic system works. It is also important to study how the system may be improved and how some of the problems and weaknesses may be eliminated or alleviated and more effective and sounder policies formulated. It should therefore be clear that economics is concerned with the workings of the total economy, with the efficiency of the economic system, and with the attempts of government to improve or control economic performance.

Citizens today need to understand economics if the intricacies of some of the basic problems facing the nation are to be grasped. Newspapers devote much space to the three economic problems that have achieved considerable prominence during the second half of the twentieth century—economic security, inflation, and economic growth. (1) Workers are striving to attain a certain degree of job security to alleviate unemployment and other economic hazards. Such maintenance of steady personal incomes is an important feature of a thriving economy. (2) Nations are struggling to prevent price levels from rising and some have been more successful than others. Also it is generally realized that individual citizens are differently affected by price changes and that, though some may gain, the overall effect of continually increasing prices is undesirable. (3) Economic growth has come to dominate much of the world's thought, with both developed and underdeveloped countries trying to increase their rate of growth in order to increase their living standards. Furthermore, the rate of economic expansion also involves a kind of contest between the capitalistic and communistic economic systems represented, respectively, by the United States and the Soviet Union. Many government decisions related to domestic and foreign policy require an understanding of economics.

ECONOMIC THEORY

Although economists have the task of describing institutions, they are also interested in analyzing economic events and predicting economic consequences of different actions. Economic theory is intended to explain economic behavior and events in the real world through the formulation of principles and "laws," and is usually based on relationships derived from past and present observations. Since economic relationships are very complex, theoretical models are constructed that simplify situations by omitting detail. What is omitted from a model depends on what is being studied and why it is being studied. Only one or a few elements making up the area of the economy studied are allowed to vary, "other things being equal." The model is good if it yields explanations and makes predictions more accurate.

Thus the usefulness of an economic theory depends on the accuracy with which it explains those facts and situations to which it applies. The greater the discrepancy between theory and practice or occurrence of events, the less valid the derived principle is. In many instances, economic theory provides valuable insights for understanding phenomena even though it may not provide perfect explanations. Though theory yields conclusions, it does not make value judgments as to their desirability. Value judgments are personal matters. The same economic theory is relevant to all countries and to all economic systems if the model on which it is based applies, even though the prevailing institutions may be quite different in each instance.

SCARCITY

There are several basic recurrent economic concepts that need to be presented and understood at the outset for subsequent discussion to be clear; probably the most basic fact in economics is that productive resources are scarce or limited in amount.

Production of goods and services requires resources. The ingredients or factors of production used by an economic system are made up of human and nonhuman components. The nonhuman factors are (1) land—consisting of the soil and certain reproducible resources, such as timber, fisheries, and water supplies, and some nonreproducible resources, such as minerals; and (2) capital—produced by people and appearing in the form of factories, equipment, and machinery available for the process of further production. The human factors consist of (3) labor—represented by physical and mental energies of people available for the productive process; and (4) entrepreneurship—established by the activities of those persons who set out to combine the other three factors in order to effectuate production and assume the financial risks involved.

None of the four factors of production is available in unlimited quantities, and each of them has many alternative uses. The type of economic system will determine what, how, and for whom goods will be produced. Each factor can be utilized in a variety of ways. Land may be used for agriculture or for a factory site. A carpenter may be employed in the construction or repair of a house, library, or factory. An automobile may be used for business or for pleasure; and a truck transports many different items. An entrepreneur must decide which good or service he should undertake to provide. There are many choices. The economic system in effect determines how the scarce resources are allocated in the production of economic goods and services.

A choice is possible at several different levels of economic activity. Entrepreneurs must combine the factors of production in one of several possible ways. Workers must decide how much of their time will be spent working and how much will be devoted to leisure. Consumers must allocate their limited amount of purchasing power. It will be seen that decisions by consumers bear heavily on the way producers allocate their resources.

Economic goods and services are characterized not only by scarcity but also by utility. Utility is the quality of a good or service that satisfies human wants. Goods that have utility but are not scarce, such as air, are free goods.

WANTS AND NEEDS

Economics is concerned with wants and preferences. Though the quantity of goods and services available to people has increased greatly over the centuries so that American consumers with a relatively low income live better than the highest income earners of past civilizations, there is no way of comparing the degree of contentment that consumers derive. Wants or demand relates to the ability of a purchaser (individual, business, or government) to buy a good or service in the market; it does not refer to hopes or dreams. Wants increase at lower prices.

The idea of need must be used with great care. Even though need connotes certain minimum physical requirements, over the course of time human needs have increased. In the 1970s, a person "needs," among other things, three nutritionally satisfying meals a day, housing with plumbing facilities, and clothing for a variety of occasions and purposes. Some of these needs are determined or established for individuals by experts or advertising. Yet the economy does not register these needs unless they are translated into wants. Individuals may or may not want what they need. "Need" enters into the orbit of economics if the government, whether federal or local, decides to meet needs that it believes individuals have, such as defense against foreign invasion, elementary and secondary school education, and inoculation against disease, despite the possibility that the person involved may have contrary feelings.

GOODS

Economic analysis differentiates between capital (producer) goods and consumption (consumer) goods. The ultimate aim of an economy is production of goods and services for the satisfaction of human wants, but in order to facilitate production men must first produce tools and equipment. Instead of planting crops by turning up soil with sharp sticks, plows are manufactured. The more advanced the civilization, the more complicated and refined the production process becomes. Instead of hunting animals to provide food, livestock is raised and marketed. Goods (including factories) used in the production of intermediate goods or of consumption goods are called capital goods. A good may be a capital good, a consumption good, or both, depending on its use. Thus an automobile used by a salesman to market wares or to seek customers is a capital good, whereas if it is used for vacation or for other nonproduction purposes, it is a consumption good.

The construction and manufacture of tools, machinery, equipment, and factories are activities that society considers highly desirable. Although such production shifts resources away from consumer goods and temporarily delays that type of production, society is willing to produce this way. People are ready to forego present consumption if such action leads to an increase in the level of future consumption.

An economy allocates its resources to the production of capital goods and consumption goods. The output, which as will be seen below roughly corresponds to the income of the economy, consists of consumption goods and goods that are not for consumption. The latter group constitutes the investment of the economy. Investment and the accumulation of capital goods are made possible by saving (i.e., a process in which income is not spent for consumption). Of course, it is possible for someone with income neither to consume nor to invest. This occurs if the saver hoards his money income—for example, he keeps it at home or in a bank safety vault. Investment in the economy takes place only if capital goods—factories, machinery, or equipment—are produced.

PRODUCTION POSSIBILITIES

The concept of allocation of resources may be clarified by examining the production-possibility curve, or transformation curve, of an economy. This relationship shows how a given quantity of resources may be used in alternative ways, assuming a fixed technology. Consider a simplified illustration in table 1-1 of an economy that devotes all its

TABLE 1-1

PRODUCTION POSSIBILITIES

Automobiles	Miles of Road
0	300,000
1,000,000	275,000
2,000,000	230,000
3,000,000	170,000
4,000,000	100,000
5,000,000	0

resources to the production of roads and automobiles. If all available factors of production are used for road construction, it might be possible to build 300,000 miles of roads; or if they are all engaged in automobile manufacturing, 5,000,000 cars might be produced. Between these extremes, various combinations of the two outputs may be had by different combinations of labor and capital resources. The fewer the number of miles of roads built, the greater the number of automobiles produced. The production-possibility curve is represented by the solid line of figure 1-1.

The graph, which shows how many units of the one item must be given up or sacrificed to produce additional units of the other item, allows intermediate points to be determined. The curve indicates that typically each increase in the number of units of output of one commodity requires the quantities of the good given up to increase by an increasing amount. The curve itself represents the frontier of the given technology, any point of which shows the maximum possible output combination of the two goods. Any point within the frontier indicates unemployment of some of the available resources, whether of labor, capital, land, or entrepreneurship.

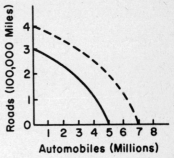

Fig. 1-1. Production-possibility curve

The production-possibility curve discloses alternative choices. It shows how many miles of roads and how many automobiles can be produced by this particular economy. Should technology advance or resources increase, a new curve (indicated by the broken line) must be constructed to the right of the first one. The output of the economy is capable of rising, but the direction of the actual increase is not predetermined. If sufficient roads are then available, most of the new resources might be used for the production of automobiles. This would be shown by a movement from point A to point B. Although increased production of both goods is possible, the choice in this case has been to reduce the amount of road construction and greatly increase the output of automobiles.

THE ECONOMIC PROCESSES

The determination of what is produced, how it is produced, and for whom it is produced is the basic task of an economic system. Such matters are determined by studying the processes of production, exchange, distribution, and consumption.

Production. Production means the creation of goods and the rendering of services people are willing to pay for and includes those activities that make goods available at the time and place desired by the purchaser. Agriculture, mining, fishing, and manufacturing therefore represent those industries that create goods. But transportation, storage, and retailing are also phases of the production process. Business efforts aimed at intensifying established wants or creating new ones are still another aspect of production.

Production is contingent upon the availability of resources and their utilization. Population and natural resources provide the sources of labor and capital necessary to produce. The state of technology, however, is the prime determinant of the level of output and depends upon labor force skills, capital accumulation, and the extent of inventions and innovations.

The labor force represents that portion of the population which is working or seeking work for pay, including those who are self-employed. The output of the economy depends upon the number of workers, and also upon those laws, customs, and dispositions of the population which influence the number of hours of labor each worker makes available. Thus, prohibiting child labor, restricting women from working on certain jobs, banning work on Sundays, and limiting the hours of some occupations are statutory impingements on output. Customs that encourage women to stay at home, children to remain in school, or workers to retire early also affect production. In addition, prosperous economic conditions, wage rate levels, and patriotic pressures during wartime bear on the willingness of people to offer their labor in the market.

But production also hinges on the quality of the labor force. Health, education, and training levels affect the kind of job workers are capable of handling and the contribution they can make to output. In the United States health and educational standards have been rising consistently; since colonial times life expectancy has increased, and the average number of years of schooling per person has gone up.

As the labor force grows, specialization and division of labor become feasible. These permit greater output with the same resources or the same output with less skilled labor. Division of labor in its broadest sense refers to the separation of production into different occupations and stages and the concentration of particular industries in different geographical locations; but in the more technical sense, as outlined by Adam Smith, it means that the productive process is divided into small parts and each of these parts of the work is assigned to a different laborer. Output rises because (1) time is saved, as each worker learns his task more rapidly and does not have to shift from one task to another; (2) special characteristics such as height, strength, and intelligence, may be employed more effectively in the performance of a task; (3) greater skill is acquired by constant repetition of the same operation; and (4) tools are utilized more fully. To some extent, however, division of labor lowers the morale of workers.

The accumulation of capital is made possible by abstinence from consumption. That part of the potential output which will not be consumed may be produced as factories, machinery, and equipment. Increases in the stock of capital lead to a rise in the productivity of labor (i.e., output per hour of labor), since workers use more machines and equipment. The availability of sources of energy and the development of mechanical power from such sources are crucial elements in modern technology, as is the existence of raw materials. Although energy sources and raw materials have been depleted over the years, basic research, new ideas, and advanced technology have opened up new and alternative possibilities. Atomic and solar energy promise new potentials; synthetic fibers have been perfected and substituted for natural materials; and nourishing food made from seaweed is now a reality. Output rises as capital increases even when the state of the technological arts is fixed, but a more impressive growth in production and standards of living occurs as a result of an advancing technology.

Technological change introduces new techniques to the process of production, including marketing, so that new products are made available, and existing products are improved or produced from fewer resources. Improvements in managerial and organizational methods are part of the concept. Thus nylon and television were new products, the electric typewriter and an automobile with power brakes represent improved goods, and mechanical picking of cotton and catalytic refining of petroleum reduce the cost of shirts and gasoline.

Though technological advance brings expansion of output, the factors leading to growth do not occur automatically. They are the result of conscious public and private decisions which depend upon the type of economic system, the attitude of the government, and the disposition of income recipients. Invention and innovation then, as well as additional machinery and equipment, are ways of increasing output, but it is usually not possible to separate the categorical contribution of each toward greater production when they occur together.

Exchange.　Individuals and families in frontier societies are highly self-sufficient and depend largely on their own efforts for the reproduction of the consumption goods they want, but more advanced economic systems utilize the process of exchange. Exchange means the voluntary transfer of goods or the performance of services in return for other goods, services, or money. When money is used, it serves not only as the medium of exchange but as an indicator of the rate of exchange. Barter—the direct exchange of goods or services for other goods or services—is practiced widely among primitive groups. It is not important in developed economies, although, of course, it does occur.

Distribution. The term *distribution* ordinarily has a specialized meaning in economics. Only rarely does it follow common usage and refer to the transportation and marketing of goods. Sometimes it deals with the way in which the wealth (i.e., property and money holdings) is apportioned among individuals or families of a society. But most often distribution concerns the way in which the income or earnings of those engaged in production are divided among its recipients. Although this division is usually related to remuneration involving the factors of production, it may also be set up according to geographical areas, industries, occupations, amount of earnings, and so on. The payment for labor is wages; for capital, interest; for land, rent; and for entrepreneurship, profit. The total output of the economy, which (with some exceptions to be noted in chapter 3) is the equivalent of total income, goes to the factors of production.

Consumption. Consumption refers to the use of goods and services to satisfy human wants. However, it concerns only that use which involves *final* consumers. For example, consumption does not refer to the use of goods in production. Items of consumption are usually classified as durable goods, nondurable goods, and services. Some goods and services, such as pens or electricity, may be used both for production and consumption.

The fact that production, distribution, and consumption are discussed in terms of money requires a distinction between money income and real income (or money value of output and real output). Money income is the income expressed in current dollars. Real income is the amount of goods and services that money income can purchase. Real income is thus affected by changes in the price level.

THE CIRCULAR FLOW

The economic processes of production, exchange, distribution, and consumption underlie what may be called the circular flow of economic activity or the circular flow of money payments. The public is paid for labor and other factors of production it supplies to business and government to produce goods and services. The finished goods and services are then purchased by the public. These two activities provide a circle of spending by the public and by business and government. Moving in the opposite direction is the circle of earning. The public earns income for contributing factors to the process of production, and business and government receive income by selling finished goods and services to the public. The picture may be broadened by saying that resources, materials, and goods are sold by one owner to another as they move toward the consumer in the process of production, whereas money payments move in the opposite direction. These relationships constitute one of the most important, though elementary, insights provided by economics: Spending serves as the source that generates income and income provides the basis of spending. Further clarification of this point will be added later on. The circular flow is represented diagrammatically in figure 1-2.

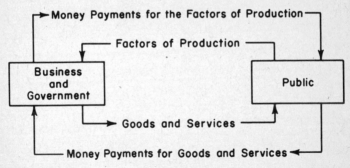

Fig. 1-2. Circular flow

Economic relationships between the public and business determine how much of what is produced. Consumers indicate their preferences for goods and services by money expenditures. More urgent demand is expressed by willingness and ability to purchase more of an item or to pay higher prices. Businessmen decide the method by which goods are produced on the basis of the relative costs of resources that can be used for the purpose of production, since substitution of one factor of production for another is often possible. Their main object is to maximize profits. Goods and services are distributed to those contributing to the process of production, whether they contribute in the form of labor or of property. Contributors receive an income related to what they have supplied and are thus in turn able to make purchases.

Chapter 2
THE ECONOMIC SYSTEM

The world has had many different types of economic systems. Today, the most important systems are either forms of capitalism or of socialism. This chapter first describes some of the highlights of the economy of the United States, essentially a free enterprise capitalistic system. It then turns to the underlying philosophy and principles of free private enterprise.

CHARACTERISTICS OF THE ECONOMY OF THE UNITED STATES

The economy of the United States is basically prosperous. In 1974 output was almost $1,400 billion; civilian employment approached 86 million persons; personal income before taxes averaged $5,430 per capita; average earnings in manufacturing were $176 per week; corporation profits were in excess of $141 billion before taxes and over $85 billion after taxes; and new private construction was valued at about $96 billion. Though the United States has only about 7 percent of the world's area and somewhat less than 6 percent of the world's population, it produces a disproportionately large part of the output and has the highest standard of living. Comparable statistics are difficult to compile and not readily available, but the general position of the United States among the countries of the world may be deduced from the fact that in 1972 it utilized almost a third of the total energy produced by the whole world.

The United States is clearly an urban nation, though the trend toward urbanization has been recent. A century ago less than a quarter of the inhabitants were living in urban areas—places with a population of 2,500 or more—and fifty years ago about half were. By 1970, 74 percent of the population resided in cities, and it is expected that by the year 2000 more than four out of every five persons will live in urban regions. Today over 40 percent of the population lives in thirty-five metropolitan areas each of which contains a million or more people.

Urbanization was intensified in the late nineteenth and early twentieth centuries by the huge influx of immigrants into the cities. Though immigration decreased by the beginning of the First World War, it was replaced by internal migration from rural to urban areas. The attractiveness of cities stems from the greater opportunities they afford for better income, but their growth has brought in its wake a host of economic and social maladjustments. Poverty, inadequate education, and low standards of health have always been important problems in rural areas. But they have become particularly prominent in central cities, where the composition of the population has changed as many persons in the upper- and middle-income groups have left for the suburbs. In addition, cities have undergone decay in their social structure associated with insufficient living space, poor housing, rising crime rates, divorce, illegitimacy, and drug addiction. Communities and businesses are faced with problems concerning efficient use of land, adequate transportation facilities, waste disposal, and water and air pollution. Government and private expenditures are attempts to alleviate some difficulties.

Income, education, and health have been improving in the United States, but with more social awareness pressures for even more rapid rises have been exerted. National income has grown from $81 billion in 1940 to $1,143 billion dollars in 1974. Even allowing for price increases, the rise has been almost fourfold in that third of a century. The average number of school years completed by persons over twenty-five years of age was 8.6 in 1940 and 12.3 in 1973. In 1973, 12.6 percent of those over twenty-five years of age had completed four or more years of college, and nearly 36 percent had had four years of high school. Nevertheless, a large fraction of the youth of above-average intelligence did not go on to college, and some of them did not complete their secondary education. The death rate has dropped from more than 17 per thousand to less than 10 per thousand since 1900, and life expectancy has risen from 47 years to 71 years; however, death rate and infant mortality statistics in several foreign countries are lower than these. Thus there are many important economic tasks to be performed.

But the United States has been fortunate in the relative abundance of its natural resources and raw materials. These resources, generally utilized in the primary stage of production (before any fabrication has occurred), are classified as related to energy (coal, oil, gas, and fuel wood), foods, and physical structure (minerals, forest products, agricultural nonfoods, and wildlife products). Since 1900 raw material consumption in the United States has risen sharply. But there has been a proportional increase in the output of energy materials while the relative share of food production has declined; physical-structure materials have remained at about the same percentage. Raw materials now support a more elaborate economic structure. During the twentieth century the gross national product has been rising more rapidly than the aggregate of raw materials produced, whereas the fraction of the civilian labor force employed in raw materials industries has declined greatly. The price of raw materials has increased more during the past seventy-five years than has the wholesale price of finished commodities. In the mid-1970s the United States began a program to achieve self-sufficiency of energy resources.

The increased volume of end products supported by the same quantity of raw materials has been made possible by (1) improvements in technology and design, (2) reduction of waste, (3) increasing complexity of consumer products that involve more processing (for example, frozen foods), (4) development of synthetic materials, and (5) expansion of scrap industries that salvage materials.

The country is naturally endowed with minerals, plant and animal life, water, and good soil. There is no reason to believe that there will be any serious limits on the growth of the economy in the foreseeable future as a result of resource scarcities. Inevitably there has been substitution of cheaper raw materials for scarcer and more expensive ones, expansion of synthetic production, and greater reliance on imports; efforts also have been made to conserve and to develop resources. New ore deposits have been discovered through advances in the methods of geological exploration. More mapping surveys have been made and research programs to develop better extraction methods of metals and petroleum have been undertaken. The government has attempted to improve timber stands on public lands and has encouraged private conservation of forests. Wildlife is increasingly protected from extinction by government regulation. Soil conservation has long been an important aspect of government activity. Water projects dealing with power generation, irrigation, flood control, navigation, pollution, and recreation have been undertaken. Progress is being made in research to convert seawater to water fit for human consumption. Prospects for resources to meet the needs of a growing economy are bright.

The favorable position of the economy of the United States with respect to natural resources is supplemented by a labor force of expanding size and skill, a rising quantity and quality of capital goods, and an increasing variety of techniques for combining the factors of production. The civilian labor force has been increasing by about a million persons a year during the past twenty-five years. In addition, the higher educational level of this force, the more frequent availability and use of training programs on and off the job, and the improved health of the population have enhanced the quality of labor. Larger investments in factories, equipment, and machinery have expanded the capacity of the economy. For example, industry has increased production of steel, aluminum, paper, and petroleum, while many additional transportation facilities have been constructed.

Greater emphasis on research and better methods of business management are other ingredients of the economic system. Expenditures for research stood at about $32.1 billion per year in 1974. A little over one-half of this money was provided by the federal government. Though a large part of the research has been directed toward military objectives, the gains accruing to civilians and business enterprises have been substantial. But the contributions of the government are large also because private enterprise is not willing to undertake enough *basic research*—research devoted to extending man's knowledge of himself and his environment with no immediate practical goal. Much basic research is conducted in universities and supported by government funds. And it is basic research that lays the foundations for many inventions and innovations. More generally, private industry does not invest a great deal of money in research when the only "product" is new knowledge. If the results of research have no immediate practical application or if other firms may costlessly appropriate for themselves the benefits of the new knowledge because such knowledge cannot be kept a secret or protected by patents, business firms are not inclined to lay out funds for research.

THE MEANING OF A PRIVATE ENTERPRISE ECONOMIC SYSTEM

The general economy of the United States is known as free private enterprise or capitalism. It is characterized by individual ownership of private property (either directly or indirectly, as shareholders of a business) and functions both to produce and to consume goods and services. Consumers are free through their expenditures to choose those goods and services they want (a process sometimes described as consumer sovereignty) and thereby influence what is produced. Producers, of course, attempt to anticipate the demand of buyers but also often try to guide consumer choices by subtle suggestion or hard-sell advertising. Workers are relatively free, within their capabilities, to choose their occupation, employer, and geographical location and to change any of them at any time they so desire.

All goods, services, and factors of production have prices, expressed as money values. They are exchanged (i.e., bought or sold) in many different kinds of markets in which both buyers and sellers compete with each other. But since the imperfections of this system of exchange give rise to a variety of problems, the government has participated to an increasing extent in regulating the economy. In general, therefore, individuals in a free private enterprise economy have a high degree of freedom of choice, but they are limited mainly by the amount of their wealth and income and by prevailing statutes and custom.

RATIONALITY OF BEHAVIOR

Theories of economics are based on the assumption that individuals act rationally in making choices among alternatives even if no deliberate mental calculation takes place on each occasion. It is not necessary for the average consumer to understand his own behavior; it is only essential that he is doing what he wants to do. Economics assumes that individuals ordinarily desire more goods and that they are willing to give up units of one good to secure additional units of another, each person having his own scale of preferences. Economic analysis puts much stress on the fact that individuals are trying to maximize some aspect of their position, but that this need not involve money, income, or wealth. Economic behavior is also influenced by political and social factors as people strive to attain more power, prestige, and leisure. But though the so-called economic man is motivated by more than greed for wealth, his actions tend to be directed toward maximum satisfaction or utility.

The consumer tries to allocate his income and resources to maximize his satisfaction. The producer attempts to combine his factors of production to obtain the greatest output with the least input. The relationship that defines the various alternative combination of inputs and resulting products for any given state of technology is called the *production function*. It is often characterized by the law of diminishing returns or, as it is sometimes known in a modified form, the law of variable proportions.

LAW OF DIMINISHING RETURNS

British economist David Ricardo (1772–1823) was the first to formulate clearly the law of diminishing returns. Although he emphasized the circumstance where increased labor is applied to a fixed amount of land, the principle has wider applications. Specifically, the law of diminishing returns says that as units of a variable factor of production are applied to a fixed factor, additional output rises by lesser amounts. More generally, the concept is expanded into the law of variable proportions and indicates that diminishing returns are present in output even if none of the factors is fixed, providing that the factors do not increase by equal proportions. But whether a variable factor is added to a fixed one or whether all factors are increased in changing proportions, it is possible that returns may first increase because of a complex relationship among the factors being combined. For example, assume a given number of pieces of machinery to which units of labor (workers) are added; each machine requires several workers to be operated most efficiently. Up to a point, the more units of labor employed, the greater the increase in the amount of goods produced. But past this point, since the number of machines has not changed, diminishing returns set in. The addition of yet another unit of labor increases the output by less than the amount which the preceding unit added. Eventually, even negative returns may follow—total output actually falls—as, for example, when so many additional units of labor are employed that one unit of it may interfere with the performance of other units.

Only if all the factors of production are increased in proportion may constant returns prevail. Nevertheless, in many cases, proportional increases in input lead to more than proportional increases in output or increasing returns to scale, because mass production is more economical. Thus doubling all the factors of production may result in more than double the output if the firm, because it is large, is able to take advantage of specialization of functions and division of labor, interchangeable parts, and more efficient power sources. This situation is seen in assembly line techniques. On the other hand, proportional increases in input may lead to decreasing returns to scale, or less than proportional increases, because of difficulties of management and lower morale of workers in a larger firm.

POPULATION GROWTH

Much of economics revolves around matters concerning population. Population is the ultimate basis of demand for goods and services as well as the source of labor. These two aspects were stressed as clashing elements for the first time by Thomas R. Malthus (1766–1834), a clergyman and economist, in *An Essay on the Principle of Population* published in 1798. Commenting on the optimistic outlook of many of his contemporaries regarding the prospects for improved economic conditions of the human race, Malthus maintained that population when unchecked tends to increase in a geometric ratio (for example, 1, 2, 4, 8, 16, and so on) but that food supply can increase only in an arithmetic ratio (for example, 1, 2, 3, 4, 5, and so on). Using the United States as a basis for his calculations, since at that time checks on the growth of population were fewest in this country, Malthus determined that the number of inhabitants was doubling every twenty-five years. He pointed out that it was not possible to increase the food supply that rapidly. Malthus based this conclusion on the principle of diminishing returns, contending that the fixed quantity of land available for raising crops and livestock could not be made to yield proportional increases to match population growth when labor units were added.

Malthus argued therefore that population growth would be curtailed either by *positive checks* or *preventive checks*. Positive checks are those that shorten the duration of human life and include extreme poverty, famine, dangerous labor conditions, inadequate child care, common diseases, epidemics, plagues, and wars. Preventive checks include moral restraint (i.e., the postponement of marriage) and various vices (for example, prostitution). Malthus favored the practice of moral restraint to reduce misery and vice. At that time birth control was not considered a preventive check, but Malthus's theory subsequently was extended and developed by the Neo-Malthusians, who stressed that misery and vice could be reduced substantially only by the use of contraceptives.

The pessimism of Malthus regarding the world's future course seemed warranted by conditions in Great Britain and in other parts of western Europe in his time because almost all arable land was under cultivation and the consequences of diminishing returns seemed inevitable. Indeed, this burgeoning of population led Thomas Carlyle (1795–1881) to call economics a dismal science, since it seemed to foreshadow a general standard of living at the subsistence level. Practically, the gloomy predictions influenced policy decisions of the British government and of many business firms during much of the nineteenth century; wage increases and improved living conditions for the lower classes were discouraged as benefits that could not endure because they would be absorbed by higher rates of survival among children.

Although Malthus and other members of the classical school of economics did realize that technological advance in agriculture might alter the production function and postpone the impact of diminishing returns, they did not anticipate the rapidity of this advance. Nor did they expect improvements in transportation, which enabled overpopulated countries to import large quantities of food from areas where new lands were being cultivated, or effective methods of birth control. For all these reasons, the gloomy predictions regarding the fate of mankind have not yet eventuated in advanced civilization. But the Malthusian principle may be seen in operation in many parts of the world today where population exceeds food supply, and it may be expected to become more important in other places now well above subsistence levels if technology ceases to advance and birth rates are not reduced further.

BACKGROUND OF FREE ENTERPRISE

British economist Adam Smith (1723–1790), who is considered the father of modern economics, published *The Wealth of Nations* in 1776. The book sets forth the argument that a free private enterprise economy operating without any overall planning by individuals, business enterprises, or government grows and flourishes to a greater extent than one marked by deliberate planning or centralized regulation. Of particular importance and central to his theme was the idea that government interference is detrimental to maximum economic growth. Laissez-faire, which means lack of government intervention in economic affairs, is conducive to improvement in output and increases in the wealth of the nation because a so-called invisible hand operates to produce order and to prevent chaos. Each individual, whether in the role of worker or entrepreneur, seeks his own interest and advantage and necessarily ultimately prefers that activity which is in the interests of society. The laborer gravitates to those employments paying the highest wages, and the employer tends to undertake business where the profit is greatest. In each instance, consumers are pressing harder for the goods and services involved.

Although the argument presented by Smith does not appear unusually profound today, it was remarkably novel in his own day, when the leading economies of western civilization were dominated by some form of mercantilism. Systems of mercantilism that emphasize protective tariffs and embargoes, subsidies, and occasionally even internal trade barriers were predicated on government interference, direction, and regulation of the economy to achieve a "favorable" balance of trade (excess of exports over imports) or increase the stock of gold and other precious metals held in the country. Mercantilism prevailed between about 1500 and 1800, a period when powerful centralized states were emerging and seeking to build up their economic and military strengths.

Smith criticized the ideas of his contemporaries. Though he proposed a system of laissez-faire as the best means of increasing the wealth of the nation and achieving national prosperity, he did recognize that there are certain essential services which must be provided by government because private enterprise finds them unprofitable and is therefore unwilling or unable to perform them effectively. These include defense, internal security, administration of justice, public education, and public works that facilitate commerce (such as roads, canals, and bridges).

Today the economy of the United States is far removed from laissez-faire. There has been a gradual and continual movement by the government into areas of economic activity reserved by Smith and his followers, the classical economists, to private initiative. The reasons for increased government participation are not difficult to ascertain. Laissez-faire functions advantageously when the economy is characterized by perfect competition. To the extent that such competition is lacking, the beneficent action of the invisible hand is inoperative, and carefully planned government involvement to prevent undesirable conditions becomes necessary.

Generally speaking, perfect competition refers to a situation where buyers and sellers in a market are so numerous and each is so negligible in the total picture that none has any influence on the price of the product. The more a participant in the market influences the price of any good, service, or factor of production, the more removed is the market from perfect competition. It will be demonstrated later that when an individual or a firm has some control over price, the benefits of free enterprise—minimum price, maximum quantity, and highest quality of goods and services in relation to costs of production—are not necessarily obtainable.

GOVERNMENT INTERVENTION

The development of business organization patterns, the expansion of industry, and the growth of enterprises and markets in the United States have introduced many monopolistic elements into the economy, and from time to time have led to public demands that required government action to modify or to control situations. Government intervention was also made necessary by the uneven performance of an economic system that has resulted in periods of severe unemployment and concomitant economic insecurity and hardship. Regulatory steps by the government have brought about an economy that is now generally called mixed capitalism. A mixed economy can range all the way from laissez-faire, where there is almost no government intervention, to varying degrees of socialism, which, when it is total, connotes full public ownership of the means of production.

The increased role of government in shaping the economy during the twentieth century has revolved around issues relating to unemployment or efficient use of the factors of production, inequities associated with a grossly unequal distribution of income, monopolistic practices, and inflationary pressures resulting from the action of producers and consumers. Statutory enactments, watchdog agencies, and policies of the executive branch of the government have been used to modify economic practices and conditions.

THE TASKS OF THE SYSTEM

The economy accomplishes certain tasks and solves some problems. Its success is evaluated by performance, but personal value judgments of desirable economic objectives and goals enter into the evaluation.

Allocation of Resources and Income. A free private enterprise system provides the mechanism that determines what, how, and for whom production takes place, but it does not assure the rectitude or desirability of the results. Those who have purchasing power may demand cigarettes, gambling facilities, or narcotics. In some cases, society does allow the consumer to buy such items even after deciding that the goods or services are not beneficial; in other instances they may be banned by statute, though they are still obtainable in an illegally operated market. Output may be increased by using more capital, even though much labor remains without employment at the time. The development of automation bears on this problem, and workers have sometimes reacted by introducing featherbedding tactics. The economy also determines the way in which wealth and income are distributed, but these results may leave much to be desired. Those with wealth or large incomes may be able to gorge themselves and live in luxurious surroundings while others, less fortunate, may go hungry and live in slums. The moral or ethical considerations associated with competitive free enterprise may be difficult to approve and accept, but certain changes have been enforced by the government to make the system more equitable.

Economics describes the workings of the system, but conditions may be changed by policy decisions at any time. Public attitudes expressed through government may ban production or sale of certain goods, may encourage private employment by approving public expenditures or tax benefits, may alter the distribution of wealth through estate and gift taxes, and may modify the distribution of income through graduated income taxes. Policy decisions are not justified or disapproved by economists, except in their role as citizens; evaluation of policy is the right of all citizens. The function of the economist in his professional capacity is primarily to analyze the operation of the economic system, judge the effects of policy changes, evaluate alternative possibilities, and recommend certain procedures. He is concerned with positive rather than normative values.

Development and Growth. Beyond description and analysis of how resources and income are allocated, economics tackles the problem of how an increase in the available resources or an improvement in current production methods can provide more output and therefore more income for the economy. This is the subject matter of economic development or economic growth. Today, many emerging nations have abysmally low standards of living, and public attitudes are gradually changing to the view that the underprivileged have a right to a minimum standard of living. Thus pressures for economic growth have increased greatly. Nations devote more of their energy to problems of development, and the world watches and compares the evolution of free enterprise in the United States and of socialism in the Soviet Union. Although the rise in output is an important gauge of growth, it is generally the output per capita that is significant in depicting progress.

For economic development particularly, the matter of allocating income between consumption and saving assumes great importance. Decisions by individuals, businesses, and government on how the allocation should be made determine in large measure the potentials or prospects of the system. Savings tend to be converted into capital goods, making a rise in future output possible. Of course, reasons for saving are diverse. They may involve accumulation by an individual of a nest egg for a rainy day or for retirement; they may represent a means by which business obtains funds for expansion without going into the capital market; or they may involve a deliberate effort by government to bring about an expansion of the capital goods available in the country.

Technological progress, as distinct from capital accumulation, is the most important element in economic advance. Although it leads to greater output and higher standards of living, it cannot be measured by income statistics alone. Technological advance can increase the length of life and improve the quality of life. Ideally it reduces illness and suffering, curtails drudgery, and affords more leisure. Nevertheless, technological change frequently imposes heavy burdens on persons whose work and way of life are affected adversely by its impact. Such change then requires difficult adjustments on the part of workers, business enterprises, and government. It is generally agreed that its overall effects are beneficial. Philosophers, however, continue to debate whether or not invention and innovation add to human happiness.

II National Income and Employment

Chapter 3
MEASURING NATIONAL INCOME

The value of measurement and the effective utilization of statistical techniques and methodology in economics are fully demonstrated in dealing with the subject of national income. Economic studies made during the past few decades to measure output and its various components have led to a clearer understanding of how the economy works and have enabled the government to formulate appropriate policies to overcome a variety of economic problems. This chapter explains the major measurements that have been developed and how they are related.

IMPORTANCE OF MEASURING INCOME

Studies of national income have always dealt with the quantity and components of the output of the economy, but since the 1930s considerable emphasis has been placed on the possibilities of using these statistics to understand why changes occur in the production and distribution of output and how these changes might be manipulated for the benefit of society. Statistics of national income can be made to yield much insight into economic trends and market prospects, and they can be used effectively by both business and government to aid in formulating economic policies and goals. Detailed and comparable national income data for the United States are available from 1929. Naturally, in most cases where important judgments of policy are made, information beyond the data provided by national income tabulations might be necessary.

Decisions regarding business operations can be made more rationally when placed within the framework of trends and fluctuations as disclosed by national income statistics. Similarly, the scope of government activity may be determined by expected tax and nontax revenues as indicated by measurements of national income. In these instances the statistics are used as guides upon which to base reasonable action. Especially during the past few decades, the vicissitudes and changes of economic activity in peacetime and the special situation prevailing in wartime have made it essential that the federal government act to direct development and growth of the economy. The effectiveness of federal policy has increased as collection and refinement of national income statistics have advanced.

National income statistics attempt to present quantitatively in a coherent and systematic fashion those categories and magnitudes related to economic activity that summarize the transactions of government, business firms, and households. Four basic sectors, each with different characteristics and peculiarities, provide the basis for broad subdivisions of the economic system. These are household (consumer), business, government, and foreign activities. The output originating in each of these units is shown in the statistics of income compiled by the U.S. Department of Commerce; the total of all sectors represents the gross national product (GNP). Transactions within and among the sectors determine the incomes of each sector. Portions of income used and saved by each sector are shown. While the account of the business sector indicates the profit or loss of all private enterprise in the economy, household and government accounts, which are essentially nonprofit in character, provide information on receipts and expenditures.

The GNP refers to goods and services produced by the labor and by the property of U.S. residents (whether or not they are citizens) and of those Americans who are living abroad temporarily. It also includes property income payments received by U.S. residents from foreign companies. On the other hand, it does not cover that part of output paid to foreigners who own property in the United States.

Much care has been taken in the development of national income statistics to provide clear and consistent definitions of terms and to decide which items belong in the aggregate of GNP. Regardless of the decisions in such cases, statistics of each category which might be useful to economists are kept. Generally, many interrelated sets of data and tables are derived that make it possible to examine the internal consistency of the material. A double entry system of bookkeeping helps check the relationships among categories. Although accounting records available for constructing the accounts of the four sectors of the economy from which national income statistics are derived ordinarily lend themselves to economic analysis because many significant classifications and categories in accounting and economics are similar in nature, there are occasions when this is not so. In such cases, special adjustments in the data or supplementary information is necessary so that the desired economic analysis and interpretation can be made.

John K. Galbraith, in *American Capitalism*, summarizes the immense contribution made by national income statistics: "At the outbreak of World War II the new system of national accounting, now generally familiar through its summary figures of Gross National Product, had just come into use in the United States, the United Kingdom and Canada. It proved indispensable for the guidance of a modern mobilization policy. It had not yet fully penetrated Germany. Partly because they were less clear than the democracies about what they were producing, how they were dividing it between military and civilian use, how they were allocating resources between immediate use and investment and how the corresponding income was being divided—all information that was displayed by the new accounts—the Germans mobilized their economic resources with considerably less skill and boldness than did England or the United States. Because they are modest men, economists never advertised the power of the weapon they had placed in the hands of their governments although its bearing on victory was considerably greater than that of atomic energy."

MEASURING OUTPUT AND INCOME AGGREGATES

The operation and performance of the economy may be examined and evaluated by analyzing the figures showing output and income of the country. It has been seen that measuring output or income represents alternative ways of looking at the totality of production—in one case it is based on the flow of goods, and in the other the flow of earnings. Production creates goods or services that have value and may be sold in the market for a price. The price received by the seller can be thought of as being shared by those who have participated in or contributed to the process of production; it constitutes their income. The idea that the flow of goods or expenditures matches the flow of income or earnings has already been identified as the circular flow.

Five basic quantities or aggregates have been developed by national income statisticians. These are gross national product, net national product, national income, personal income, and disposable personal income.

Gross National Product. The gross national product (GNP), which is probably the most widely used measurement in national income accounting, consists of the total production of final goods and services in the nation during a given period of time or the total expenditure for (market value of) final goods and services in the nation during that period. Final goods and services include all purchases by households (consumers) and government. Business investments—purchases of factories, machinery, and equipment —are counted as final products, but items used or altered in the production process are considered intermediate goods. The actual calculation of GNP must be made in money terms because this is the only convenient common denominator that makes it possible to combine or add the many different classes and kinds of goods produced.

It is necessary to distinguish between final and intermediate goods to avoid duplication in compiling the gross national output. For example, if the process of production involves the growing of cotton, the manufacture of cloth, and the making of dresses purchased by consumers, then the value added to total product should equal the value of the dresses but should not include in addition the value of the cloth or of the cotton used in manufacture. Duplication is avoided by counting only the final or end product. The distinction between final and intermediate goods depends on whether or not they are used in further production. Thus cloth would be a final product if purchased by a housewife intending to make her own dress. Put differently, goods that are not resold and therefore do not enter into the value of other goods and services are counted as part of GNP, but goods resold and used in further production become part of the value of other goods and services and must not be counted separately. The cost of intermediate goods becomes part of the price of final goods and services, but the cost of investment goods does not. Thus capital formation, purchases by government, and purchases by consumers are included in GNP, but raw materials used by business firms are not.

Since the gross national product can be obtained by adding together the value of the total output of each firm or producing unit and subtracting therefrom the value of intermediate goods purchased from other units, duplication or double counting is avoided by this method also. Value added by the government sector to GNP is limited to wages and salaries paid to government employees. Interest payments are not counted because they are not necessarily connected with current production. Unlike the case of owner-occupied houses, an imputation (i.e., an estimate of the value of a good or a service when no market transaction occurs) for the rental value of property owned by the government, such as the road network, is not made because a realistic market valuation is lacking. The essence of the procedure is that it considers only the actual value added to a product by each producing unit.

The major categories making up the gross national product for precise computational purposes include the amount of goods and services purchased by consumers (C) and by government (G), the gross private domestic investment (I), and the net export of goods and services. Each of these groups accounts for part of the expenditures in the economy.

Consumption accounts for nearly two-thirds of the GNP. It is divided for convenience into durable goods, nondurable goods, and services. Nondurable goods are the largest component, and durable goods are the smallest. Interest paid by consumers as well as personal transfers to foreigners are not part of consumption.

Investment involves those goods called capital goods or producer goods that are used in further production. They are factories, machinery, equipment, and (for statistical convenience) the change in inventories from the preceding period. It also includes the homes constructed during any period even though they are owned and occupied by consumers. Investment in the economy refers only to the current production of real goods. It does not include financial transfers between businesses or persons of goods produced in prior periods.

Investment includes the replacement of worn-out capital (capital consumption allowances or depreciation) and net additions to stock. Gross investment less capital consumption allowances is called net investment. In recent years gross private domestic investment has been about 16 percent of GNP, and capital consumption allowances under 60 percent of gross investment.

Net export of goods and services (expenditures by foreigners) is considered part of the gross national product of the economy. It consists of the excess of exports of goods and services over the sum of imports of goods and services and foreign transfer payments of the U.S. government. Exports represent output. Imports are deducted from total output, however, because they have been included in personal consumption expenditure. In 1974 exports were $140.2 billion and imports were $138.1 billion. The difference ($2.1 billion) is accounted for and may be divided into net foreign investment and net transfers and grants abroad.

The net foreign investment consists of the excess of foreign assets acquired by U.S. residents over U.S. assets acquired by foreigners. It may be computed from international balance of payments statistics (discussed in chapter 19) as the numerical difference between the value of exports of goods and services and the value of the sum of imports of goods and services and net unilateral transfers.

Government purchases of goods and services constitute about a fifth of the gross national product. Government expenditures are a broader category. They include goods and services purchased by federal, state, and local governments; transfer payments to persons in the United States and to foreign sources; net interest; and subsidies less current surplus of government enterprises. Such spending is balanced against government receipts. Receipts are made up primarily of federal, state, and local personal taxes; corporate profits taxes; indirect business taxes; and social insurance contributions of employees, employers, and self-employed persons. Some nontax receipts should be added. In 1974 federal government receipts were $264.9 billion and expenditures, including transfer payments and interest, were $268.4 billion. The difference between receipts and expenditures constitutes surplus (saving) or deficit.

Output accounts only for economic production and avoids, with a few exceptions, those activities that are not reflected in market purchases or sales. For example, painting one's home, shining one's shoes, or cooking a meal for one's family are not economic pursuits, whereas the same type of output derived by employing a painter, a bootblack, or a cook would involve a market transaction and appear in the output figures. The output that housewives render to their families and, generally, output that results when people do things for themselves are not counted. Nor does the shifting of wealth between persons affect the GNP. (Shifts of secondhand assets among households, firms, and government involve only offsetting changes in output.) Thus buying a share of stock or a used car may add the services of the stockbroker or salesman to the total output, but the value of the assets themselves is not included. Nevertheless, it has been decided to impute a value to the rental value of owner-occupied dwellings and include it as part of output; similarly the value of food and fuel produced and consumed on farms is estimated even though no market exchange takes place in these cases. On the other hand, tradition has decreed that illegal transactions are excluded from output regardless of their amount or whether there are accurate figures available. Furthermore, though the product of commercial radio broadcasting and television industries is of considerable importance as a form of pleasure and recreation, it is not counted in GNP because no direct payment is made by consumers for the service. As a result, only the costs of these industries as borne by business are included. Many other arbitrary or conventional decisions are made in calculating GNP.

Net National Product. Capital goods depreciate or are used up in the production of other goods. When capital consumption is deducted from GNP, the remainder is called the net national product (NNP). Capital consumption, however, is difficult to measure accurately. Figures used by business firms are based on the original cost of the producer durable goods and are usually written off, using an arbitrary formula. Depreciation allowances are not very realistic because of changes in price levels and practices permitted by the government for tax purposes to encourage investment. The result is that although net national product is sometimes considered a better measure of the amount of current production, the economist's inability to estimate capital consumption with sufficient accuracy leads to the more general use of GNP figures.

In the past few decades the rates of gross capital formation and net capital formation have been declining in the United States. Despite increases in both wealth and income and the generally established principle that higher income recipients save more than lower income recipients, the rate of saving in the United States has not been going up. This has been due to the pressures of conspicuous consumption (i.e., keeping up with the Joneses), the higher levels of income taxes, and the declining proportion of small businessmen and farmers who save larger portions of their income than do wage earners. Moreover, in some years poor profit prospects lessened the desire to invest. This led to a reduced GNP and a lower level of saving.

National Income. Reduction of the net national product by indirect business taxes, such as excise and sales taxes, leaves the national income (NI). (This concept of national income is most useful for accounting purposes. The economist generally considers national income as the equivalent of gross national product.) Indirect taxes are those that are chargeable as business expenses. Employment taxes, however, are included as supplements to wages and salaries, not as indirect taxes.

National income is the sum of the earnings of the factors of production (also known as inputs or resources) during a period. It measures receipts of land, capital, entrepreneurs, and labor in the form of rent, interest, profit, and wages. Since statistics of income do not exist for such clearly defined categories, national income figures are broken down into compensation of employees, proprietors' income, rental income of persons, corporate profits modified by inventory valuation adjustment, and net interest. These factor earnings, which are given before payment of income taxes, may be subdivided to provide very useful information, including the income produced by different industries in the economy and the amount of labor and property incomes derived from each industry.

Compensation of employees includes all fringe benefits and social security taxes paid by employers. The category of proprietors' income refers to the returns received by all unincorporated enterprises. It is considered to include, in addition to the profits earned by these businesses, the explicit or implicit wages of the owners, the interest on the money supplied by the owners, and the net rent paid for the property provided by the owners for use in the business. Statistical difficulties make it necessary to combine these factor payments in one figure. Corporate profits, which show the earnings of all corporations and mutual institutions, may be subdivided into corporate income taxes paid to government, dividends paid out to stockholders, and undistributed earnings retained by the firm. Since 1947 corporate profits have fluctuated between 9 percent and 16 percent of national income. Rental income of persons comprises the net rents received by individual landlords whose primary economic activity is not the real estate business. However, it does contain an element representing a labor payment to the extent that owners perform supervisory and other functions. Rent includes the imputed rental value of owner-occupied housing. Net interest is the total interest received less interest paid by the government and interest paid on the consumer debt. The reason for these exclusions from GNP is that most such payments are associated with the financing of wars and purchases of final goods and services; there is almost no current production resulting from the money borrowed.

It should be clear from the discussion above that gross national product may be expressed in two ways—either (1) as the expenditures for the output (the flow of product) of the economy or (2) as the payments to factors for participating in the production (the flow of income) of the economy:

(1) GNP = Consumption (C) + Gross Investment (I) + Government Expenditures (G)
(2) GNP = Wages + Rent + Interest + Profits + Indirect Business Taxes + Depreciation

Both methods of calculation yield identical results except that, in practice, imperfections in collection of data lead to a difference between them that is called statistical discrepancy. GNP in 1974 is broken down in table 3-1.

Personal Income. Personal income is the amount of money received from all sources by individuals and unincorporated businesses. Corporation and government receipts are excluded. Transfer payments (payments made that are not for current contributions to production) from government and business are part of personal income, but transfers from other persons (except consumer interest) are excluded. Government transfers are made up primarily of social security outlays, welfare payments, and interest on the public debt. Business transfers consist mainly of corporate gifts and allowances for bad debts by consumers. Some nonmonetary items are included in personal income, such as wages and salaries paid in the form of food and lodging, the value of food and fuel produced and used on farms, and the rental value of homes to owner-occupants. Furthermore, though interest paid by government and by consumers to persons is not part of the national income, it is considered part of the personal income. Payments made by individuals for social insurance, mainly old-age retirement, are excluded.

Recipients of personal income spend part of it and save the rest. Personal income is equal to personal outlay (personal consumption expenditure, interest paid by consumers, and consumer transfer payments to foreigners), personal taxes, and personal saving. Table 3-2 classifies personal income in 1974.

Disposable Personal Income. Disposable personal income is the amount that remains after income taxes, property taxes, and government fines are deducted from personal income. It includes personal

TABLE 3-1

GROSS NATIONAL PRODUCT, 1974
(BILLIONS OF DOLLARS)

Personal consumption expenditure	876.7	Compensation of employees	855.8
Gross private domestic investment	209.4	Proprietors' income	93.0
		Corporate profits	106.2
Net exports of goods and services	2.1	Rental income of persons	26.5
		Net interest	61.6
Government purchases of goods and services	309.2	Indirect business taxes	135.0
		Capital consumption allowances	119.5
		Statistical discrepancy	−0.2
Gross National Product	1,397.4		1,397.4

Source: *Federal Reserve Bulletin,* April 1975, pp. A 54–A 55. Minor categories have been included in related items: Corporate profits include inventory valuation adjustment, and indirect business taxes include business transfer payments and current surplus of government enterprises less subsidies.

TABLE 3-2

PERSONAL INCOME, 1974
(BILLIONS OF DOLLARS)

Personal taxes	170.8	Wages and salaries	754.7
Personal consumption expenditure	876.7	Proprietors' income	93.0
Durable goods	127.5	Rental income of persons	26.5
Nondurable goods	380.2	Dividends	32.7
Services	369.0	Personal interest income	103.8
Interest paid by consumers	25.0	Transfer payments	139.8
Transfer payments to foreigners	1.0		
Personal saving	77.0		
Personal Taxes, Outlay, and Savings	1,150.5	Personal Income	1,150.5

Source: *Federal Reserve Bulletin,* April 1975, pp. A 54–A 55. Wages and salaries differ.

TABLE 3-3

GROSS INVESTMENT AND GROSS SAVING, 1974
(BILLINGS OF DOLLARS)

Gross private domestic		Personal saving	77.0
investment	209.4	Gross business saving	136.5
New construction	98.1	Government surplus	5.9
Producer durable		Statistical discrepancy	−0.2
equipment	97.1		
Change in business			
inventories	14.2		
Net foreign investment	−5.6		
Gross Investment	207.8		207.8

Source: *Economic Report of the President*, 1975, p. 262 and *Federal Reserve Bulletin*, April 1975, p. A 54.

outlay and saving and indicates the purchasing power in the hands of consumers.

Savings. The resources available to produce investment goods are those that have not been consumed by households, used by the government, or expended by corporate firms. In effect, therefore, these resources are that part of the national output saved by private individuals, businesses, and government. Saving by persons, including owners of unincorporated business, is that part of disposable personal income that is not personal outlay. Personal savings comprise the difference in the net assets of persons over the period involved. Net investment in factories and equipment by unincorporated enterprises is therefore included. Corporate savings are corporate profits after taxes that have not been distributed as dividends. Government savings are the excess of government revenues over government expenditures for goods and services and outlays for transfer payments. Investment and savings figures are given in table 3-3.

LIMITATIONS ON THE USEFULNESS OF THE GNP

Changes in gross national product over a period of time provide a useful approximation of growth in the volume of goods and services produced by the economy as well as changes in living standards. But the relationships are not precise; distortions arise for a number of reasons: (1) Total output has several weaknesses as a measure of well-being. Since total GNP figures do not reveal the effects of population changes, per capita output is often a better measure of social welfare. Moreover, a higher output does not necessarily mean greater well-being. For example, a complex urban society that devotes much of its resources to an adequate system of transportation (and thus generates GNP) does not provide a better living standard than a rural economy where GNP is lower because it devotes fewer resources to transportation. But even if GNP remains unchanged over a period of time, redistribution of income in the population can increase well-being. (2) Gross national product is affected by the size of the labor force. (The term *labor force* refers to that part of the population which is employed or available for employment, i.e., unemployed.) The more people working, the larger the GNP may be expected to be. Conversely, if unemployment rises, the GNP may be expected to fall. A decline in available jobs was responsible for the sharp contradiction in output and income that prevailed during the decade of the 1930s. It is therefore important to remember that as employment rises the GNP will rise even if methods of production do not change substantially. (3) Price movements rather than differences in real output may be responsible for changes in the money value of GNP. These movements may be accounted for by converting dollar values into dollars of constant purchasing power; the procedure is discussed in the next chapter. (4) Much of the output in GNP does not increase welfare immediately (items included in investment); other output items may be of little value in growth (wartime production). (5) A substantial part of the output does not pass through the market and is not counted. This is especially true of what people make and do for themselves. Furthermore, if consumers shift from baking bread at home to buying bread in the bakery, GNP rises even though no more bread is eaten. (6) Satisfactions derived from leisure do not enter into the GNP, yet the trend has been clearly toward more leisure for employees. Nor is psychic income—pleasure and other non-material advantages that some persons derive from their work—included in the gross national product. (7) Consumer durable goods are counted only in the year in which they are purchased, so that the addition that they make to the welfare of their purchasers in subsequent years is not computed. Thus the GNP must be adjusted to yield more precise and useful measures of economic growth or the standard of living of the population.

GROWTH OF OUTPUT

The growth of the gross national product offers abundant evidence of the strength of the economy of the United States since the Second World War. The average annual rate of increase in GNP beginning in 1948 has been about 6.6 percent. The rate of *real* growth (corrected for the rising price level) during the same period has been about 4 percent; economists consider this a fairly rapid rate. The annual rate was high between 1948 and 1953, was somewhat lower between 1953 and 1960, and higher thereafter. Statistics reveal that the rate of growth of output in the United States during the past two decades is higher than the rate of estimated growth during the past century.

The substantial increases in the GNP have been made possible by

TABLE 3-4

SELECTED NATIONAL INCOME STATISTICS,
1929–1974
(BILLIONS OF DOLLARS)

Year	Gross National Product	National Income	Disposable Personal Income	Con-sumption	Gross Invest-ment	Govern-ment Purchases
1929	103.1	86.8	83.3	77.2	16.2	8.5
1933	55.6	40.3	45.5	45.8	1.4	8.0
1940	99.7	81.1	75.7	70.8	13.1	14.0
1945	212.0	181.5	150.2	119.7	10.6	82.3
1950	284.8	241.1	206.9	191.0	54.1	37.9
1955	398.0	331.0	275.3	254.4	67.4	74.2
1960	503.7	414.5	350.0	325.2	74.8	99.6
1965	684.9	564.3	473.2	432.8	108.1	137.0
1970	977.1	800.5	691.7	617.6	136.3	219.5
1971	1054.9	857.7	746.4	667.1	153.7	234.2
1972	1158.0	946.5	802.5	729.0	179.3	255.7
1973	1294.9	1065.6	903.7	805.2	209.4	276.4
1974	1397.4	1143.0	979.7	876.7	209.4	309.2

Source: *Statistical Abstract of the United States*, 1974, pp. 373, 374, 377 and *Federal Reserve Bulletin*, April 1975, p. A 54.

the rising productivity of workers (higher output per worker) and the increasing size of the labor force. Higher productivity has been brought about by increased capital, advancing technology, innovations, better education of workers, more training of workers, and improved managerial techniques. The relationships of the components of output and income are illustrated in figure 3-1.

Growth of national income is shown in table 3-4.

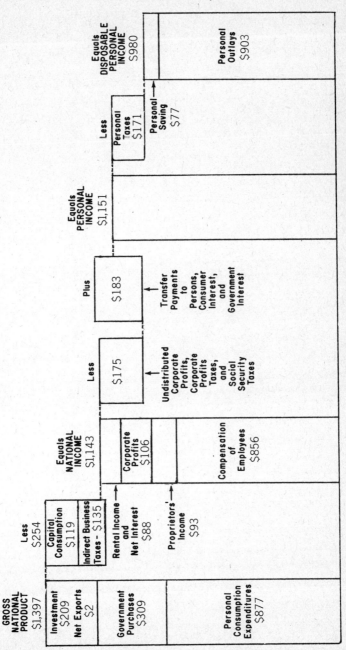

Fig. 3-1. The national income and product accounts, 1974 (billions of dollars)

Chapter 4
MONEY AND PRICES

Modern civilization revolves around money economies. Households, business firms, and government spend money to purchase goods, services, and factors of production at various prices. A knowledge of the meaning and role of money, the relation of money to prices and their movement, and the links between money and spending helps in understanding how the economic system functions.

A MONEY ECONOMY

Each good and each service has a market value. In a barter economy the value of one item may be expressed in terms of every other item. For example, a one-pound loaf of bread may be worth two pounds of table salt or one-sixtieth part of a particular pair of shoes. In a money economy every good and service has a price. Price is the money value of any purchase or sale made.

Background of Money. Many of the difficulties associated with barter were eliminated with the introduction and use of metallic money. Precious metals served for many centuries as a convenient source of the money supply; they were frequently used for decorative and ornamental purposes, did not wear out easily, and fulfilled most requirements of money. Coins were introduced later to standardize the amount of metal and eliminate the necessity of measuring and weighing the payment at each purchase or sale. Nevertheless, care was required in accepting coins because of the practice of clipping or sweating them by dishonest persons. Furthermore, occasional debasing (introducing more base metal) of the coinage by the government or the ruler lowered the value of the coin and coincidentally tended to raise prices.

The use of paper currency began when goldsmiths, and later banks, were given metal and coins for safekeeping. Persons depositing these metals received receipts that were readily accepted as money if the safekeeper was known to be reliable. However, since the goldsmith or bank rarely needed to have all the metal left for safekeeping available at all times to meet the demands of its depositors, techniques of using some of the metal for profitable investment by lending it out or buying securities were soon developed. This action made it impossible for the safekeeper to meet obligations on demand if all depositors requested their metal at once. But such requests almost never came, and a money system of fractionally backed paper currency evolved.

Gradually central banks in each country took over the function of printing paper currency from commercial banks. For a long time this currency continued to be backed fractionally and to be convertible into gold. But by 1940 most countries had abandoned the gold standard. Paper currency became fiat money. This means that it was not convertible into anything but other paper currency. Yet even as fiat money, currency remains valuable because (1) the public continues to accept it in payment for goods and services and (2) the government designates it to be legal tender.

Supply of Money. It may appear that the idea of money is a simple one, but it becomes clear upon close examination that the subject presents many complexities. To begin with, money is widely used and commonly accepted in payment for goods or as a measure of value, but different societies and civilizations have employed diverse media for these purposes. Generally, money has been characterized historically by being readily and easily recognizable, divisible, portable, and storable. In our own economy the categories of money consist of currency, which is paper dollars and coins of various denominations, and bank money, which is the total value of checking accounts or demand deposits in commercial banks. Paper currency now in circulation is issued by the U.S. Treasury or by Federal Reserve Banks. Money arises out of debt incurred by the government and banks.

Demand deposits are available and acceptable for payment almost as readily as currency and are therefore classified as money. Some types of relatively liquid assets that involve little or no risk of decline in value, such as time deposits or savings accounts, government bonds, and insurance certificates with cash surrender value, ordinarily lack instant convertibility, ready acceptance, direct transferability, or definite value. They are usually categorized as near money, but some of these items may be counted as money for specific purposes.

Demand deposits, which are subject to withdrawal by check, constitute more than 75 percent of the money supply of the United States. It is the demand deposit account, not the check, that is considered money.

The supply of money and of near money in the United States has followed a consistent upward movement over the past century.

Until 1933 gold played a major role in determining the nature and value of money in the United States; thereafter it gradually lost its importance in that connection. Although gold no longer serves as backing for currency, it is still used in international trade. The value of the stock of gold of the United States rose from $1.5 billion in 1914 to just over $4 billion in 1933. In January 1934 the price per fine ounce was raised from $20.67 to $35 by the government and the value of the stock of gold rose to $8.2 billion. The increase continued slowly, reaching a peak of nearly $24.6 billion in 1949. Since then the value of gold has reached $42.22 an ounce in government markets. U.S. gold reserves, however, have declined gradually during the past twenty-five years.

Uses of Money. Money serves as a medium of exchange (or means of payment) to avoid the difficulty of barter and as a standard of value (or unit of account) to permit the direct comparison of the value of different goods and services by their prices. Money also serves to store value, i.e., to accumulate purchasing power for future use, and to standardize deferred payments, i.e., to be used as a measure or yardstick for the future repayment of debts. Some kinds of money may be designated by governments as legal tender. Unless a

TABLE 4-1

SUPPLY OF MONEY AND NEAR MONEY
(BILLIONS OF DOLLARS)

Year	Currency Outside Banks	Demand Deposits	Time Deposits (Commercial Banks and Mutual Savings Banks)
1895	1.0	3.0	2.1
1940	6.7	32.0	26.2
1975	67.8	213.0	805.4

Source: *Historical Statistics of the United States, Colonial Times to 1957,* 1960, p. 646 and *Federal Reserve Bulletin,* April 1975, p. A 12.

contract specifies otherwise, creditors must accept payment of debt in any legal tender proffered. Of course, a contract for another kind of payment cannot be satisfied by legal tender. Nor must the seller accept legal tender at the time of sale if he wishes another type of payment. In the United States both paper and coin currency in unlimited amounts are legal tender.

THE PRICE LEVEL

The average price of goods and services is generally affected by changes in the prices of individual commodities. The average price moves upward or downward and rapidly or gradually. Fluctuations in the general price level affect the value of money and, for this reason, are usually studied in relation to money.

A rising general price level (inflation) or a falling one (deflation) affects the value of goods produced or consumed but need not necessarily alter the quantities available in the market. Because of changing prices, it is possible for the income of a person to rise without improving his ability to consume or for the product of the nation to rise without a corresponding increase in the value of the output. Price changes are measured by price indexes.

Index Numbers. The measurement of price movements over time is not simple because the values of different goods are changing at different rates. Indeed, even when the prices of most items are rising, those of some commodities remain stationary and those of others are falling. The construction of price indexes therefore becomes a problem of determining which goods and services to include in the index and the appropriate weight, based on relative economic importance, to attach to each. After the selection and the appropriate weighting are completed, the items are averaged. The base year, the year with which the comparison is made, is assigned the value of 100, and the indexes for other years are based on this number. Generally, series of wholesale prices or consumer prices taken over a period of time are used to construct indexes reflecting price movements, although many other kinds of price series may be used. Since price indexes compare prices, care must be taken that identical goods are used in all periods so that changes in quality or product do not affect the index level. It is thus difficult to compare prices over a great number of years, as there are very few goods and services that remain unchanged over long periods of time. For this reason, consumer prices are even harder to compile than are wholesale prices; in the latter case, goods for the wholesale market, such as agricultural staples, tend to be of constant standard quality.

Price Movements. During the past two centuries wholesale prices have fluctuated sharply in the United States. Price peaks occurred during or immediately after the Revolutionary War, the War of 1812, the Civil War, and the First World War. In each instance substantial declines followed. Actually the lowest wholesale price level of the past two hundred years occurred in the mid-1890s. Although the upward movement of prices that took place during the Second World War was not unexpected, there has been no drop in the price level in the more than thirty years that have elapsed since. On the contrary, the upward movement has persisted and prices, having passed all previous peaks, are currently at the highest level in the history of the United States. The resistance of prices to a downward movement has been associated with both the vigorous action of the government to prevent declining prices for fear that depression would follow and the policy of unions to block any cuts in wages (which is responsible for sticky costs of production).

Over a long period of time, consumer prices and wholesale prices follow the same trends. In the short run, however, they may move at greatly different rates or, occasionally, in opposite directions. Table 4-2 shows that consumer prices have quadrupled in the sixty years subsequent to 1913. Since 1933 the consumer price index has risen each year, with the exception of very small declines in 1938, 1939, 1949, and 1955.

An index of price changes is used to correct or deflate a series given

TABLE 4-2

CONSUMER PRICE INDEX, 1913–1974
(1967 = 100)

1913	29.7	1945	53.9
1920	60.0	1950	72.1
1925	52.5	1955	80.2
1930	50.0	1960	88.7
1933	38.8	1965	94.5
1937	43.0	1970	116.3
1940	42.0	1974	147.7

Source: *Handbook of Basic Economic Statistics*, May 1975, pp. 101–102.

in current money prices if real values are desired. The use of the proper deflator is important. Although both national and personal income dropped between 1929 and 1933, changes in real income were not quite as sharp because prices also fell. Similarly, income rose substantially between 1950 and 1975, but part of this rise was due to a higher price level. When total income remains unaltered, purchasing power increases if prices fall and decreases if prices rise.

Inflation and Deflation. Price movements affect various groups in the economy differently. The creditor's income from previously negotiated loans is fixed; he loses real income when the prices rise and gains real income when they fall. The debtor has an advantage when the price level rises because his task of paying off obligations is lighter, but he is at a disadvantage if the price level moves down. Those persons whose incomes are rising, but at a slower rate than prices, suffer setbacks in their standard of living. Inflation and deflation thus have arbitrary redistributional effects on income. Mild or creeping inflation is sometimes considered a stimulus to business activity and economic growth because businessmen typically are debtors. However, if a country experiences more rapid price increases than its competitors, foreign export markets will decline and a less favorable balance of trade and reduced purchasing power will result.

Inflation lessens the willingness of lenders to extend credit. It is ordinarily foolish for a person to lend money at 5 percent a year (or deposit money in a bank at that rate) if the price level is rising at 6 percent each year. In effect, he has less total purchasing power at the end of the period than he had at the beginning. Instead, if possible, the money should be placed in assets that are likely to appreciate in conjunction with the upward movement of prices or it should be spent for consumption. Thus a person buying a ten-year federal government defense bond (savings bond) in 1940 for $75 and receiving $100 at maturity in 1950 was really getting a negative interest rate on purchasing power because prices rose by much more than $33\frac{1}{3}$ percent during this period. In 1950, for $100 he was able to get goods worth less than $60 at 1940 prices.

A demand for goods at a price level that exceeds the quantity available produces inflation. This situation leads to a rise in prices and is called demand inflation or demand-pull inflation. Inflation is also produced as a result of increases in the costs of factors of production. For example, a decision by unions to push wages up or by business firms to increase profits may exert an upward pressure on prices. This kind of inflation is called cost inflation, cost-push inflation, or sellers' inflation. The major checks on continued inflations in advanced economies are the monetary controls used by the government, the declining demand of those groups whose income is not rising as fast as prices, and the expectation that prices which are too high will not continue to rise.

Hyperinflation. Government anti-inflationary policies stem in part from many unhappy experiences with rapidly rising prices. The concept of inflation ordinarily is not defined with sufficient precision to differentiate whether the price rise is slow or rapid. Generally, however, very rapid inflation, with increases of many thousands of percent in relatively short periods of time, occurs when the demand for goods and services or the national income continues to rise though physical output cannot be expanded much or at all. This case is termed *hyperinflation, runaway inflation,* or *galloping inflation.* Naturally since the downward movement of prices cannot fall below zero (i.e., a decline of 100 percent), there is no corresponding deflationary counterpart for hyperinflation.

The most important element in hyperinflation is an increase in the quantity of money in a country, although other factors have a bearing on the situation. These include changes in the demand for money, in the size of the population, and in the stock of physical goods. Usually the situation is one in which the government finds it more convenient to finance its operations by creating additional money than by raising taxes. Typically, hyperinflation is an event associated with war or its aftermath. The vast issue of paper currency was responsible for the incredibly rapid increases in prices in the early 1920s in Germany, Poland, Hungary, and the Soviet Union, in the 1940s in China, in 1944 in Greece, and in 1946 in Hungary again. In the German inflation prices doubled about every two weeks; in the Hungarian inflation of 1946 prices doubled almost two times each week of the year.

Government Policy. Since the mid-1950s special attention has been paid by the U.S. government to policies designed to prevent any rapid movement upward in the price level. For the decade ending in the middle of the 1960s the problem was not unusually difficult to meet because unemployment remained fairly high even during booming business conditions. The cost of living rose about 1½ percent each year. But maintaining stability of prices became more difficult in 1965 as the United States became involved in the Vietnam War and the economy began to approach full employment of labor and machinery. The guideposts set by the government for noninflationary wage and fringe benefit increases of 3.2 percent based on the estimated annual gain in productivity were under great pressure in labor-management negotiations and were exceeded in various contract agreements.

Utilization of standby and older equipment as output approached plant capacity raised the cost of production. (Though expansion of capacity helps reduce the pressure of demand on supply over the long run, initially such spending means increases in demand.) Higher prices also resulted from the lack of excessive inventories that would have served to absorb strong demand. These factors have been bolstered since 1965 by the continuing and persistent upward trend in the prices of services, particularly medical care, public transportation, and household costs. Moreover, in some years bad weather reduced the supply of many agricultural products and led to higher consumer prices.

In the 1970s prices began to accelerate even more rapidly. The federal government undertook to check inflation by using monetary, fiscal, and price controls, but in 1974 a severe recession ensued. In 1976 the unemployment rate was near 9 percent, but the rate of inflation had subsided somewhat.

Recent studies have shown an inverse relation between changes in the price level and changes in unemployment. The Phillips curve relates the inflation and unemployment rates in graphic form. In the past few years the trade-off between rates of inflation and unemployment has worsened; that is, at any rate of unemployment the rate of inflation is higher than it used to be. (For many analytical purposes, economists substitute wage increases for inflation or price increases.)

SOME RELATIONS BETWEEN MONEY, PRICES, AND SPENDING

It is now clearly realized that the total volume of money and changes in its volume affect the price level, total income, and total employment. Different schemes and models have been worked out to show various combinations of these relationships.

The Equation of Exchange. One of the earliest and best-known relationships was suggested by Irving Fisher and is known as the quantity theory of money or the equation of exchange. This equation, also called the transactions-velocity model, is written $MV = PT$; where M is the amount of money in the hands of the public, V is the velocity or rate at which money changes hands, P is the average price of all exchanges transacted, and T is the number of transactions taking place in a given period. MV therefore represents the total expenditures on goods and services and must equal PT, which corresponds to the total receipts for goods and services sold during the same period.

The equation of exchange may be calculated for all transactions in the economy, including intermediate goods and transfer payments, in which case V refers to all money turning over, or transactions velocity. Of the equation may refer only to exchanges involving the measurement of final outputs, where V is the income velocity of money and PT corresponds to GNP. In either case, the two sides of the equation are equal by definition. Obviously this must be so because the amount of money paid out by one person must exactly equal the amount received by someone else. The equation reveals nothing about causal relations. But the usefulness of the relationship stems from the opportunity it provides to compare the effects of a change in one variable upon other variables. It is clear that the price level varies directly with the supply of money (MV) and indirectly with the number of transactions (T) where the equation is written $P = \dfrac{MV}{T}$.

If it is assumed that velocity is relatively constant and that T changes only gradually, then changes in M must bring about changes in P. On the other hand, if receipts, or PT, are considered to be an inactive or a passive element and V is fairly constant, then changes in M may be used to bring about a higher level of expenditures. The supply of money, which is influenced by government, banks, and other sources determining its availability, becomes an important factor in total output. While the equation of exchange has some usefulness in linking M and P if applied with care, difficulties arise because V is not constant, even in the short run. The degree of stability in V is related to how confident people are of retaining their jobs, how much they expect prices to change, how regularly they receive income, how favorable investment opportunities are, and how easy it is to borrow money. Moreover, T also fluctuates as business conditions change.

The Cash-Balances Equation. The Cambridge (University) theory of money, or cash-balances equation, which is associated with the work of Alfred Marshall, can be used instead of the equation of exchange. It is built upon the premise that the quantity of money a household or firm wishes to hold depends upon the need of the household or firm to purchase commodities or services. The cash-balances equation is written $M = KPT$, where M is the amount of money held by the public, K is the proportion of the total value of transactions that the public (households and firms) wishes to hold in the form of cash balances, P is the average price of all transactions, and T is the total number of transactions taking place in the economy in a given period. $\frac{M}{K} = PT$ is a relationship that says the amount of money held by the public divided by the fraction of the value of transactions the public wishes to hold in the form of cash during any period of time is equal to the total value of the transactions during the same period. It follows that if the number of transactions and the amount of money remain constant, the price level varies inversely with the demand for money (K). This may be seen more clearly by writing the equation $P = \frac{M}{KT}$. A change in the demand for money indicates a change in the desire to hold purchasing power in the form of cash balances, not in the quantity of cash. Thus changes in the demand for money cause prices to rise or fall. The cash-balances equation, like the equation of exchange, may be used to represent income transactions or total transactions.

The cash-balance equation yields the same conclusions as the equation of exchange. This is true because K is only the reciprocal of V, i.e., the velocity of money. It means that the fraction of the value of transactions for which the public wishes to hold cash (K) is equal to one divided by the number of times that quantity of cash must change hands to account for the total value of the transactions $(\frac{1}{V})$. Therefore $M = KPT$ is the same as $M = \frac{PT}{V}$. This may be rewritten as $MV = PT$, the equation of exchange. K and V represent the same concept and therefore have the same characteristics. Nevertheless, the cash-balances equation is generally more helpful than the equation of exchange because it explains more directly why people hold money and how such holding of money relates to spending processes. These matters are central to an explanation of changes in the national income.

Liquidity Preference. The Keynesian liquidity preference theory is more recent. It maintains that the stock of money held by the public will vary inversely with the rate of interest (price of money). The higher the return on income-yielding assets, the less likely it is that cash will be held. That some relationship exists between the supply of money and the interest rate can be seen from relevant statistics, if adjustments are made for changes in prices, output, and population and if war years are excluded. The liquidity preference theory provides more insight than the cash-balances equation as to why the public holds money.

Demand for Money. The holder of money incurs a cost in the foregone profit or interest that might be earned if it were converted into other assets. He also gives up the alternative of buying consumer goods and services and deriving immediate satisfaction or utility. Nevertheless, individuals wish to hold money balances. This demand for money, which indicates a desire not to spend currently, is now usually associated with three motives. First, money is held for *transaction* purposes so that payments may be made more conveniently in meeting the obligations incurred by daily expenditures for goods and services. Money as a medium of exchange also avoids the higher cost of holding many items for barter, as future needs cannot be foreseen with accuracy. Second, money serves as a store of value for *precautionary* purposes so that it is immediately available for whatever reason at any time in the future. It gives holders a sense of security as it enables them to meet emergency needs. Third, money is held for *speculative* motives if the expectation is that prices will fall. Spending is postponed in the belief that money will provide more purchasing power in the future. Transaction balances held will vary directly with incomes and indirectly with interest rates. Precautionary and speculative balances will be affected, in addition, by the wealth of the individual and by price expectations. The total demand for money is equal to the total supply of money.

Generally, however, the relation between money and prices and between money and spending cannot be established with much precision. Although historically there has been a rough relationship between the growth of the money supply and the output of the economy, there is little basis to establish cause and effect. Other models to be discussed later will link consumption and saving decisions to income receipts.

Statistics clearly reveal that the stock of money changes continually. Since most money today consists of demand deposits in commercial banks, an examination of the banking system is appropriate at this point.

Chapter 5
THE BANKING SYSTEM

Business activity in the United States is dependent upon an efficient banking system. The commercial bank is the basic unit in this system, but there are other types of financial institutions. The Federal Reserve System supervises much of the banking system, particularly the commercial banks, and has considerable authority to expand or restrict the availability of credit. Such power over credit is the key to monetary policy.

COMMERCIAL BANKS

A commercial bank obtains a charter by incorporating as a federal or state institution. Generally the promoters must show the authorities granting the charter that a bank is needed in the city or the community and that the bank is likely to be successful. At the end of 1974 there were just over 14,400 commercial banks in the United States, of which about 4,700 were federally chartered. Of more than 9,700 state-chartered banks, about 1,100 voluntarily had become members of the Federal Reserve System and over 8,400 others were insured by the Federal Deposit Insurance Corporation. Fewer than 200 commercial banks, therefore, were outside direct federal control, and these held a very small fraction of total deposits.

Although many nations have a system of branch banking, where a few large banks dominate the entire country, the prevalent system in the United States is unit banking, where a bank with branches is limited to a prescribed geographical area. This limitation is enforced by banking legislation specifically designed to restrict expansion and results in an evolution quite different from the development of branch operations normally found in other enterprises.

Functions. Among other activities, commercial banks accept savings accounts or time deposits, make loans, act as trustees and fiduciary agents, provide currency, and sell money orders, but their most important function is to handle demand deposits and process checks drawn upon these deposits. Demand deposits arise and are maintained by customers who (1) bring in currency or checks drawn on other banks, (2) borrow money, or (3) sell the bank investment or corporate securities. In the latter two cases it will be shown that commercial banks may create money. But the power to create money involves decisions regarding the allocation of credit in the economy, and commercial banks therefore have a profound impact on the course of business and economic development.

Other financial institutions, such as mutual savings banks, savings and loan associations, investment banks, and life insurance companies, are not in a position to create money. Although they too may affect the volume of credit by making loans and buying securities, they turn over cash or provide near money (in the form of time deposits) to borrowers and sellers so that there is no increase in the amount of money in the economy. Thus commercial banks operate in a unique way: They actually expand the amount of money.

Creation of Money. When an individual or business borrows from a commercial bank, a checking account is opened for the amount of the loan or an addition to an existing account is made. (Cash is sometimes paid out.) This demand deposit becomes a liability of the bank, but it is offset by a promissory note as an asset. Similarly, a security purchased by the bank is an asset that balances the checking account extended to the seller. In each case the volume of demand deposits, and hence of money, increases. If the holder of a demand deposit pays a bill by check, the recipient ordinarily will deposit the check in the same bank or in another one so that the total amount of demand deposits in the system does not change. Contrariwise, if a borrower pays off a loan or a bond held by the bank when it matures, assets are reduced, but the check received by the bank curtails liabilities by an equal amount because demand deposits decline.

The process of expansion of the money supply by banks is essentially limited by the probability that the owners of demand deposits will call for cash instead of using checks for transactions. As a result, a bank is basically restricted in its loan operations by the fraction of the money supply that the public wishes to keep in the form of currency. Thus if the public wants to hold 20 percent of its money in cash, money creation that increases demand deposits cannot exceed cash deposits by more than five times. But a fivefold expansion is the outside limit because such expansion does not provide a margin of safety should there be a greater than usual demand for currency. Obviously, if all depositors wanted to withdraw their deposits at one time, the bank would find it impossible to satisfy them.

In practice the government sets a legal reserve requirement that commercial banks must meet. This means that the bank must keep a specified fraction of its deposits in cash form. Thus there is a certain margin of safety if a depositor wishes to make withdrawals. But more important, there is a limit imposed on the amount of credit a bank may extend. Since loans or purchases of securities by a bank increase demand deposits but not cash, they must be geared to the amount of cash available above the legally required reserves (excess reserves).

Although in theory a commercial bank may expand its demand deposits to the limit imposed by the reserve requirement, in practice credit cannot be extended much beyond the excess reserves held by the bank. This is so because loans above that amount would involve losses of reserves both to borrowers who withdraw cash and to other banks in the process of clearing balances. Suppose that a bank has $5,000 in cash assets and $20,000 in demand deposit liabilities; and that the legal reserve requirement is 20 percent. Excess reserves are $1,000 since only $4,000 is required by law to be held as reserves. In theory, therefore, the bank can extend another $5,000 in loans. Should it do so, however, it would be unable to meet any demand for cash. But even if loans were increased by only $2,000 (and other banks were not expanding demand deposits at the same rate), the chances are that borrowers would write checks against their deposits that would be placed mainly in other banks and thereby cause a drain of cash of almost the entire $2,000 when interbank balances are cleared. Demand deposits created by loans usually remain in the bank in the proportion of its own demand deposits to the total demand deposits in the community. A safe practice for the bank therefore would be to extend additional credit of no more than $1,000—that is, the amount of its excess reserves.

The banking system as a whole, however, may engage in multiple credit expansion; that is, it is not limited in expanding loans to the sum of *excess reserves* held by all banks at any moment of time. Instead each dollar of excess reserves may be expanded to the full limit allowed by legal requirements. Such is the case because a second bank, receiving an individual's check drawn on the demand deposits of a bank that loaned him money, is adding to its cash assets and is thus able to extend additional loans. Demand deposit expansion is cumulative because those receiving payments for goods and services from borrowers at various banks are depositing the checks (representing cash) at other banks. This means that an initial deposit of $1,000 in cash in any bank enables it (with reserve requirements at 20 percent) to extend loans or buy securities up to $800. Deposit of the $800 in another bank (which receives this money as cash assets in the clearing operation) allows the latter to increase its demand deposits by an additional $640. Repetition of the process leads to the addition at another bank of $512 in demand deposits. Eventually therefore it is possible for the banking system to add a total of $5,000 in deposit liabilities and $4,000 in assets (consisting of loans and securities) as a result of the initial cash deposit of $1,000.

The increase in demand deposits may be derived by formula.

$$\frac{Increase\ in}{Demand\ Deposits} = \frac{Original\ Cash\ Deposit}{Legal\ Reserve\ Requirement\ Percentage}$$

The value of loans made and securities purchased by the banking system is equal to the volume of excess reserves. The only important limitation on the process of credit expansion in the banking system outlined above arises from the failure of those receiving checks from borrowers to redeposit all or part of the payment received. Such currency leakages or withdrawals from banks for hand-to-hand circulation must be deducted from the initial deposit before computing the amount of expansion possible.

If banks have made loans to the full extent of the legal reserve limit and reserves are then lost because of withdrawals or for other reasons, credit contraction must occur. With a legal reserve limit of 20 percent, each dollar of reserves lost by the bank requires a reduction of $5 in loans or in securities held. If many banks are losing reserves at the same time, they may be forced to call in loans previously extended to customers; such action may intensify a deteriorating economic situation responsible for the original loss in reserves. The problems faced by government monetary authorities stem in part from the tendency of the banks in a period of expanding economic activity to increase the availability of credit and stimulate business even more but to reduce loans when business in general is contracting. Such behavior intensifies economic instability.

Insurance. Government protection of deposits has been available through a federal agency since 1934. All federally chartered (national) banks and state banks that are members of the Federal Reserve System must insure with the Federal Deposit Insurance Corporation (FDIC). Other state banks that satisfy specified requirements may also obtain insurance coverage. Banks pay premiums to the FDIC; each bank account (demand deposit or time deposit) is protected to $40,000. Mutual savings banks are also eligible for insurance, and almost two-thirds of them have subscribed.

THE FEDERAL RESERVE SYSTEM

The general public is served by commercial banks. But commercial banks need many of the same services that they themselves offer. Such functions are performed for them by the central bank, or the banker's bank. In the United States the central bank was set up in 1914, under the Federal Reserve Act of 1913, as part of the Federal Reserve System.

Background. The Federal Reserve System (frequently called Fed) attained its present structure and functions as a result of several statutory changes in the original law, particularly those made by the Banking Acts of 1933 and 1935. At a time when no central bank existed in this country, the Federal Reserve System was created to replace the national banking system that had been in operation since the Civil War. The scheme by which national banking had been organized was weak because currency, consisting of national bank notes (based on federal bonds), U.S. notes (greenbacks) from the Civil War period, coins of silver and gold (or silver and gold certificates), and minor coins, was relatively *inelastic*. This meant that often neither cyclical nor seasonal demands of business for currency could be properly met. Furthermore, the reserve requirement regulations, which were intended to protect depositors, did not in fact do so satisfactorily because they linked reserves to the size and financial importance of the city in which the bank was located. The primary defect in this arrangement was that banks in smaller cities were permitted to hold part of their reserves in banks located in larger cities. Such *pyramiding* of reserves sometimes led to money drains in New

York City and Chicago when relatively mild reserve shortages occurred elsewhere in the country and could thereby bring about financial difficulties and restrictions on loans. The recurring financial panics, particularly the one in 1907, led to public pressure for revision in the banking structure and the resultant adoption of the Federal Reserve System.

Structure. The central banking institution in the United States consists of the Board of Governors, the Federal Reserve Banks and their branches, the Federal Open Market Committee, and the Federal Advisory Council. These units in combination with the member banks constitute the Federal Reserve System. The system provides the main commercial banking facilities of the nation.

The system divides the United States into twelve districts, Each district has a Federal Reserve Bank located in one of its major cities, although some regions also have branches. All national banks and those state banks that meet specified requirements and desire to join are members of the system. In each district, member banks, who are the sole stockholders of the Federal Reserve Bank, elect six of the nine directors. Although the FR Banks pay dividends to their owners, they must operate primarily in the public interest.

The Federal Reserve System is run from Washington, D.C., by a board of governors of seven members, formerly called the Federal Reserve Board, appointed by the president for overlapping terms of fourteen years. The effective powers of the board have been gradually increased so that today the system is centralized. The board, among other duties, appoints three of the directors of each of the twelve regional banks. Each of the twelve banks is headed by a president elected by its nine directors, but the Board of Governors has veto power over the selection.

The Federal Open Market Committee is an important part of the system because it controls the purchase and sale of government securities by the twelve Federal Reserve Banks in the open market and is therefore able to act as a powerful force in determining the expansion and contraction of credit. The committee is made up of twelve persons; the seven members of the Board of Governors and five others chosen annually to represent the FR Banks. Each of the twelve banks selects a well-known commercial banker as a member of the Federal Advisory Council. The council meets at least four times a year to present its views regarding business conditions to the Board of Governors. The board is free to accept or reject the recommendations, but the opinions expressed by the council receive wide public attention.

Functions. The central bank serves the commercial banks and the government. It collects and clears checks of its members, supplies them with paper currency and coins, makes loans and advances to them, advises them on portfolio investment and banking operations, and holds their legally required reserves. The central bank issues and redeems federal government securities, holds much of the funds in the checking accounts of the government, and generally acts as the fiscal agent of the federal government. But the most important function of the central bank is to control the supply of money and credit in the economy.

Although both the Federal Treasury and the Federal Reserve Banks may issue currency, the latter is responsible for almost all the paper currency in circulation today. (The U.S. Treasury has gradually withdrawn the various currency certificates that it had issued.) Coins are still minted by the federal government, and are put into circulation through the facilities of the Federal Reserve System. The paper currency currently in use consists almost entirely of Federal Reserve notes, which are issued as liabilities of the FR Banks. They are backed by government bonds or by specified types of commercial paper (business loans). The FR notes are designed to be elastic so that the seasonal business needs of the community may be met readily. The FR Bank supplies whatever currency its members request, by cashing checks and by reducing reserves of the drawers. The reserves of members are correspondingly increased when they return currency to the FR Bank.

Federal Reserve Banks own gold certificates (which represent claims against gold held by the U.S. Treasury). In 1968 Congress repealed the provisions of the law that required at least 25 percent of the backing of FR notes to be kept in gold certificates. (Until 1965 gold certificates were also required to the extent of 25 percent of the reserves held by FR Banks against the liabilities of deposits made with them by member banks.) Such certificates are acquired by FR Banks as a result of either the production or international shipment of gold. When a person mines and sells gold to the Treasury he receives a check. The check is ordinarily deposited in a commercial bank and then finds its way into the reserve account of that bank at the FR Bank. The Treasury issues a gold certificate for the amount purchased and deposits it at the FR Bank, thus restoring its balance.

The mechanism is similar when gold is imported and turned over to the Treasury. Gold certificates held by the FR Banks are eliminated if the Treasury sells gold for use in domestic production or if gold is exported.

CONTROL OF CREDIT

The Federal Reserve System has considerable influence over monetary policy because of its ability to alter the money supply of the United States. Beyond its general powers to supervise the operations of member banks, it establishes and directs monetary policy through a number of major and minor controls over credit expansion and contraction. The three main controls are intended to affect the total supply of money and are therefore considered quantitative controls. Other controls influence the flow of credit in specific areas or for special purposes and are referred to as qualitative or selective controls.

Quantitative Controls. (1) The most important credit control of the Federal Reserve System is the open-market operations. The Federal Open Market Committee decides the timing and volume of all open-market purchases or sales of government securities by FR Banks. Transactions are executed for the committee by the FR Bank of New York and are then apportioned among the portfolios of the twelve banks. Although sometimes the purpose of the open-market activity may be to support the present price of government bills (short-term obligations) or bonds, or to achieve a desired price, it controls credit by altering the reserves of member banks. The securities that the FR Bank sells in the open market are purchased by individuals or commercial banks, and the reserves of the commercial banks are reduced when payment for them is made. If, on the other hand, securities are purchased by FR Banks, payments ordinarily find their way into the reserves of member banks. But the amount of reserves held by commercial banks determines the volume of loans that may be made. This means that the committee will order FR Banks to sell securities when credit tightening is desired and to purchase them when it wishes to make credit expansion possible. Although there are no practical limitations on the powers of the monetary authorities to expand credit facilities through open-market operations, the ability to contract credit is restricted by the volume of securities available to the FR Banks for sale to the banks and the public, the attitude of the Treasury to the lower market price of government securities brought about by sales (and the consequent increase in the cost of financing the public debt), and the extent to which FR Banks are willing to reduce their earning assets.

(2) The Federal Reserve System also affects the money supply by controlling the rediscount rate. Changes in this rate are proposed by each of the FR Banks, but they must be approved by the Board of Governors. It is possible therefore for some variation to exist among the rates in different districts. But the board may compel a specific rate to be established, if it so chooses.

Member banks needing reserves borrow from the FR Bank. They may rediscount the promissory notes or commercial paper of their customers or borrow (discount) on some of the government securities they hold. Though the FR System may encourage borrowing by commercial banks when it lowers the rediscount rate or discourage borrowing when it raises the rate, the initiative nevertheless lies in the hands of the members. High rates may not discourage bankers from applying for loans nor may low rates encourage them to do so, especially since banks in the United States have traditionally shown a resistance against borrowing. The action of the FR System in changing rediscount rates, however, has a psychological impact on banks and on the rest of the economy. In extreme cases, the FR Bank may restrict credit by refusing to renew loans or extend borrowing privileges to member banks.

(3) A powerful instrument available to the Board of Governors to control credit is provided by the statutory requirement for legal reserves that member banks must hold against demand deposits and time deposits. The law authorizes the board to fix reserves on demand deposits held by city banks at a level between 10 and 22 percent (formerly different requirements were set for central reserve or large city banks and reserve or smaller city banks) and of those held by other (country) banks between 7 and 14 percent; reserves on time deposits at all member banks may be varied between 3 and 10 percent. Changes in requirements can drastically and quickly alter the excess reserves that banks have available for making loans. Though this technique of restricting credit is very effective, it is also very unpopular among member banks, especially since competitive nonmember banking institutions may be required to hold lower reserves. Of course, when reserve requirements are at a legal maximum the board is not able to restrict credit further by this technique; con-

versely, when reserves are at a minimum credit restrictions cannot be eased. The reserve requirements in effect in mid-1975 were between 7.5 percent and 16.5 percent on demand deposits, depending on the amount of deposits held by the commercial bank, and between 3 percent and 6 percent on time deposits. Since the end of 1960 all vault cash held by banks is included with deposits at the FR Bank as legal reserves.

Selective Controls. The volume of credit may also be controlled through qualitative or selective devices. However, criticism has been expressed that such regulation is discriminatory.

(1) Moral suasion and the power of bank supervision exercised by FR authorities may be used in cases where it is desirable to limit the extension of credit of particular banks. Pressure may be applied by warning banks and sending examiners to check books. Public opinion may be molded to support the position of the FR System. The efficacy of this technique is doubtful.

(2) The regulation of stock market credit is an important selective control. Purchasers of stock do not always pay cash in full. Instead they borrow part of the money they need, using the stock as collateral. Should the stock fall in price, however, the collateral may become insufficient to protect the lender. A general price decline in the stock market results in many calls upon buyers for additional cash and intensifies the downward pressure on prices. Under the Securities Exchange Act of 1934 the Board of Governors may set the down payment (margin requirement) purchasers of stock must make. The regulations affect the extension of credit by brokers and dealers as well as by commercial banks for securities listed on the exchanges. If the margin is raised, it becomes increasingly difficult to purchase stock or speculate as more cash is required. On the other hand, stock market activity may be encouraged if margin requirements are reduced. In mid-1975 the margin required was 50 percent of the market value of the stock.

(3) During the Second World War and the Korean War, the Board of Governors was empowered to regulate consumer installment credit. The minimum down payment to buy specified consumer durable goods and the maximum period for repayment of loans were regulated to reduce the volume of credit and inflationary pressures. This power lapsed in 1952.

(4) Between 1950 and 1952 the board was also authorized to regulate credit to finance residential construction. Requirements

were imposed on the minimum down payment and on the number of years for which the mortgage could be written. Such action affected the extension of credit and the rate at which homes were constructed. This device, like consumer installment credit regulation, was intended to check inflation during the Korean War.

(5) Some control over the extent of credit in the economy is exercised by the Board of Governors through its ability to determine the maximum interest rates payable on time and savings deposits. Since the interest rate level affects the volume of deposits, there is an obvious impact on the availability of funds for loans. The Board of Governors has ruled that the interest rate payable by member banks may not exceed the maximum rate that state banks may pay on similar deposits under the laws of the state in which the member bank is located. Furthermore, the Federal Deposit Insurance Corporation has set the same maximum interest rates for insured nonmember commercial banks as those imposed by the Board of Governors.

Limitations of Monetary Policy. The task of regulating the availability of credit in order to reduce cyclical movements of the economy has been assigned by Congress to the Federal Reserve System. The influence that the system exerts on the money supply enables the government to use monetary policy as a device to control economic fluctuations. But though such policies have been useful, they have not been able to prevent depressions, unemployment, and inflation. Many reasons for this situation are evident.

Although the Federal Reserve System can control the volume of credit that the commercial banks may issue, other sources of funds are free from any direct control. Savings and loan associations, insurance companies, and personal finance companies—institutions not under the supervision of the FR System—are able to make loans. In addition, various government agencies, such as those involved in providing mortgage credit for housing and in making agricultural loans, affect the volume of credit outstanding and are not subject to the authority of the FR System. In recent years many firms have relied to a greater extent on internally generated funds and undistributed profit for investment money, and their operations are thus outside the purview of regulations that apply to borrowers from banks. Near money and highly liquid assets that are readily available and convertible into cash by businesses and households also limit the monetary authorities from exercising more effective control of the supply of money.

Nor is the Federal Reserve System always able to predict accurately whether inflation or recession is threatening the economy. Various indicators and indexes sometimes conflict so that a clear business trend is not evident. Furthermore, even though the Federal Reserve authorities have much influence over the quantity of money available to the public, they have very little say over the velocity of its movement. As a result, the effectiveness of action affecting quantity of money may be reduced substantially.

There are other more specific weaknesses in the monetary actions of the Federal Reserve System. Tightening credit is likely to limit small businesses more than larger firms since the latter have stronger credit positions and are better able to borrow. It is also evident that whereas restriction of credit is likely to contract business activity, availability of loanable funds does not insure that individuals or companies will borrow. Expansion in the volume of investment is more difficult to achieve through credit manipulation. Moreover, different regional needs throughout the country cannot conveniently be met by the application of uniform regulations throughout the system. Thus easing credit facilities may help a distressed area but harm a region that is already flourishing. In general, inflationary pressures and unemployment require different policies. The steep price increases that occurred simultaneously with high unemployment rates in the early 1970s added to the difficulties facing the monetary authorities of the system.

Various policy conflicts have arisen as the Federal Reserve has endeavored to carry out its functions. Attempts by the system to restrict credit by raising the interest rate when inflationary pressures occur tend to increase the costs to the U.S. Treasury of borrowing money for the repayment of debt or for other financial needs. Similarly, the sale of bonds by the banks, at the direction of the Open Market Committee, makes it more difficult and costly for the Treasury to sell bonds. It is also possible that the efforts of the Federal Reserve System to stimulate domestic economic activity by lowering interest rates may result in money in the form of gold flowing abroad as individuals and businesses seek higher rates of return. A reduction in the country's gold stock may weaken the status of the dollar as an international monetary standard.

Thus the incomplete power that the Federal Reserve System exercises over the supply of money and the volume of credit in the economy limits the effectiveness of monetary policy in controlling business conditions, employment, and price levels. But the state of the economy and the gross national product also are affected by factors other than the quantity of money in circulation, making possible other governmental control policies. Generally, decisions that determine the volumes of consumption, investment, and government expenditures are beyond the control of the Federal Reserve System, though not of the government. Actions designed to affect or determine these decisions are the basis of fiscal policy.

Fiscal Policy. Fiscal policy involves the manipulation of the government budget to affect the level of economic activity and relates primarily to matters concerning taxation, government expenditures, and government transfer payments. It comprises both automatic and discretionary mechanisms and programs. Automatic or built-in stabilizers include progressive income tax receipts that vary directly with national income, unemployment compensation, and other transfers that get larger as income declines and smaller as income rises, and those corporate dividends that remain fairly constant over the course of business cycles. Discretionary action refers to public works programs, welfare spending, and changes in tax rates that may be used to supplement the inadequate effects of automatic responses to counteract instabilities in the economic system. The long lags and political controversies involved in introducing various kinds of discretionary fiscal policy in times of need make their use in short recessions ineffective.

A primary function of fiscal policy is to maintain full or maximum employment and prevent the economic hardships of inflation. Often these objectives involve a growth in the public debt, as money must be borrowed by the government to increase expenditures or meet reduced tax collections. If this debt is held domestically (or internally) rather than by foreigners (or externally), it will tend to shift consumption from one group to another. The public debt will lead to reduced future consumption to the extent that it currently involves borrowing from abroad or reducing capital formation in the present.

Monetary policy and fiscal policy must be used to complement each other as the government strives to maintain economic growth, high employment levels, and stable prices.

FINANCIAL INSTITUTIONS OTHER THAN COMMERCIAL BANKS

There are various institutions other than commercial banks that extend credit or act as intermediaries between lenders and borrowers. Generally these institutions serve particular groups of individuals or have special purposes. They include banks or other companies primarily concerned with savings, mortgage credit, agricultural credit, consumer credit, securities, and life insurance.

Mutual savings banks are organized to provide for the safekeeping of small amounts of funds. They accept time deposits primarily, but in recent years a few savings banks have begun to permit accounts similar to checking deposits. Unlike demand deposits that are subject to withdrawal by check at any time the depositor wishes, time deposits are covered by rules under which banks may require at least thirty days' notice before funds may be withdrawn. This regulation, however, is rarely enforced. Depositors are paid interest on their savings, the rate depending upon prevailing market conditions. Savings banks use their deposit funds to purchase conservative securities and to extend mortgage loans. Ordinarily they are set up as mutual institutions, being owned by their depositors. Although commercial banks are primarily concerned with demand deposit accounts, many of them have savings departments also.

Savings and loan associations may be mutually owned or stock companies and may be chartered either by the federal or the state government. On the one hand, they provide a place for the deposit of savings on which interest is paid; on the other hand, a source of mortgage money for the purchase or building of homes. Deposits to $40,000 in any account are insured by the Federal Savings and Loan Insurance Corporation (FSLIC).

A large part of credit available to farmers is supervised by the Farm Credit Administration. It extends long-term mortgage credit through twelve Federal Land Banks and short-term loans through twelve Federal Intermediate Credit Banks. Other institutions provide loans for the production and marketing of agricultural commodities.

Consumer credit, most of which is for installment buying, is extended not only by the retailers themselves and by personal loan departments of commercial banks but also by specialized organizations. These include credit unions, which are set up as cooperatives, sales finance companies, personal finance companies, and pawn-brokers.

Investment banks are underwriters that float large stock and bond issues for corporations. They buy securities from the issuers and attempt to sell them at a profit to other institutions and to the public.

Life insurance companies are giant financial middlemen. A large part of the premiums paid by policyholders constitutes savings. These funds are used by the companies to extend loans of many kinds to business and to purchase government bonds. Trust companies act as fiduciaries for persons unwilling or unable to perform the services for themselves and for corporations that require a public inter-mediary. In these cases, funds often become available for the extension of credit.

Chapter 6
INCOME AND OUTPUT

The income and output of the economy are determined by spending decisions of households, business, and government. The volume of output varies from year to year, and economists have tried to explain the nature and causes of these fluctuations.

DETERMINATION OF INCOME

The theory of income determination, postulated by John M. Keynes, one of the most influential modern economists, has been used as a basic tool in formulating economic policy. His thinking received special attention because it could be better applied to the problems of the depression years than could the older, extant theories. The theory, vastly modified and amplified since Keynes first set it forth in 1936 in *The General Theory of Employment, Interest, and Money,* involves relationships of income, consumption, saving, investment, and employment. The underlying ideas are that national income is generated by expenditures of households for consumption, business firms for investment, and government for goods and services and that the total or aggregate amount of this spending is not necessarily large enough to assure a volume of output sufficiently high to provide full employment. It thus becomes the task of the government to raise the level of expenditure.

The Consumption Function. Household expenditures for consumption constitute about two-thirds of the gross national product of the United States. The volume of consumption depends on a number of factors, the most important of which is disposable personal income. The relationship between consumption expenditure (or personal outlay) and disposable personal income (or national income) is called the consumption function. The sum of household consumption functions gives the consumption function of the economy. Generally, several types of aggregate consumption functions, each with its own peculiarities, are analyzed. These depend upon data showing the ratio of consumption to income of all households at any moment in time (cross-section data), of a single household over a period of time, or of all households over a period of time.

The average propensity to consume (APC) measures the proportion of disposable personal income spent on consumption. (The concept of national income rather than disposable personal income sometimes is used in connection with the propensity to consume, but in such cases it should be clear from the discussion.) The marginal propensity to consume (MPC) is the amount of additional consumption that is generated if there is an addition to income. (MPC applies also to a decline in consumption.) The average propensity to save (APS) is the ratio of saving to income and the marginal propensity to save (MPS) is the fraction of additional income saved. Since all disposable income is consumed or saved, it follows that at any income (1) the average propensity to consume plus the average propensity to save are equal to unity and that (2) the marginal propensity to consume plus the marginal propensity to save are equal to unity. These relations may be written:

$$(1)\quad \frac{Consumption\ (C)}{Disposable\ Personal\ Income\ (DPI)} + \frac{Saving\ (S)}{Disposable\ Personal\ Income\ (DPI)} = 1$$

$$(2)\quad \frac{\Delta C}{\Delta DPI} + \frac{\Delta S}{\Delta DPI} = 1$$

For example, if disposable personal income is $3,000, consumption $2,700, and savings $300, then the average propensity to consume is 0.9 and the average propensity to save is 0.1. If income changes to $3,200, consumption to $2,850, and savings to $350, the marginal propensity to consume is $\frac{\$150}{\$200}$ or 0.75 and the marginal propensity to save is $\frac{\$50}{\$200}$ or 0.25.

Although much variation in the consumption expenditure of different households is independent of income, on the average, spending does rise with income, although not as rapidly. At very low personal incomes consumption is greater than income. As income rises it becomes equal to consumption at some point and thereafter exceeds it.

Attempts have been made to determine the basis of consumption expenditure in households at any time. The consumption of a family unit is affected by factors other than income, including total wealth or previously accumulated savings, money borrowed, future income expectations, price change expectations, differences in tastes, durable goods available, and customary behavior. Whether a household at a particular income level has had that income for a period of time or has just risen or fallen to it also affects consumption. The permanent income hypothesis suggests that family consumption during any period is related to the expected income over the lifetime of the income recipients.

The consumption function measured over time is also affected by the changing size and composition of the population, fluctuating prices, unequal distribution of marginal income among households, and even when income remains fixed, changing consumer tastes and habits that result from advertising or other reasons. The function may be applied to the short run and comparisons made between total consumption and total income for a series of consecutive years or to the long run and comparisons made of averages of consumption and income for successive periods of about five to ten years. The short-run consumption function shows a high correlation between consumption and disposable personal income. The APC falls as income rises. The MPC is less than the APC, but for similar incomes the MPC derived from time data is greater than the MPC derived from cross-section data. The long-run consumption function also shows a high correlation between consumption and income. However, in this case the APC does not fall as income rises. APC and MPC are just about equal to each other. The various relationships between consumption and disposable personal income are illustrated graphically in figure 6-1.

The consumption functions show great stability. Although the volume of savings was unusually high during the Second World War, outlays by consumers have remained very close to 94 percent of disposable personal income since 1948. The balance has been saved.

Investment. The volume of investment is less stable than consumption and thus more difficult to predict. Investment spending by business enterprises consists of new factories, machinery, and

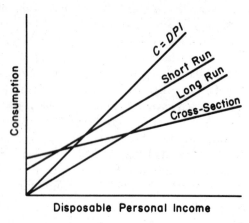

Fig. 6-1. Consumption function

equipment that are added to the stock of capital. Changes in inventories (produced and purchased raw materials, goods in process, and finished products ready to be sold) are also counted. Households acting as consumers do not add to the investment of the economy except when they purchase newly constructed residential dwellings.

The volume of investment depends largely on business firm activities. Decisions to spend for capital formation are based upon expectations of profit and the availability of funds. Although investment in inventory and investment decisions in general may be changed quite rapidly, expenditures for factories and larger pieces of machinery and equipment at any time reflect decisions made in a prior period.

A firm is concerned with the likelihood of greater production and consumption in the economy as well as the potentialities of increased demand for its own product. Judgment regarding the growth prospects of a firm depends upon many factors, including current technology and possible technological advances, prevailing and prospective taxes, and general attitudes of businessmen. The firm must also consider the cash flow of funds, its ability to borrow money from banks, and the desire of the public to supply funds by purchasing stocks and bonds. A firm that is averse to borrowing may use its own accumulated funds, consisting of undistributed profits and depreciation reserves. Of course, it is possible that business savings (accumulated funds of any period) may remain uninvested.

The firm that attempts to maximize profit uses capital to the point where the marginal revenue product of capital (revenue added by the output derived from the employment of the last unit of capital) is equal to the price of capital (interest rate). It should be clear therefore that there are three elements that must be considered in determining the profit to be derived from investment: These are the cost of the investment goods (including maintenance), the rate of interest paid for the funds used to make the purchase (including implicit interest if the firm uses its own funds), and the revenue derived as a result of the investment. If the cost plus the interest is less than the expected revenue (or yield of the capital asset), then the investment is profitable. Put another way, investment is a desirable undertaking for the firm if the expected percentage yield of the asset (rate of return or marginal efficiency of investment) is greater than the rate of interest. Generally, because of the risk factor, the rate of return must be *well above* the rate of interest before an investment is made.

Although investment and saving are undertaken by different people for different motives, it is clear that the basic source of investment funds is linked to the savings of households and business firms. If current saving is inadequate to meet current investment, additional money may come out of previous accumulations of wealth or out of purchasing power created by banks. It is possible also that all savings is not absorbed and that idle funds become available. Prior to Keynes, the generally prevailing notion, which still finds some support among economists, was that the volume of saving and investment are equalized by the interest rate. If investment exceeds saving interest rates tend to go up, thereby lowering the volume of investment and raising the volume of saving until they are equal. The reverse role is played by the interest rate when the volume of saving is larger than the volume of investment.

Keynes used income fluctuations rather than interest rate to equilibrate saving and investment. In his analysis the interest rate is kept fairly constant by bondholders who sell or buy bonds when changes in investment or saving affect the prices of bonds. As will be seen in the following discussion, income changes function to equate saving and investment.

Government Expenditure. Spending by the federal, state, and local government is part of the gross national product. Although most of this spending is undertaken without regard to anticipated rises and falls in tax receipts or national income but is rather a result of the commitment of government to provide certain services to the public, some outlays are geared to move contrary to the national income. Particularly at the federal level, spending for such items as public works, unemployment compensation, and agricultural subsidies is intended to bolster national income when unemployment is high. Local and state governments, on the whole, have tended to continue spending gradually increasing sums of money regardless of general business conditions.

Equilibrium.   It is now in order to inquire how the level of national output is determined and maintained. The sum of expenditures by households for consumption, businesses for investment, and government for goods and services constitutes the gross national product. The money or income associated with the GNP may be considered to be dispersed among or to flow to households, businesses, and government (whose revenues are the taxes received from private persons and businesses). This chain of events is simply the circular flow of output and of income.

The level of output remains at equilibrium (it tends to remain unchanged from one period to the next) if the expenditures in the new period are exactly equal to the expenditures of the preceding period. The details follow. The output of the first period may be divided among the categories of consumption, savings of households and businesses (undistributed profit), and government tax collections. The output of the second period is generated by consumption, business investment, and government spending. Thus for equilibrium of income to be maintained, if it is assumed that there is a relatively stable relationship between consumption and income, the volume of saving plus government taxation must equal business investment plus government expenditure. It is for this reason that, when the government budget is balanced (taxation equals government expenditure), saving must equal investment at equilibrium. Otherwise, if the amount of investment in the second period exceeds saving in the first, then the level of GNP and employment are expanding; whereas if the amount of saving is larger than investment, the level of GNP and employment are contracting. A restatement of the notion of equilibrium is that the flow of income generated by any output must be utilized to purchase that output.

If individual and business savings exceed investment so that the total output of the economy (and therefore employment) tends to decline, government expenditures above the level of taxation (deficit financing) to provide a difference exactly equal to the excess of savings over investment, which does not reduce the volume of consumption or investment, restores equilibrium. The alternative possibility of expanding output and employment—that businessmen will increase investment (and thus raise aggregate demand) when profit expectations are low—is unlikely. The government must therefore assume responsibility to increase expenditure and output.

Modern economic analysis stresses that equilibrium may be achieved at an income below full employment of labor and other resources. Under such circumstances, the GNP is not sufficiently high to absorb all the unemployed. Greater expenditures, however, will lead to increased employment. If business has no incentive to invest more, government deficits alleviate the problem of an economy not operating at full capacity. Naturally such injections of money are sensible only if unemployed labor or capital factors are put to use. Should the resources of the economy be fully utilized, additional government outlays or business investment only serve to bring on inflation because of the higher prices resulting from the competitive demand for the factors of production.

The *deflationary gap* and the *inflationary gap* are terms associated with full employment. The deflationary gap occurs when the economy is in equilibrium below full employment. It measures the additional amount of investment and government spending that is necessary to achieve full employment. The inflationary gap measures the amount of demand in excess of what can be produced when all resources are employed. In this case, prices rise unless consumption, investment, or government spending declines.

The equilibrium of output and expenditure is presented graphically in a simplified form in figure 6-2. If the line *DD* (representing the aggregate demand function) indicates expected expenditures for consumption, investment, and government purchase at different levels of GNP (the upward movement is linked primarily to the fact that consumption varies with output) and $800 billion constitutes the amount of GNP necessary to maintain full employment, unemployment occurs at equilibrium in this case (shown by the intersection of the *DD* and GNP lines). This means that GNP will tend to remain at $600 billion unless additional outlays by the government are made. If the outlays are sufficient to raise aggregate demand to $D'D'$, then full employment is reached. Equilibrium is achieved where the demand line crosses the line that equates GNP and expenditure because any expenditure falling below the latter line will lead to lower GNP in the next period and any expenditure above it will lead to a higher GNP.

The paradox of thrift (i.e., a desire of individuals to save more leads to reduced savings in the economy) may be explained with the help of equilibrium analysis. When individuals wish to save more, they decide at the same time to consume less. But if the resources of the economy are not fully employed and there is no inducement for additional investment, reduced consumption results in a lower GNP. A concomitant of a smaller GNP is reduced savings. Contrariwise, an attempt to lower savings and in effect to raise consumption brings about higher income. The effect in such cases is greater savings. When the economy is operating at full capacity, however, increased efforts to save may result in greater investment and thereby lead to higher GNP. In such cases, the paradox of thrift may not manifest itself. At full capacity, increased efforts to save also reduce inflationary pressures.

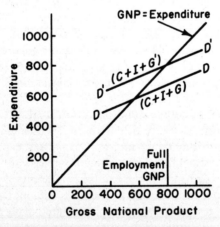

Fig. 6-2. Equilibrium of output and expenditure (billions of dollars)

THE MULTIPLIER AND THE ACCELERATOR

Much of the spending that occurs in the economy is dependent on income, but other factors, as indicated, are also relevant. An *induced* change in the expenditure of consumers, business, or government occurs if the new amount spent is the result of a change in income. If more or less is spent though the income remains constant, the change is termed *autonomous*. This distinction is used in the definition of multiplier and accelerator, concepts which help explain movements in the level of national income.

The Multiplier. The multiplier relates changes in autonomous expenditure to the resultant changes in income. Such spending may involve, among other possibilities, increases in consumption resulting from tax cuts, advertising campaigns, or the marketing of new products; greater private investment because profit expectations rise; or government decisions to undertake public projects. For example, a decision by the federal government to build a road system provides jobs if there is unemployment and increases the income of the economy. But the effect on GNP does not stop there because the recipients of that income spend part of their receipts (depending on the marginal propensity to consume) on consumption. This latter consumption expenditure again adds income to various households and is divided once more into consumption and saving. Thus if autonomous government spending involves $1,000,000 and the MPC is 0.9, then consumption expenditures at the second level are $900,000, at the third level they are $810,000, and they continue diminishing for an indefinite number of steps, gradually approaching zero. It is demonstrable mathematically, however, that the total increase in income would be $10,000,000—the original injection of $1,000,000 and the new consumption spending of $9,000,000. The multiplier measures the number of times that income increases as a result of the original autonomous injection. The mathematical formula is:

$$Multiplier = \frac{1}{1-MPC} = \frac{1}{MPS}$$

If the MPC is 0.6, then the multiplier is 2.5, so that an injection of $1,000 would add $2,500 to GNP. (The multiplier is the reciprocal of the marginal propensity to save.) It should be clear that an autonomous reduction in spending lowers the GNP by an amount greater than the autonomous reduction. The decline also may be measured by the multiplier.

In judging the amount of expenditure necessary to produce a particular increase in income and thus provide a certain amount of employment, the government must make allowances for the multiplier effect. This means that sufficient time must elapse before consumption at the different stages takes place and the full impact is felt.

Of course, changes in expenditure are not always autonomous; often they are based upon income changes. In such cases, the increase or decrease in income is the same as the increase or decrease in expenditure. The multiplier in effect is 1.

The Accelerator. The acceleration principle is used to relate the volume of investment to changes in income. It can be applied to a single firm, industry, or the economy; it demonstrates how the demand by entrepreneurs for capital goods depends upon changes in income. If income is constant, investment is essentially limited to replacing depreciated machinery at a relatively constant rate. A rise in income, however, leads to an increase in demand for the output of the firm. If idle capacity exists or the businessman waits to make sure that the increase in demand is permanent, acceleration does not occur. Assuming that the firm is operating at capacity and the entrepreneur decides to meet the increased consumer demand, existing plant and equipment must be expanded. But under such conditions demand by the firm for investment goods increases more sharply than demand for output. Thus a firm operating at full capacity and without inventory stocks, which is replacing 10 percent of its machinery annually as a result of depreciation, requires twice as many machines (100 percent increase) during a year in which demand for its product rises by only 10 percent. The increase in demand necessitates additional machines to meet production requirements superimposed on the machines being purchased for replacement. For example, if the yearly output of shoes is 100,000 pairs and the number of machines necessary to produce the output is 100 (the ratio thus being 1,000 pairs of shoes to each machine), an increase in demand for shoes by 10,000 pairs requires the firm to have another ten machines. The total for the period therefore increases from the ten ordinarily required for replacement to twenty. In order to maintain the new investment level at twenty per year, demand for the output of the firm must continue to rise annually at the rate of 10 percent. If the increase is less than that or if the demand becomes stable, the volume of investment decreases with a consequent downward impact on GNP. Furthermore, a decline in demand for the product could reduce investment to zero if idle capacity makes it unnecessary to replace depreciated equipment.

The ratio of additional investment to change in income is called the accelerator coefficient. In the example above, if each pair of shoes increases the income of the firm by $10 and each machine costs $100,000, the increase in income of $100,000 requires an investment outlay of $1,000,000. The accelerator coefficient is 10.

The acceleration principle helps to explain changes in the volume of investment. It is a useful tool in business cycle analysis, particularly when it is used to follow the continuing process of economic expansion that occurs after an initial injection of autonomous spending and the associated multiplier effect. It can be seen that an increase in consumption stimulates more investment through the acceleration effect and thus accelerator and multiplier interact.

BUSINESS CYCLES

Fluctuations in general economic activity, which are most clearly indicated by changes in income and employment, are usually called business cycles. These movements began in the nineteenth century with the development of industrial economies in all the countries that comprise Western civilization, although financial crises and other fluctuations in business had been seen earlier. Production, consumption, and employment rise for a time (expansion) and reach a peak, then, following a crisis, they decline (contraction). At some point the fall reaches a low point or trough and a revival or rise begins. The cycle is complete and will begin again. The expansion phase is called prosperity, the contraction phase depression. Long and severe depressions occurred in the United States in 1837–1843, 1873–1878, 1882–1885, and 1929–1933; there have also been short and severe depressions in 1857–1858, 1907–1908, 1920–1921, and 1937–1938.

Generally, analysis of economic data for business cycle purposes requires the elimination of seasonal influences and of long-term or secular trends. Irregular or random impacts on business, such as major strikes, floods, and earthquakes, also need to be considered and make adjustments in the data necessary. Seasonal influences are removed by using annual data, and secular influences may be reduced by employing per capita figures. It then becomes evident that fluctuations have occurred regularly, although the amplitude or percentage of change in economic activity within cycles has varied substantially. While the average length of the cycle during the past 150 years has been somewhat over eight years, each of these longer or major cycles is marked by several shorter or minor ones that extend about three years. Some economic series, particularly in construction, have longer cyclical periods. Since the Second World War there has been a persistent and upward movement in economic activity. Only a few minor cycles have occurred, a very unusual situation.

Characteristics. The individual economic series are related to business conditions, although changes in some series may come before, and in others lag behind, the general pattern. Series may be divided into three categories. Leading series, which move up and down before general business activity does, include building construction contracts, new orders for durable goods, business failures, certain sensitive wholesale prices, new business incorporations, length of the manufacturing workweek, and stock prices. Coincident series, which make their turns in economic activity at about the same time that business in general does, include gross national product, industrial production, employment, unemployment, corporate profits, freight car loadings, and wholesale prices. These series therefore tend to represent the core of the business cycle. Lagging series, which fall behind the pattern of economic activity, include retail sales, personal income, consumer installment debt, bank interest rates on business loans, and inventories of manufacturers.

Economic series vary in amplitude. Production of durable goods, such as steel and other metals, machinery, and equipment, shows great cyclical fluctuations. Business firm expenditures for these goods and consumer expenditures for durable goods, such as automobiles, household appliances, and furniture, also fluctuate widely. Great changes take place in employment, unemployment, business profits, business inventories, interest rates, and taxes collected by the federal government in the course run by business cycles. Economic series that fluctuate very little in relation to general business conditions include consumer spending for services and nondurable goods, purchases of goods and services by government (particularly states and municipalities), wage rates, and price level. Since the end of the Second World War these series have moved upward at a slow rate, even during periods of recession.

Theories. Most of the fluctuation that occurs in minor cycles may be explained by changes in inventory. Although additions and subtractions from stock ordinarily constitute much less than 1 percent of total output, increases in inventory rise to 3 percent or more near the peak and decline by 3 percent near the trough. This behavior, which involves a difference in output of 6 percent or more over the course of a cycle, generally represents a substantial fraction of the change in output during minor cycles.

Theories of major business cycles may be divided into six categories as follows: (1) Theories that emphasize psychological factors. Optimistic or pessimistic attitudes of businessmen and consumers determine the state of the economy. Confidence or anticipation that conditions will improve leads to increases in investment and consumption, but feelings that conditions will deteriorate affect expenditures adversely. Turning points occur when it becomes evident to some that expectations will fail to materialize. Arthur C. Pigou was a leading exponent of these theories. (2) Theories that contend cycles result from underconsumption. This situation arises either because sufficient purchasing power is not available to the public, particularly those with lower incomes, to purchase the total output or because people save too much. This leads to business failures and unemployment. As purchasing power is built up and stocks of goods decline, new pressures to increase output are created. John A. Hobson has written on underconsumption. (3) Theories that maintain cycles occur because of overinvestment. Investment opportunities resulting from innovations are responsible for expansion. Such impact is especially important when several important inventions are made at the same time. As output piles up, there may be a decline in investment leading to a downturn and contraction. Then the cycle is repeated. Joseph A. Schumpeter and Wesley C. Mitchell have made important contributions to these theories. (4) Monetary theories of business cycles that emphasize that expansion in economic activity stems from increases in the money supply and availability of credit. For example, the banking system is in a position to encourage upswings until excess reserves are eliminated. Declines in borrowing and spending induce a contraction. But the deposit of inactive funds in the banks increases reserves and allows the cycle to change direction again. Ralph G. Hawtrey has been a leading exponent of this school. (5) Theories that place emphasis on external or exogenous factors as the cause of business cycles in contrast to the internal or endogenous factors considered in the four groups of theories above. Endogenous causes arise out of changes in or operations of the economic system. External factors, such as climatic changes, wars, political upheavals, changes in population growth, and migration, are considered to be traditionally beyond the scope of economics. Some economists consider these occurrences sufficient to generate cyclical movement. William S. Jevons and Henry L. Moore have contributed to these theories. (6) Theories that draw upon elements from several others(i.e., eclectic or synthesizing) are commonly used today to explain the behavior of cycles. The theory of national income determination described in the first section of this chapter, including the interactions of the multiplier and accelerator, provides one of the more general explanations of the business cycle. Autonomous expenditures produce the multiplier effect that may lead to acceleration of investment. It is thought that such expenditures generate fluctuations in economic activity. Particular emphasis is usually placed on changes in the volume of investment, and many economists give attention to technological advances, innovations, and inventions. Furthermore, different factors and elements used to explain cycles may be given different weights, depending on the business cycle under consideration.

Even though the causes of business cycles are uncertain, it is evident that various factors taken together tend to keep expansions and contractions moving in the same direction. These include psychological factors, the acceleration principle, and expansion of bank credit. There are, however, other factors that serve to slow down and arrest expansions and contractions because they retard movements of general activity. These include the effect of built-in or automatic stabilizers—such as the progressive income tax, social security taxes, and unemployment compensation payments—on spending by individuals and business and the relative stability of consumption expenditures and disposable personal income. Turning points are brought on by changes in such factors as prices, inventories, costs, plant capacity, bank reserves, consumer durables, business expectations, and the impact of acceleration.

Forecasting.   Because businessmen and government officials have a vital interest in the progression of the business cycle, economists are asked to work out ways and means to forecast its movements. Entrepreneurs need estimates of likely changes in the volume and components of total economic activity to determine the impact of these movements on their own businesses and to be in a better position to make decisions regarding construction of new facilities, purchase of new machinery and equipment, and accumulation of inventories. Such estimates provide the firm with the general setting. Government officials require sound estimates of future outlays of consumers for goods and services, and businesses for investment, as well as their own probable expenditures, in order to have some knowledge of aggregate demand. In this way, it can be determined whether additional government expenditures are necessary to provide the level of employment considered desirable under the policies in effect at that time. Presently, the government strives to keep the rate of unemployment just high enough to maintain a relatively stable price level.

It is readily apparent that forecasting tends to be more reliable when undertaken for a near rather than a distant period. Small but unanticipated departures from expectations in the near future may have profound effects on long-range predictions.

Four methods of economic forecasting have been used. The effectiveness of each varies, depending upon economic circumstances. (1) Inertia predictions are those made under the assumption that the economy is moving along in a fairly regular and consistent pattern. Trends are watched and estimates are geared to extrapolate changes at rates currently in effect. For example, if consumption expenditures have been increasing at a rate of 2 percent every half year, the forecast may be that consumption will increase 2 percent in the next six months. Forecasts of this type are less likely to be accurate when business activity changes its direction. (2) Barometric predictions are based upon the use of certain economic series as indicators. Various series of economic activity, some of which have been studied for more than a century, have been found to move up or down before the rest of the economy moves. These leading series include new business incorporations, business failures, stock prices, building construction contracts, new orders for durable goods, and length of the manufacturing workweek. Nevertheless, no series has invariably moved ahead of general business conditions, nor has the entire group in combination done so. Furthermore, barometric prediction at best is useful only in anticipating turning points, not in determining the amplitude of business fluctuations. (3) Analytical predictions are related to the gross national product and deal with the components of GNP. The major subdivisions of consumption, investment, and government expenditure are broken down further and are examined not only in terms of trends in the immediately preceding periods but also in terms of dependent relations with other sectors in the economy. Thus consumer spending in one period depends on disposable personal income in the preceding period. Surveys of expected outlays also are made. For example, the U.S. Department of Commerce and the Securities and Exchange Commission check business firms to gain information on expected investment spending; Dun and Bradstreet and *Fortune* survey expected inventory changes; and the Survey Research Center of the University of Michigan questions consumers about their intended spending. Proposed governmental budgets are examined. Account is taken of the availability of the factors of production and the likelihood of price increases. Totals of subdivisions are then checked for internal consistency. The final result is an estimate of gross national product of some future period. (4) Econometric predictions depend on a more complicated and precise form of analytical model building. Mathematical relationships are established between variables on the basis of analysis and study of relevant statistical records. Equations are derived and used to estimate some economic variables when others are known.

Fluctuations in economic activity seem likely to continue in the future. Nevertheless, it is safe to conclude that a depression of the magnitude experienced in the early 1930s will not recur because the government can act in many ways to forestall it.

Chapter 7
ECONOMIC GROWTH

The subject of economic growth and development has become an increasingly important area of interest. Growth and development are concepts that deal with changes in the real per capita income or consumption of a country. They may be studied in relation to economies that are already developed or advanced as well as those that are underdeveloped or economically backward. Economists use standard techniques to analyze the growth processes of developed economies (i.e., those using the most modern methods of production and possessing well-established economic institutions). But since conscious efforts to bring about the development of underdeveloped economies require many systematic alterations in culture, substantial contributions are necessary from social scientists as well as from engineers.

Although economic growth and development are terms that are generally interchangeable, and they will be used interchangeably throughout the text, a distinction is sometimes made between them. Thus growth is associated with increases in population and the quantity of goods produced, and development with improvements in the methods and techniques of production (which implies that the productivity of labor must be rising). Growth and development, as individually defined, ordinarily take place at the same time, but they need not. For example, primitive societies may expand without developing, while countries with stationary populations may develop without growing.

Income per person varies markedly among the countries of the world. For comparative purposes, nations may be classified according to gross national product per capita to indicate the level of affluence or poverty. (Statistics of output are more readily available than those of income.) At the present time high development may be associated with a GNP per capita of $2,000 a year or more; intermediate development with a GNP per capita between $1,000 and $1,999; and underdevelopment with a GNP per capita of less than $1,000. Per capita output figures of leading countries are given in table 7-1.

TABLE 7-1

GNP PER CAPITA IN SELECTED COUNTRIES, 1971
(IN U.S. DOLLARS)

United States	5,160	Rumania	740
Sweden	4,240	Yugoslavia	730
Canada	4,140	Mexico	700
Kuwait	3,860	Saudi Arabia	540
Switzerland	3,640	Cuba	510
France	3,360	Albania	480
Germany (West)	3,210	Brazil	460
Australia	2,870	Iran	450
New Zealand	2,470	Taiwan	430
United Kingdom	2,430	Malaysia	400
Israel	2,190	Algeria	360
Germany (East)	2,190	Turkey	340
Japan	2,130	Rhodesia	320
Czechoslavakia	2,120	South Korea	290
Italy	1,860	Ghana	250
Puerto Rico	1,830	Philippines	240
Ireland	1,510	Egypt	220
Libya	1,450	Thailand	210
U.S.S.R.	1,400	China	160
Poland	1,350	Nigeria	140
Greece	1,250	Pakistan	130
Argentina	1,230	Haiti	120
Hungary	1,200	India	110
Spain	1,100	Malawi	90
Venezuela	1,060	Indonesia	80
Hong Kong	900	Burma	80
Bulgaria	820	Ethopia	80
South Africa	810	Burundi	60

Source: International Bank for Reconstruction and Development, *World Bank Atlas: Population, Per Capita Product and Growth Rates,* 1973, p. 5. The gross national product is based on market prices; multiyear weighted exchange rates are used for converting domestic currencies into U.S. dollars.

FACTORS OF GROWTH

A country that attempts to grow does not need to direct the primary effects of its economy toward urbanization and industrialization. In less advanced economic systems, where farm production comprises the bulk of the output, investment expenditures might be concentrated on agriculture. Advancement in an agricultural economy is the degree to which mechanization takes place and new and more equipment is added.

Measurement. The most meaningful indicators of economic growth and progress currently used are based upon the per capita output of consumer goods and services in the economy. Thus, they arbitrarily exclude a number of noneconomic factors, such as happiness, cultural progress, aesthetic considerations, and the spiritual values of the people. (Nor do such measurements indicate the existence of depressed areas or of underprivileged segments of the population.) The measurement of development in terms of material well-being means that the most important specific element in the process of growth is the volume of investments in the economy, a conclusion derived from national income analysis. The growth of the economy therefore may be related to such factors as inducement to invest, propensity to save, growth of population, availability of physical resources, and advances in technology.

Since growth is compounded or cumulative, small differences in the rate of economic expansion of two countries starting at the same level of output result in wide divergences in the GNP after several score years. Though the redistribution of income may raise the standard of living of a nation, this process has limited scope unless the economy is also expanding. Small increases in growth rate ordinarily provide a much more feasible way of improving standards than does income redistribution in a stationary economy. Growth is associated primarily with expansion in productive capacity and supply rather than increases in demand. Changes in the degree to which productive capacity is utilized may bring about increases in output that do not truly measure growth.

Population. A modern growing economy is ordinarily marked by an increasing population and invariably by technological advance and expansion in the stock of capital. Population changes in any country depend on the relation of birth and deaths (as well as on immigration and emigration). The rate of population growth among the countries of the world varies from those in which almost stationary conditions prevail to those in which the increase is more than 3 percent per year. As a rule, the rate is lower in the more advanced countries. In growing economies, increases in population need not have an adverse effect on per capita output because they provide a growing market for business and encourage expansion of facilities and capacity. Furthermore, with business expansion there is a need for more labor to match the greater volume of capital if a decline in the productivity of capital is to be prevented. In less developed countries, however, rising population may make growth more difficult because more food is required and also because unemployment, usually already in evidence, may be intensified (and absorption made more difficult).

Capital. Growth of capital depends upon the volume of personal saving, business saving, and government saving. (A country may also increase its capital by using the savings of another country.) The element of saving in any period indicates abstention from consumption, or the portion of output that is not consumer goods or services. The government provides most of the saving in communist countries; democratic nations depend mainly on the saving of both government and private business for their increases in capital. The United States presents an exceptional case in that personal saving accounts for a substantial part of capital formation. In growing economies the rate of increase in capital is greater than the rate of increase in the labor force (population). Over the past century the amount of capital per worker in the United States has increased at about 1.5 percent per year.

The increase in capital as a factor in growth may be measured as the ratio of gross capital formation to gross national product or net capital formation to net national product. Although the latter figure is possibly more significant since it deals with the actual changes in the supply of capital over a period of time, it is frequently less meaningful in practice because estimates of the amount of depreciation or capital consumption are not very accurate at present. In more advanced countries, annual gross capital formation varies between about 15 and 30 percent. In less developed countries, the rate lies between 5 and 15 percent so that net capital formation may not be much above zero.

Capital formation includes new physical structures, machinery, and equipment, and increases in inventory. In communist countries all new capital belongs to the government. In noncommunist nations generally about one-third to two-fifths of all new capital is purchased by government. Recently a little more than half of capital formation has been in the form of construction of roads, factories, public buildings, dams, commercial establishments, and houses; a little more than one-third is made up of different kinds of equipment; and about one-tenth constitutes additions to inventories.

Several terms are used to describe the relationship between the supply of labor and the supply of capital. In advanced economies particularly, capital accumulates more rapidly than the labor force expands, so that on the average each employee works with more capital. The process is called *capital deepening*. When, however, the rate of increase in capital corresponds to the rate of increase in labor, the process is termed *capital widening*. *Capital shallowing* generally refers to the spreading of a relatively scarce amount of capital more uniformly over a relatively abundant labor force. The latter two terms apply more to less advanced economies than to more advanced ones.

Output. Economic growth usually involves increasing supplies of labor and capital, each of which is expanding at its own rate. In less advanced countries the potential labor supply generally is sufficiently large to provide all the manpower necessary to employ a rising stock of capital. With no advances in technology the rate of expansion of output tends to be the same as the rate of expansion of capital. In advanced economies, where the supply of labor cannot be increased as readily, especially when conditions of near full employment prevail, the amount of increase in output depends upon how the factors of capital and labor combine in the process of production. Technological change is an element affecting output which must be considered separately—irrespective of modifications in capital and labor supplies.

The relationship of the amount of capital to annual output is called the (average) capital-output ratio. Another concept, that of marginal capital-output ratio (increment in stock of capital during one period to added output in the following period) is often used because statistics of changes in capital are more pertinent in analyzing the problems of planning and more reliable than those of the stock of capital.

A country with a stock of capital valued at $300,000,000 and an annual product of $100,000,000 would have a capital-output ratio of three to one. Assuming that these figures apply to a less developed economy in which the marginal capital-output ratio is also three to one, an increase in capital of $12,000,000 would raise output by $4,000,000, or 4 percent. The 4 percent figure may be used to identify economic growth. Working backwards it is possible to determine the volume of additional capital necessary to obtain any rate of growth. Thus, in order to achieve a rate of growth of 6 percent, or a rise of $6,000,000 in output, capital formation of $18,000,000 (or 18 percent of the volume of output) is required. The rate of growth desired by the economy multiplied by the marginal capital-output ratio yields the rate of investment necessary. These overall relationships between capital and output, however, are only averages. They vary sharply for specific expenditures. For example, increases in the output of agriculture are generally considerably greater for specific amounts of capital outlay than they are in the output of housing or railroad construction.

In advanced or well-developed economies the rate of growth in output does not vary proportionately with the rate of increase in capital because the impact of the changing supply of labor must be considered. The rate of expansion of output is equal to the proportion of total output received by labor, multiplied by the rate of increase in labor supply, added to the proportion of total output received by capital, multiplied by the rate of increase in capital. For example, if three-fourths of GNP is paid to labor and one-fourth is paid to capital, and if labor is growing at the annual rate of 2 percent and capital at the annual rate of 6 percent, then output will increase by 3 percent. (This may be computed as follows: $\frac{3}{4} \times .02 + \frac{1}{4} \times .06 = .03$.) Doubling the rate of capital expansion, however, will not increase output twofold because of the dragging effect of the lower rate of increase in the labor force.

The rate of increase in output is greater than that of labor but smaller than that of capital in the illustration given. The standard of living therefore tends to rise, while the marginal productivity of capital (i.e., the ratio of the added output to the added input of capital) and therefore the rate of interest (i.e., the return to capital) tend to fall. The lower cost of capital relative to wages, however, encourages its use as a substitute for labor. Eventually, under the condition in which a sufficiently low interest rate prevails, saving and investment would decline to the extent that a stationary economy would emerge.

Technology. It is mainly the process of technological advancement that prevents the emergence of a stationary state. Technological change makes it possible to use the same quantity of input factors to increase the volume of output. Marginal productivities of these factors are raised by advances in scientific and technical knowledge, innovations, and inventions. If technological change increases marginal productivity of capital more than that of labor it is called a laborsaving innovation, whereas if marginal productivity of labor rises by a greater amount it is termed a capital-saving innovation. A laborsaving advance acts as if the supply of labor has been increased, so that more capital may be used without lowering its marginal productivity. The effect is that labor's share of national output is reduced. The use of machines to replace bookkeepers is an example of this process. A capital-saving advance, on the other hand, appears to increase the supply of capital, thereby raising the marginal productivity of labor relatively; and the relative share of national product received by capital falls. Sending messages by radio rather than by wire or cable is an example of a capital-saving advance. A neutral innovation leaves unchanged the relative marginal productivities of labor and capital, as well as the relative shares of national output each receives. Although the nature of technological progress over the past century has been such that there has been no substantial change in the relative shares of labor and property incomes, it seems to have been sufficiently laborsaving to prevent both interest rates and profits from falling. The increase in capital therefore has not caused the marginal productivity of capital to decrease (i.e., diminishing marginal returns to capital) as the economy expands.

Aggregate Demand. In less advanced or underdeveloped economies and in communist countries the problem of growth is essentially one of expanding the facilities used for production. Free enterprise and socialistic advanced industrial nations however must also take into account the adequacy of aggregate demand. Economic growth implies that the volume of investment is rising, though not necessarily as a percentage of gross national product. Over a period of time, the percentage of income saved does not necessarily increase even if output rises, since the consumption schedule may shift upward. Investment therefore must keep pace with the increased amount of saving as the economy expands if full employment is to be maintained and capacity is to be enlarged. But the needed increase in investment depends upon the growth of saving. However, if aggregate demand falls below the level of output or if planned investment is less than planned saving, economic growth will cease.

The changing proportions in output of different goods and services of an expanding economy arise from a variety of factors. (1) There is a change in the types of expenditures made by consumers because of different income elasticities of demand for the things they buy. For example, higher income consumers generally reduce the proportional outlay for food but increase that for entertainment or education. (2) New products are placed on the market while others are displaced or otherwise lose their desirability. (3) The more rapidly rising productivity associated with some goods lowers their relative price and increases the quantity demanded. Such goods tend to gain larger portions of the purchasing power in the market. (4) The altered pattern of foreign trade affects the nature of output.

DEVELOPED ECONOMIES

The economic growth of the nations of the Western world during the past two centuries has been without historical parallel. Although there was economic expansion in other periods, such as in the reigns of Emperor Augustus Caesar in Rome and King Louis XIV of France, the best information regarding those eras is that the living standards of the masses rose very slowly. Furthermore, this growth did not last long.

Characteristics. It is generally agreed that the growth of an economy requires certain environmental conditions. These conditions are ordinarily found in countries where the economic system is advanced. The government must be stable, interested in economic progress, and able to enforce law and order, so that productive property and other wealth may be protected and accumulated. It is important that the programs instituted for the purpose of growth should be administered by persons willing and able to carry out necessary policies. Efficient means of transportation, communication, and trade, such as good roads, an adequate telephone system, and sufficient currency, are essential for the expansion of markets. Entrepreneurs and executives able to organize businesses must be available; they should have freedom to move the factors of production and final products about the country without too many restraints. Effective educational and training facilities should be commonplace. Furthermore, the population must have the desire to increase its standard of living, and the labor force must have sufficient incentives to work efficiently; adequate penalties for inefficiency should be imposed. In the absence of these factors growth does not appear feasible. The introduction of foreign investment funds into a country or a rise in the price of export goods tends to produce a temporary increase in growth, but stability and stagnation in the volume of output are likely to follow in a relatively short time.

Problems. In many ways, economic growth in advanced economies presents more complex problems than does growth in underdeveloped countries. Advanced countries, far more than countries in the early stages of development, must be concerned with the search for new techniques as a way to greater growth. Matters related to unemployment, redistribution of wealth and income, and foreign trade balances are more troublesome. Furthermore, the process of growth becomes much more difficult to describe. Changes in gross national product must be evaluated in relation to the depreciation of capital, the quality of goods produced, price movements, population differences, altered distributional patterns of wealth and income, modifications in leisure time, and noneconomic considerations (for example, current psychological, sociological, and religious values).

The economic growth rate may be increased by reducing idle capacity and unemployment. But full utilization of resources is a technique that can be used only once in the process of expansion. The significant ways to achieve growth available to advanced economies are (1) to engage in more public and private technological and management research, (2) to increase the amount of education and training of members of the labor force, and (3) to pursue vigorous monetary policies and use appropriate fiscal policies to encourage capital accumulation at the expense of current consumption and maintain relative price stability. Nevertheless, in practice, some compromises must be made concerning policies set by the government to influence the rate of economic growth, the level of unemployment, the degree of price stability, and the existence of foreign trade deficits.

Growth of the economy emphasizes increases in output and does not automatically preclude the emergence of serious unemployment problems. Almost invariably, the output of a good or service rises as expansion occurs. But unless demand increases more rapidly than the productivity of labor in the industry, employment falls. Thus, since output, demand, and productivity of industries do not expand uniformly, factors and resources are reallocated in the economy. This has happened in the United States. For example, though agricultural output has been increasing, the size of the labor force in that sector has been contracting. In the service sector, however, both the output and the number of employed have been rising. Reallocation may involve a higher rate of structural unemployment. Workers may be technologically displaced in certain industries and not able to use their skills elsewhere. Or they may find employment disappearing in a certain region and lack mobility to find work in another location. There is no clear evidence that these factors have been important in recent years in raising the national rate of unemployment in advanced economies.

The United States. The economic expansion of the United States illustrates changes taking place in an advanced economy. The rate of real growth, measured by the gross national product and corrected for price changes, has been about 3 percent over the past century, although, since the end of the Second World War, it rose and leveled off at about 4 percent. (Growth of production adjusted for population increases—i.e., put on a per capita basis—reduces the figures to 2 and 3 percent, respectively.) Nevertheless, at the present time there is some evidence that the average rate of growth during the past three decades has been lagging behind that of several other advanced countries—West Germany, the Soviet Union, and Japan, for example. The particular rate prevailing in any country must be considered in terms of the factors that stimulate growth and the obstacles that slow it.

UNDERDEVELOPED ECONOMIES

The economic objectives of many underdeveloped countries, to alter their economies with great rapidity in order to achieve outputs comparable to those in more advanced countries, cannot be fulfilled in a short period of time. The process of development is extremely complex and includes many phenomena outside the scope of economics. Social, political, legal, religious, and cultural transformations, along with a change in the economic behavior of the population, are necessary to economic growth. Successful growth in a modern economy requires understanding of money and credit relationships by government officials, development and improvement of educational facilities and training of skilled workers, enforceable standards of health, urbanization, accumulation of investment goods, construction of public roads and other means of transportation, establishment of public assistance schemes, and economically motivated consumers and workers.

Characteristics. The characteristics bearing on economic growth of the less developed countries differ widely. These countries vary with regard to type and abundance of natural resources, amount of accumulated capital, area, number of residents, rate of population growth, and length of experience with an independent government (ranging from a few years to many centuries). Yet these countries are marked by a uniformity of certain other characteristics which leads to the designation of "less developed." A major part of the labor force is engaged in agricultural production, and labor productivity is low. In some cases the marginal product is zero, because the excess of farm labor contributes nothing to total output. Much of the agricultural produce provides food only for those working on the farms and members of their families. Export goods, which are an important part of the total output for commercial markets, are produced in limited quantities. The economy is seriously affected by changes in foreign demand. Government revenues are derived mainly from duties imposed on foreign trade and excises on domestic output. Income taxes, the most likely source of governmental funds to meet the needs of a growing economy, are not emphasized in fiscal programs or are readily evaded. Native entrepreneurial ability is limited and successful business activity is conducted by foreigners. In part, this situation stems from the limited scope and amount of education and training, particularly at higher levels, available to the population. It is also due, in many backward economies, to the fact that even when businesses are owned and operated by citizens, control is kept within the family unit. Occupational and social mobility therefore is relatively uncommon.

Problems. The obstacles to economic development are immense. In many less developed countries, entrenched interests resist change. Monopolistic enterprises do not wish competition. Owners of vast land estates struggle to maintain the status quo to continue to receive a substantial portion of the national income. Military and other leaders desire to maintain power and thus oppose modernization and change. A small middle class, traditionally associated with economic progress, is weak. The prospects for sound economic development therefore are presently limited to a handful of countries that have been able to overcome enough of these difficulties to advance. These countries include some that are imbued with the British tradition of a fine class of civil servants, such as India, Pakistan, Ceylon, and Singapore, and some others whose development has been assisted to some extent by the United States, such as Brazil, Venezuela, and the Philippines. In addition a few countries with extensive petroleum reserves, such as Iran, Saudi Arabia, and Nigeria, have been able to accumulate substantial foreign trade balances. Very few nations outside of these groups are as yet on the road to progress.

In the second half of the twentieth century problems of economic development are high on the agenda when world leaders meet to discuss urgent matters. The intensive rivalry between capitalism and communism to win the ideological allegiance of those nations not yet decided on what path to follow has made the growth issue important. Two-thirds of the people of the world live in underdeveloped countries and not even one-sixth in the highly developed ones. Hungry and poor people of less developed countries recognize the sharp contrast and increasing difference in living standards between themselves and more prosperous and fortunate groups living in more affluent nations and this has intensified the need for universal economic progress. Careful consideration of history, however, belies efforts to associate advanced development with location in a temperate climate, domination of the region by the white race, or a culture geared to the Protestant ethic. It is now assumed that within the proper framework economic development is possible in any country.

Government Policies. Planning in poor countries involves considerable government participation. The kind of production and investment which the government is most clearly justified in undertaking is adding social overhead capital such as roads, sanitation and other health facilities, and irrigation projects. Spending for these purposes is essential for development but cannot be done by private enterprise for profit, particularly in the early stages of growth. Many of these activities give rise to external economies (i.e., the product or benefit gained by society is larger than the product or satisfaction for which a direct charge can be made to the purchaser). For example, when one person in a village is inoculated, the danger of disease to the other persons in the village is reduced. Thus the value to a group of inoculating one of its members is greater than is the value to that member. But the price that individuals are willing to pay for inoculation may not enable private enterprise to recover costs. In many of the less developed economies the government must establish new enterprises and industries because private entrepreneurs are unwilling or unable to do so. Yet it is possible and may be desirable in many of these instances to turn over the operation of the business to private ownership once it has begun to function well so that government capital and labor resources are released for other undertakings. There are other cases in which government participation may expand the scale of production and bring increasing returns; socialization of output may thus be appropriate.

It is also the role of government to determine whether a policy of *balanced growth* involving the expansion of the economy in all sectors should be pursued. Such growth may be useful even if the country is not entirely suited for certain types of production because objectives other than maximum output may be desired. But this goal requires care in timing investment activity. For instance, it would be foolish to build a steel mill if there were no iron ore for processing. In some cases, however, the completion of some projects encourages the construction and the growth of others. Nevertheless, *unbalanced growth* or emphasis on those sectors of production in which the country has the greatest international advantage could lead to a more rapid expansion of output.

Economic progress in less developed countries depends upon the resources available to the economy for formation of capital, the potential labor supply, and the possibilities for improving production techniques. Agricultural yields may often be increased by changing established land patterns, for example, breaking up estates that are too large or combining parcels that are too small. Such action may provide incentives toward higher production. Owners who are confident of reaping the rewards of their work and of property improvements are more likely to contribute to an increase in output. A stronger and more vigorous labor force bolstered by more education and better training is another means of improving production. In addition, the efficient utilization of the labor supply is essential. Underemployment of some persons because there is insufficient productive work to perform and idleness of others in both rural and urban areas because there is no work at all for them are conditions that must be eliminated by appropriate policies. Projects with low marginal capital-output ratios are generally preferred because the scarce capital may be used more effectively and the abundant labor supply more advantageously in increasing output. This means that preferred investments are those which yield high ratios of return.

The difficulty of capital accumulation and investment stems in part from the relatively high level of consumption and the relatively low level of personal saving. This problem ordinarily can be met effectively only by appropriate government fiscal, investment, and monetary policies. Many poor countries have been unable to enact and administer an efficient income tax program. Evasion of payment has been extremely common. Nevertheless, a policy of progressive income taxes must be vigorously pursued to speed capital formation. In addition, the government must try to increase the income of those persons and corporations likely to undertake large investment expenditures.

One of the barriers to economic growth is the vicious circle of poverty. Since the proportion of output which is saved in many underdeveloped countries is very low, only small amounts of investment funds are forthcoming. Furthermore, the saving is in a form that does not lend itself to domestic growth. Precious metals and minerals are accumulated, funds are deposited abroad for safety, and durable goods and land are purchased and held as a hedge against potential inflation. Only a limited fraction of the saving is converted into investment and used for growth.

Although capital from abroad could serve to meet some of the investment requirements of less developed nations, foreigners are often reluctant to provide capital because nationalistic policies tend to discourage foreign supervision and control of enterprises. Moreover, the investors may feel that the risk of expropriation or the failure of business is too great to permit the native population full operating discretion. It is therefore often necessary for a government, rather than private persons, to invest in economic enterprises of less developed nations and for international lending agencies and facilities to be established.

One of the great advantages available to poor countries is that they may imitate many production techniques utilized by advanced economies. They may also call upon foreign experts for advice and assistance in carrying out programs. But it is very important for the less developed nations to strive to achieve the cultural pattern, the political structure, and the economic behavior necessary for growth.

Capital accumulation can be expected at a relatively low cost to the economy because some of the excess labor supply available in agriculture may be utilized for social overhead capital construction, and the profits of some private enterprises in the early stages of development may be readily invested; however, the government must participate directly in the process of creating the necessary financial milieu conducive to growth. Without causing inflation monetary and fiscal policies must stimulate private enterprise and provide sufficient tax revenues for other investment projects to be undertaken. The economic climate must be sufficiently favorable to attract foreign capital needed to finance imports.

Strategy. The strategy of economic development requires the government to emphasize either investment in social overhead capital industries (sometimes called economic infrastructure) or in agriculture, mining, and manufacturing (sometimes called directly productive activities). Social overhead capital includes structures and facilities of public utilities, generally recognized as within the usual scope of government ownership and operation. But it encompasses more than physical overhead capital; it extends to expenditures that make for a more highly qualified labor force. These outlays may be called investment in human capital. An advantage of increased social overhead capital is that the development of manufacturing industries is encouraged by the existence of a good network of transportation, power, and communication facilities and a skilled labor force. Nevertheless, undue expansion of social overhead capital leads to the possibility of excess facilities and a consequent waste of resources. Many economists believe that despite the long period necessary for the completion of infrastructure projects, such construction should not take place until agriculture and manufacturing activities have expanded sufficiently to require more social overhead capital.

Good strategy also requires an appropriate balance between agriculture and manufacturing. An advancing economy almost invariably requires greater agricultural output and technological advance. Higher incomes earned by urban workers increase the demand for food. Moreover, as industrialization advances it draws primarily upon the labor supply of the rural areas and intensifies the pressures for mechanization and other improvements in agriculture to raise productivity. Beyond these considerations, the production of agricultural surpluses for export provides a source of foreign exchange (purchasing power) for the importation of capital goods. In many backward countries the level of agricultural output can be raised substantially by teaching native farmers to use production techniques already employed in more advanced economies. It should be clear that agricultural production of a variety of goods other than food, such as cotton, wool, and tobacco, is necessary for the expansion of the economy.

Tactics also require government decisions to determine priorities in manufacturing. The extent of the domestic market, modified by possibilities of finding foreign outlets, is basic to a determination of desirable economic activities. Smaller countries generally must steer clear of heavy industries. Encouragement should be given to the type of production using relatively much labor and little capital. Furthermore, economic enterprises that stimulate related activities should be encouraged. For example, the construction of a plant to produce shoes may lead to the establishment of a leather industry. Establishing a factory to process leather, on the other hand, is less likely to induce the manufacture of shoes. The government must try to see that imports are reduced and exports are increased. Beneficial international trade requires encouragement of those industries which take advantage of the resources provided by nature and the skills of the labor supply.

Chapter 8
ALTERNATIVE ECONOMIC SYSTEMS

This book is mainly concerned with the description of a capitalistic economy that incorporates the amount of government intervention necessary to regulate monopolies in some sectors and prevent restraint of trade in other sectors. Such a system is called mixed private enterprise or competitive capitalism. But there are very few countries, other than the United States, in this category.

THE MAIN TYPES

In recent years several types of economic systems other than capitalism have developed. These may be classified as fascism, socialism, and communism. Careful analysis, however, reveals that there are many similarities in the economic institutions and operations of all these systems, including capitalism. Also, countries identified by the same economic label may not be alike in many important respects.

Fascism. Over the past half century, fascism has dominated several governments—first in Italy under Benito Mussolini after the First World War and later in Portugal, Germany, Spain, and Argentina, among other countries. Fascism operates in the form of a dictatorship intent upon maintaining its power and emphasizes nationalism at the cost of individualism, civil liberties, democracy, and humanity. The state exercises supremacy over the economy and economic groups, but it does not seek ownership of the land or the means of production. Private enterprise is permitted to exist, but it must ally itself with the government. The state stands ready to intervene in economic activities and direct their course whenever its political interests are involved or private entrepreneurs are not performing to its satisfaction. Generally, the military needs of the government receive the highest priority in production. Disputes between labor and management are subject to arbitration procedures and strikes by workers to improve working conditions are prohibited.

The most thorough development of fascism was reached in Germany (where the system was called national socialism) under the regime of Adolf Hitler. The defeat of the fascist powers in the Second World War led to the end of fascism as an important world movement. However, vestiges of this form of political and economic system have survived, particularly in Spain.

Socialism. Socialism, a somewhat nebulous concept characterized by divergent philosophies, has evolved as a series of movements during the past two centuries. It has assumed different forms as a result of varying historical, political, and economic conditions. There are, however, a number of elements common to all forms of socialist philosophy. These include: (1) Public ownership of basic industries in order to control those goods and services upon which the welfare of the community depends. Such government proprietorship is compatible with private ownership in agriculture, relatively small industrial establishments, and retail trade. The degree of public control depends upon the economic structure and the state of development of the country. (2) Governmental planning of production to assure full employment and rising output. Some capitalist characteristics, such as the concentration of economic power in the hands of a relatively few private entrepreneurs and the profit motive as the driving force of industry, become unacceptable. Industrial growth is not an end in itself but a means to increase the welfare and happiness of society. (3) Fair distribution of income and property to provide economic security and a rising standard of living. Shifts in the ownership of property for these purposes are in order. (4) Political and economic democracy is usually a feature of socialism. Extension and strengthening consumer organizations and trade unions and forging close links between labor and management are encouraged. Democratic institutions in all countries and voluntary cooperation among nations are ordinarily considered necessary to assure world peace.

Despite many identical underlying principles, socialist thinking may be associated with several different schools. (1) Utopian socialism constituted the first widely recognized body of socialist thought. It had its adherents in the first half of the 1800s, but thereafter its influence waned. Utopian socialism did not comprehend the workings of economic forces. It visualized a new economic society based on moral principles, reason, and utopian ideals and comprising communities of relatively small groups. Experiments to implement these goals generally failed. (2) Christian socialism was popular in the middle of the nineteenth century. It stressed the establishment of producer cooperatives and cooperative workshops to alleviate the terrible conditions in the factories. Often, however, this movement is associated with social reform rather than with socialism. (3) Marxian socialism provides an economic interpretation of history. It stemmed from the *Communist Manifesto* of 1848, which was somewhat expanded and modified later. Marxian socialism stresses that industrial progress concentrates wealth into fewer hands, brings about the elimination of the middle class, and leads to the exploitation of workers by the capitalist class. Periodic depressions and chronic unemployment provide the incentive for the class struggle which eventuates in the overthrow of capitalism and the establishment of socialism. (4) Fabian socialism, which arose in Great Britain in the 1880s, was based on the belief that socialism is necessary to improve the welfare of the general public and reduce the adverse effects of monopolistic elements in the economy. These objectives were to be achieved through the operation of political democracy, a gradual increase in public ownership of the means of production, and an increase in trade unions and consumer cooperatives. Heavy stress was placed on the usefulness of political activity to gain desirable goals. (5) Revisionist socialism was conceived near the end of the nineteenth century. It modified some Marxian doctrines, and in many ways was similar to Fabian socialism. Revisionism propounded the idea that prospects for the success of socialism are greater if working-class conditions improve gradually rather than as a result of abrupt or violent change. Noneconomic forces were acknowledged as influencing the course of history. (6) Guild socialism had its supporters during the 1920s and 1930s. It postulated that the needs of individual workers in an industrial society could be met only if guilds, made up of all those employed in any industry, controlled the operations of the industry. An industrial design of this type would enable employees to develop their full potential. Though the state would still own the means of production, its domination of enterprise would be reduced.

Communism. The economic system of communism is based in part on the socialistic ideas suggested by Karl Marx, but many others, particularly Nikolai Lenin (1870–1924), have contributed to its practical implementation. The main goal of communism is to satisfy the material and cultural requirements of society rather than to achieve the maximization of profit. Workers are paid according to their needs rather than amount produced or type of work done. Productive resources are publicly owned and output is based on planned goals, not on prices determined by demand and supply.

Under communism the political system is intertwined with the economic system. The notion advocated by some early proponents of communism that workers should control the government and dictate policy has been sidetracked for a dictatorship that is not representative of the people. Democracy to the communists means equality of opportunity, distribution of income according to need, and economic security rather than personal and political liberty.

SOME IMPORTANT ALTERNATIVES

The ability of U.S. entrepreneurs to channel savings into investment and to limit the amount of resources used for consumption goods industries, with little government help, has stemmed from the prevailing relatively high standard of living, the desire of businessmen to innovate and to become wealthy, the ratio of population (low) to other resources (high), and the lack of government and public concern with the need to stimulate the growth of the economy. For all these reasons growth and development in the United States were spontaneous, and for a long time no economic regulation was necessary. Currently, however, the United States system of competitive capitalism is not used as a guide by any underdeveloped nation trying to achieve rapid economic growth. Indeed, very few countries have the means and resources to operate under a system of competitive capitalism.

Government intervention in economic affairs is common throughout the world and almost invariably follows socialist or communist philosophy. Among the more advanced economies intervention is exemplified by Great Britain, where attempts are made to bring about expansion in both the public and private sectors through relatively limited government participation and regulation, and by the Soviet Union, where nationalization of industry and planning of output are almost complete. All the underdeveloped countries face great difficulties in achieving growth; and India and China, which to a large extent follow the economic patterns of Great Britain and the Soviet Union, respectively, exemplify alternative ways of economic expansion.

British Socialism. Most governments of western Europe, including Great Britain, operate under economic systems with many of the characteristics of socialism. Generally, regardless of the political party in power, whether socialist, labor, liberal, or conservative, extensive government participation in economic affairs is recognized to be desirable and is practiced.

Great Britain, with an area somewhat smaller than the state of Oregon, has a population of about 55,000,000. Socialism has evolved slowly in this nation.

At the turn of the twentieth century, the Fabian socialists, together with many trade unionists and others seeking reform, organized the Labour party in Great Britain. During the next two decades the Labour party gradually gained strength in Parliament. Indeed, for relatively short periods at the beginning and at the end of the 1920s, it had a sufficient number of parliamentary seats to form a government in cooperation with the Liberal party. It was not until 1945, however, that the British electorate gave the Labour party a mandate to inaugurate major economic changes in the country. For the first time, a majority of the voters of Great Britain had approved a socialist government.

Major programs of nationalization were undertaken leading to governmental ownership of about 20 percent of British industrial assets. The government took over the Bank of England; the electric, gas, telephone, telegraph, and coal industries; air transportation; and the inland transportation facilities comprising railroads, canals, and trucking. Just compensation was paid to stockholders; their certificates of ownership were replaced with bonds paying fixed yields. The iron and steel industries were also nationalized by the Labour party; they were returned to private ownership after the Conservative party resumed control in 1951 but renationalized by the Labour government in 1967. Wages and working conditions continued to be set by collective bargaining. Furthermore, the nationalized industries, on the whole, remained autonomous and devoted to the goals of profit making and minimizing costs. Although there is much more planning in Great Britain than in the United States, both economies are guided by the pricing mechanism rather than the predetermined goals of physical output that mark the Soviet Union economy.

The Labour party instituted an extensive and costly program of socialized medicine providing, with minor exceptions, free medical services for the entire population. Widespread improvements have been made in housing accommodations, unemployment insurance provisions, relief payments, and employment exchange facilities. All the major British political parties agree on the desirability of maintaining the various programs now in effect. But there is no strong sentiment in any group for substantial further nationalization.

The main emphasis of socialism in Great Britain today, as expressed through the Labour party, is no longer on planning or nationalization. It is rather oriented toward a redistribution of income and wealth to bring about greater equality. Progressive taxation and the provision of extensive social services have tended to increase the degree of equality. Yet inequality in wealth, which is much greater in Great Britain than in the United States, has not been declining when considered in terms of the assets of family units rather than individuals.

Soviet Communism. The background of the economic policies of the Soviet Union is found in the writings of Karl Marx (1818–1883), particularly the *Communist Manifesto* written jointly with Friedrich Engels (1820–1895) in 1848 and the subsequent three volumes of *Das Kapital* (Engels put together the third volume from Marx's notes). These works, however, are more of an analysis and critique of capitalism, emphasizing the "inevitability" of its destruction, than a portrait of socialism in operation. Soviet leaders have had to work out actual policies and plans of action of Soviet communism.

The Soviet Union is the largest country in the world. It has a sixth of the land area of the world and ranks third in population—about a quarter of a billion people. The Russian Revolution started in October 1917, shortly before the end of the First World War, when the Bolsheviks, or Communists, seized power from the more moderate revolutionists who a few months before had overthrown the czar. The Communist party set out to establish a socialist state. Landed estates were divided among the peasants who had been cultivating them, and large factories, transportation systems, and banks were nationalized. The state attempted to direct and control the economy by appropriating raw materials and intermediate goods from farms, mines, and factories for assignment to other producers and by rationing consumer goods. But poor and inexperienced management as well as strong opposition by those whose output was being requisitioned led to rapid inflation and economic confusion. As output declined in many sectors and barter replaced money transactions, the Soviet Union in 1921 instituted a New Economic Policy (NEP) that permitted small-scale enterprise, retail trade, and farming to operate under private ownership. During the next six years only large-scale industry and foreign trade were under the complete control of the government. As the economy gradually regained some of its vitality, private ownership of the means of production other than agriculture was eliminated.

In 1928, when Stalin had achieved complete political control of the country, the first of a series of comprehensive five-year plans was introduced. Only the nationalization or collectivization of farms remained as an obstacle to the complete achievement of central economic planning. The process of collectivizing the farms was begun in 1927. Though the strong resistance of the peasants necessitated severe action by the government, the process was effectively accomplished by the early 1930s. Collective farms were essential for the success of planning, because the government needed control of agricultural output to feed city factory workers and their families and to allocate raw materials necessary for meeting the goals set for industry. Furthermore, large-scale farming seemed more likely to achieve higher productivity. Nevertheless the problems concerning adequate agricultural output have remained among the most vexing facing the Soviet planners. Farm workers as a group have refused to look with favor on the process of collectivization.

In the United States each person is permitted to use his wealth and income to produce and consume as he wishes, subject only to the existing legal framework. The Soviet Union has adopted a different approach. The Soviet system is marked not only by a considerable centralization of political power but by a high degree of economic planning. Thus the sovereignty of the consumer and the independence of the producer are not given much weight. Although the process of planning which was introduced in 1928 has been associated with many difficulties and errors over the course of the years, there is now a coherent and relatively effective system in operation. The political leaders of the nation completely dominate the economy. The objectives of the economic system of the Soviet Union are in a large measure similar to those of the United States—a higher standard of living, economic security, better health, more leisure time, and strong national defense. The attainment of these goals depends on full utilization of resources and expansion of the capacity of the economy to produce goods and services. Private property is limited almost entirely to consumer goods. Central planning provides the Soviet Union with the means by which it is able to enforce higher rates of saving than would otherwise be acceptable to individuals. The public is forced to consume less and thus a higher level of investment is effected.

The overall plan of the economy in terms of political and economic objectives is set by the political authorities—the Presidium and the Central Committee of the Communist party. More precise details to implement output goals are determined by the Gosplan, or State Planning Commission, which depends upon the Central Statistical Administration for information on the available resources or inputs and techniques of production. Though the plan generally is prepared for a five-year period, alterations in goals are made yearly or even monthly as production progresses and reports come in revealing unforeseen difficulties in some sectors and unexpected progress in others. In recent years longer planning periods have been in effect.

The Gosplan pays particular attention to about 1,500 commodities. Resources available and needed are broken down geographically in each case. As a result, a picture of shortages and surpluses in the country becomes clear and plans can be adjusted as required. In addition, special attention is given to approximately fifty basic industries or commodities that underlie the entire plan. The production of other commodities is worked out around these.

A tentative plan is sent to regional and local administrators, who may raise questions regarding the output expected of them or the inadequacy of inputs or equipment and machinery that have been assigned to them. After negotiations that may or may not lead to changes, the Gosplan secures the approval of the political authorities and sends the completed plans back to the localities to be carried out. Execution of plans is under the supervision of Communist party officials, the Gosplan, and the Gosbank (the state banking system).

Able managers are essential in the system and incentives in the form of relatively high pay are offered to bring forth their best efforts. In addition, managers who exceed their quotas are given special benefits, such as automobiles, superior housing accommodations, and vacation expenses. Special bonuses may be given. However, those who fail may be demoted and severely reprimanded. It is the risk of failure that has reduced the incentive to innovate in the Soviet

Union. Ownership of property is not an important source of income, but salaries extend over a range comparable to that in the United States.

Wages provide the main incentive for workers in the Soviet Union, although leaders give much attention to patriotic appeals. The majority of workers are paid on the basis of piecework (in the United States a minority are). Wage differentials between the low and the highly paid workers appear to be much greater in the Soviet Union than in the United States. Generally workers have freedom to move from one job to another to the extent that their financial resources permit; they are also limited by prior commitments given to the government in exchange for special education or training. Although most members of the labor force belong to trade unions, the functions of these organizations do not include collective bargaining. Unions in the Soviet Union help carry out the goals of the economic plan; they assist in the adjustment of plant grievances and are largely responsible for the administration of social security programs.

The economic plan is developed in terms of physical quantities of input and output, but it is supervised by the Gosbank on the basis of a set of money values, supplied by the Gosplan, which accompanies the physical units of input and output. The Gosbank provides managers with money needed to acquire inputs or resources specified in the plan; all receipts from sales of output must be deposited in the Gosbank. Verification of the amount of input used and the amount produced by each factory or establishment is thus available. All money transactions other than retail purchases and wage payments are made by check. The Gosbank itself is supervised by the State Control. Commission and officials of the Communist party.

The main sources of revenue for the operation of the government, including social services, are the turnover tax (sales tax) and the profits derived from state enterprises. The personal income tax is relatively small and is in the process of being even further reduced. Turnover taxes on consumer goods, which may change from time to time and vary over an extremely wide range, are adjusted to discourage consumer purchases when supply is low relative to demand and encourage them when supply is large relative to demand. Prices of goods need not cover costs of production but may be set to subsidize low income recipients; this arrangement is used in the case of housing.

The gradual rise in the standard of living has increased the ability of Soviet consumers to purchase goods selectively and has forced the authorities to change prices more frequently (as an alternative to changing the turnover tax) in order to reduce accumulated stocks of some items. In a few cases, factory output of consumer goods is now based on demand registered by consumers at retail stores. Voluntary saving is rather low in the Soviet Union, and inflationary pressures resulting from consumer demand have been a persistent problem. In 1957 the government attempted to reduce purchasing power and repudiated much of the public debt held in the form of bonds which workers had been compelled to buy in the preceding years.

Although Soviet industrial output has shown unusually rapid expansion since 1950, agricultural progress has been slower. Productivity in this area is generally lower than in other advanced economies. Many vast state farms operated by hired farm labor are in existence, but much of the agricultural output is produced on collective farms. There are many forms of collectives, ranging from those where all property and labor are shared to those where only major pieces of equipment are used in common. In many instances, families are allotted small plots of land to use as they wish. Farmers have apparently been reluctant to do their best work on collective farms.

Although personal freedom has increased in the Soviet Union in recent years, the economy is still planned and operated by the state. A small group of men control the government and make the decisions guiding the economy. It should be clear that the concept of democracy in the Soviet Union refers primarily to economic equality and security whereas in the United States it is associated with personal and political freedoms and only secondarily with freedom from want. The key to Soviet economic activity has been the deliberate curtailment in the output of consumer goods in order to expand the volume of investment and thus increase the rate of growth. This decision was made without the consumers' consent. But the rapid economic advances of the Soviet Union have also come about because many resources were assigned to technological modernization, specialized manpower training, higher education, and scientific research.

Chinese Communism. China has the third largest land area but is the most populous country in the world, containing about one-quarter of the human race. Although roughly three of every four inhabitants dwell in rural regions, only one-sixth of the country lends itself to cultivation. The supply of capital and equipment is low, and human energy provides the main source of productive power. There is considerable overcrowding and agricultural yields are low. The Chinese standard of living is very low.

The Communists who gained control of China at the end of the 1940s have undertaken a number of economic programs modeled along the lines followed by the Soviet Union. Efforts have been directed especially toward building heavy industries and increasing the number of factories and the quantities of machinery produced. Elimination of private ownership in the agricultural, commercial, and industrial sectors of the economy and its replacement by public ownership has been vigorously pursued. For a time much technical assistance and equipment were provided by the Soviet Union, but in recent years the strained relations between these countries has greatly reduced the volume of aid.

Overall central planning and control is under the direction of the State Economic Commission, which sets forth the long-term goals of each of the five-year plans under which the economy has operated. But local and regional planning bodies, which take into account conditions prevailing in their areas, implement objectives and determine the specific output of particular firms.

The agricultural program has been developed in three phases. (1) A substantial portion of farmland was redistributed among the peasants. (2) The peasants were urged to join cooperatives and collectives, the inducements being agricultural equipment, supplies, and cheap loans. (3) People's Communes were set up through a merger of cooperatives to bring about greater integration of community activity and higher output. More than 70,000 communes, each averaging many thousands of people, are responsible for the development of agriculture and the decentralization of industrial output. More women have been brought into the labor force by freeing them from normal routines through the establishment of communal kitchens and of nurseries for children. The success of the commune system, however, is not yet evident.

The Chinese government has also nationalized heavy and light industry and has increased industrial output, particularly iron, steel, and electrical energy. Since the early 1950s a rising portion of the gross national product has been allocated to investment. Vigorous attempts have been made to upgrade the quality of the labor force by increasing literacy and providing more advanced educational opportunities. As a result there has been a steady and substantial rise in gross national product, particularly in the 1950s, although per capita output is still relatively low.

The ambitious development program received a series of setbacks about 1960 as a result of the withdrawal of Soviet aid, a number of natural calamities adversely affecting agriculture, the problems of complicated planning and interindustry imbalance, and a deterioration in the quality of products. Starting in 1960 Chinese economic policy shifted emphasis from heavy industry to agriculture and attached more importance to training for managerial and professional positions and securing greater amounts of capital from the West and Japan. From all indications the Chinese economy had resumed its expansion at a reasonably rapid rate by 1970, after experiencing some political struggles in the 1960s.

Indian Socialism. The land area of India is a little over one-third that of the United States, but it has more than twice as many people, more people than any country other than China. Nearly three-quarters of the labor force is engaged in agriculture, but the marginal product of many workers is very low and unemployment among the urban population is high. Total population is currently rising because the birth rate is high and the death rate is declining.

Indian growth efforts also revolve around planning. Careful and detailed plans are made for the public sector of the economy; regulations and controls of several kinds are imposed on the private sector. The near-term goal of India is to raise the level of real consumption through an increase in social services and establishment of greater equality of opportunity and income for the population. Until 1975, the development and protection of democratic institutions received a high priority. Since then, many personal freedoms have been severely restricted. As is the case in Great Britain, India has no intention of collectivizing agriculture or nationalizing all its industries. Economic growth therefore cannot be expected to increase as rapidly as it does in countries that are devoting their full efforts to expand the volume of investment.

The series of five-year plans in India, which began in 1951, have been devised to facilitate urgent investment projects. The sources of funds available to the government are expected to grow as tax revenues increase, internal borrowing is facilitated (as public savings levels rise), and more grants and loans are obtained abroad. Private investment in the private sector provides less than half the total spent for capital goods. Such investment is expected to increase in industry, agriculture, retailing, and handicraft operations.

Economic growth in India, however, depends mainly on a decline in the birth rate. Population growth makes it difficult for per capita output and the standard of living to rise. Per capita income is very low, housing is typically substandard both in rural and in urban areas, illiteracy is unusually high, food consumption (calorie intake per person) is well below the level in the United States, and little or no purchasing power is available to the vast majority of the population for clothing. Various plans for birth control have been introduced, including a scheme for voluntary sterilization of men.

But it is also essential that effective use of the unemployed and the underemployed workers is made. This labor should be employed on projects that do not require extensive capital equipment, such as building roads, constructing public works, improving irrigation facilities, and helping to introduce new agricultural techniques.

Economic planning in India is more moderate and involves far less coercion than in China. Most observers believe that Indian economic growth is now slower than that of China.

III The Price System

Chapter 9
THE ORGANIZATION OF BUSINESS

There are nearly 12,500,000 firms of varying structural forms and sizes in the United States. Firms, generally defined as organizations under a single management (they may have more than one plant), engage in many kinds of economic activity; they include a large number of professional persons, practicing as individuals or in partnerships, and 3,300,000 agricultural units. Turnover or failure in business is high; most firms survive only a few years. Typically several hundred thousand businesses are begun each year, and almost the same number are discontinued. Poor management is the underlying cause of many business failures.

Small establishments have been an American tradition that has served many purposes. A small business permits an owner to work without supervision, perform a greater variety of tasks, use family labor more efficiently, find outlets for ambition, and secure higher financial rewards. Some business activities, such as farming, businesses catering to local customers, and professional services of physicians, dentists, attorneys, and engineers, perform more effectively as small enterprises.

A major portion of productive activity, however, is carried on by a relatively small number of large firms. Several hundred enterprises dominate the economy and account for a substantial part of the output, income, and employment of the nation. Industrial giants have flourished because the state of technology requires mass production of output, most markets are nationwide, and vast sums of capital are needed to operate efficiently and profitably.

Most business firms are primarily concerned with profit. In practice, profit is computed by well-established accounting techniques and procedures. Economists, however, modify this concept somewhat for use in economic analysis.

FORMS OF ENTERPRISE

The three main forms of business organization in the United States are the sole proprietorship, the partnership, and the corporation. Variations of these basic types include the limited partnership and the cooperative. In 1971 there were about 9,750,000 sole proprietorships, 950,000 partnerships, and 1,730,000 corporations. Each form of business may be described in terms of a long list of advantages and disadvantages. Yet the form chosen for a business in specific cases usually depends upon very few considerations. The paramount factors in its determination generally are tax obligations and debt liabilities.

The Sole Proprietorship. The sole proprietor assumes full responsibility for the conduct of the business he sets up. The business usually begins as a small enterprise, but in many instances it grows much larger. There are no formalities involved in starting a sole proprietorship, although a local or state license may be necessary for some types of activity. Ordinarily, it is not easy for the owner to raise capital if he should need it. The sole proprietor, however, does have the advantage of paying the regular personal income tax on the profit of the business. For this reason, he is willing to assume the legally required burden of unlimited liability for the debts of the enterprise. This means that all his personal wealth may be used to pay any financial obligation that the business incurs to any creditors, suppliers of raw materials or merchandise, and employees. Nevertheless, despite these financial dangers, a few large enterprises operate under the sole proprietorship form of organization.

The Partnership. Sometimes, the sole proprietor needs help in managing or financing the business and finds persons willing to assist him and join the enterprise. At other times, several persons start a business venture together. But in either case if the owners wish to avoid paying any special taxes they must be willing to assume unlimited liability. This form of business, in which two or more owners have made a written or an oral agreement to engage in some enterprise, is called a partnership. The disadvantages of the partnership are that each partner is legally liable for all the debts of the business (beyond the share that he owns) if the other owners are unable to pay their share; that each partner has considerable authority to make commitments that bind the others; and that the death, resignation, withdrawal, or addition of a partner requires a new agreement to be executed.

The danger to the personal fortune of a partner when the enterprise is huge and complex has led to limited partnerships. State statutes permitting this form of organization provide that one or more partners may have their financial obligations limited to the extent of the amount of money or property contributed to the business so long as they do not participate actively in the operation of the enterprise.

The partnership permits joint ownership based on contributions of money, special abilities, or knowledge, but it is most suitable in professional fields that require relatively little capital, such as law, accounting, and medicine. Indeed, in a number of professions state laws do not permit incorporation, which would reduce financial protection for users of the services. Although the sole proprietorship and the partnership are sometimes subjected to government supervision because of the nature of the enterprise, the form of organization adopted by the corporation implies regulation by the government.

The Corporation. The corporation is one of the symbols of the twentieth century. Although it has been used as a form of business enterprise for many centuries, until modern times government incorporation charters were granted to each applicant by special legislative action and were considered a privilege. Beginning about 1830 in the United States general incorporation laws were introduced that made it possible for all to incorporate on an equal basis. There are now few difficulties facing those seeking to form corporations. Indeed, state competition to attract business enterprise has resulted in extremely liberal requirements for incorporation and has led to extensive grants of power to the corporation. Except for the area of banking, the federal government has made little use of its authority to charter corporations.

The corporation represents an important modern institution because it allows a firm to accumulate large sums of capital and establish and operate the giant type of enterprise that dominates the U.S. economy. Nevertheless, by far the greatest proportion of firms that incorporate do so to achieve limited liability, that is, to limit the financial obligations of the owners to the sum constituting their investment in the business. In most respects these corporations are indistinguishable from sole proprietors in the conduct of their business. Customers entering a retail establishment are neither aware nor concerned in most cases with its form of business organization. Indeed, corporations are frequently small; they are owned or dominated by a single individual; and they have greater difficulty in raising capital because banks, and even relatives, are less likely to extend credit to borrowers whose liability is limited.

Firms often are reluctant to adopt the corporate form of enterprise because they then must assume added tax burdens. But businesses requiring vast aggregates of capital to operate have little choice. It is only by incorporating and turning to the general public for assistance in supplying capital that such enterprises can attract a large number of investors. It should be clear, however, that the corporate form is not the solution for the ordinary firm requiring financing. Organizers of a new corporation who go to the public for funds must generally be well-known and respected if they are to succeed in selling the ownership capital issued. Usually only established and profitable firms that need additional capital for expansion are in a position to attract funds from investors who want to be owners. A cursory examination of the financial pages of newspapers that list stock market transactions will indicate that only a few thousand companies have any substantial number of owners.

States issue corporate charters when at least three persons file appropriate applications stating the nature of the business to be undertaken and the number of shares they wish to authorize for sale. The incorporators must pay a fee. The powers of shareholders include electing a board of directors, approving charter amendments, authorizing changes in capitalization, and agreeing to the terms of merger and dissolution. State law confers power to manage the business on the board of directors. The chairman of the board of directors is frequently the most powerful person in the corporation, but the board normally delegates appropriate authority to each executive officer it selects to operate the company. Ordinarily the president is the chief executive officer of the firm.

Most corporations have only one kind or class of ownership shares and provide that each share outstanding should have equal voting rights at annual meetings. Occasionally, however, in order to permit minority representation on the board of directors cumulative voting procedures are used. Under this arrangement an owner of one share may cast as many votes as there are directors to be elected in any way he wishes. For example, if ten directors are to be elected, a shareholder may vote ten times for one candidate, or six times for one candidate and four times for another, or once for each of ten candidates. (Many other combinations are obviously possible.) Though shareholders may vote in person or by proxy, directors must be present at board meetings to cast their ballots.

A corporation is a legal entity or a legal person and may perform in its own name all business activities that the individual proprietor or partnership carries on. It may own property, enter into contracts, and sue and be sued. Since securities representing corporate ownership may be transferred from one person to another, the life of the company continues even if any or all the stockholders should die or sell their shares.

There are four types of corporations: (1) business corporations that issue stock; (2) business corporations that do not issue stock, such as mutual savings banks and mutual insurance companies; (3) private nonprofit corporations, such as universities, charitable foundations, and social clubs; and (4) public corporations, such as cities and government agencies.

Stock corporations include business enterprises that are free to maximize their profit, firms whose operations and profit are closely regulated by the government (public utilities), and cooperatives. Cooperatives may be formed by producers, distributors, or consumers. They are designed to spread the control and the benefits of a business among a relatively large number of persons. Cooperatives are organized under laws that prescribe the maximum amount of stock any person may hold, limit the dividends that may be paid to stockholders, and require the profits in excess of dividends that are not reinvested in the business to be distributed among the owners. Cooperatives of producers and distributors divide profits above dividends in accordance with the relative proportion of the product contributed by each owner, and consumer cooperatives apportion them in accordance with the purchases made. The cooperative movement, which has its greatest strength in agriculture, is of relatively little importance in the United States.

Mutual savings banks and mutual insurance companies are nonstock corporations. The former are owned by their depositors and the latter by their policyholders. These enterprises, as well as private nonprofit corporations, are usually controlled by a self-perpetuating board of directors. Public corporations, of course, are headed by elected officials or their appointed subordinates.

FINANCING BUSINESS OPERATIONS

Corporations raise capital by issuing or floating securities. These financial documents are either stocks or bonds. Each type of security is intended to attract specific groups of investors. Stocks or equity capital shares represent ownership in the corporation, whereas bonds are held by creditors of the corporation. The usual kind of security issued by a corporation is common stock, each share of which represents an equal fraction of ownership. Holders of these shares vote at meetings and receive dividends as declared by the directors; they may purchase additional shares if issued by the company and, upon termination of the business, are entitled to a proportion of the assets remaining after creditors are paid. Investors may buy common stock for two reasons. They may anticipate a rise in the market price of the stock if they have reason to expect that company profits are likely to increase. They also look forward to dividends paid from the earnings of the company. Naturally, stocks and all other corporate securities entail risks. The amount of risk depends upon the volume of creditor claims to the assets in the event of business failure and the extent to which the company may sustain a loss or decline in earning power. Stockholders cannot normally recover the value of their equity from the company. They must sell their shares to persons willing to buy them.

Other classes of stock may be available. Occasionally nonvoting common stock is issued; these shares do not permit persons holding them to vote for directors or on certain other specified matters. Preferred stock assures a greater degree of certainty that investors will receive dividends as no payments ordinarily may be made to common stockholders until a stipulated dividend per year has been declared for the preferred shares. If these dividends are cumulative, omitted payments must be made up in subsequent periods before common shareholders receive anything. This arrangement affords preferred shareholders more protection than common stockholders since the directors of the company may decide to bypass a dividend payment regardless of the size of company profits. In some cases, upon liquidation of the company, preferred stockholders have the added advantage of recovering their original investment before common stockholders do. A holder of convertible preferred stock may exchange each of his shares for common shares at a specified ratio. For example, the owner of a share of convertible preferred stock may have the option of exchanging it for two shares of common stock. Thus if the value of the common stock rises, there will be an induced increase in the price of the convertible preferred stock even though the dividends of the latter are fixed.

The original equity capital may be insufficient to meet the needs of an expanding business. The directors have several alternatives. They may sell more stock. They may also choose to retain part or all of the earnings in the business rather than distribute the profit as dividends. This technique of reinvesting undistributed profit has been used to an increasing extent in recent years, but it also may prove inadequate. The company may have to resort to other ways of obtaining funds, such as borrowing.

Corporations may meet their long-term capital requirements by issuing several types of bonds. These may take the form of mortgage bonds, which involve a first lien on the property of the firm; debentures which have no specific security; and convertible bonds, which the holder at his option may exchange for the common stock of the company. Bonds are usually sold in denominations of $1,000 each and pay a specified rate of interest to their holders for a fixed period of time. At the end of the period the principal must be repaid by the debtor company. Failure to make interest payments on the bonds or to repay the principal when it falls due shifts control of the company to the bondholders. Sometimes income bonds are issued by a corporation. In this case interest is paid only if sufficient profit is earned by the company during the year. Many types of complicated mortgage bonds have been floated by the larger corporations, especially railroads and public utilities.

The ease of transferring securities and their liquidity are important features in attracting purchasers among the public. After the initial sale has been completed, the securities of most leading business enterprises are bought and sold through organized exchanges. Although there are some regional exchanges, the New York Stock Exchange and the American Stock Exchange are national in scope and account for the bulk of transactions involving listed securities.

Brokers who are members of the exchange conduct the business of buying and selling for their customers, for which they charge specified commissions. Securities of some large national companies, of firms having regional or local reputations, and of almost all banks and insurance companies, are traded in the over-the-counter market, where brokers and investment bankers buy and sell securities by telephone or telegraph.

Sale of stocks and bonds and reinvestment are not the only ways in which corporations raise capital. The methods of financing used by a business depend not only on the situation in the money market at the time but also on the characteristics of the firm, including size, product or service, age, and prior experience in fund raising. Short-term financing of business takes several forms. Trade credit allows the business firm a specified period of time to pay for the goods it purchases. Commercial banks may limit loans to the extent of the net worth of the firm or net working capital, whichever is smaller. Inventory, accounts receivable, and equipment may also be used as security for loans to finance short-term financial needs. As is already evident, different means are used in raising capital, depending on whether it is needed for short or long periods of time. In addition to borrowing and internal expansion, enterprises can expand by combining or consolidating with other firms.

The separation of ownership from control has become inevitable as corporations have grown in size in the United States. Stock ownership is now spread widely among the population. A 1970 survey showed that one out of every four adults in the United States, or 30,850,000 persons, owned stock. Each of the largest corporations has many hundreds of thousands of owners. Holders of stock are generally not concerned with management and operations of a company. A small group of active investors owning a minority of stock, therefore, is usually able to exercise control. Since a controlling minority is also interested in the profit and prosperity of the corporation, conflict of interests is not frequent. There are many occasions when widespread ownership has enabled management to take over control of a corporation. But in these cases too managers and stockholders are likely to be in agreement regarding the objectives of the firm. Salaries, bonuses, and expense accounts to be paid to the executives of the firm, however, may give rise to controversy between owners and managers.

Some indication of the size of corporations may be gathered from statistics showing that in 1974 Exxon Corporation had $31.3 billion in assets and over $3 billion in net profit, and General Motors had $20.5 billion in assets and almost $1 billion in profit. Seventeen other industrial corporations each held more than $5 billion in assets. In the latter-size category there were twenty-three commercial banks, ten life insurance companies, one retailing firm, no transportation companies, and five utilities (including American Telephone and Telegraph Company with more than $67 billion). Twenty-two industrial corporations each employed more that 200,000 persons.

FINANCIAL STATEMENTS

Business enterprises are complex organizations. The accountant tries to explain the affairs of the firm in an orderly and coherent way. Two important tools for this purpose are the balance sheet and the income statement. Knowledge of these financial statements is helpful in understanding the operations of the firm and the different analytical approaches used in economics and accounting. It is also useful to stockholders and creditors who wish to decide whether to buy or sell the securities of the firm or to extend credit to it.

The Balance Sheet. The balance sheet shows the financial position of a company at any time. It is based on books kept by the double entry method, which means that all items are recorded in two places. The value of a firm is analyzed in terms of the kind of item involved and its source.

A business must possess various kinds of tangible and intangible resources and property, called assets, in order to function effectively. The owners of the business do not provide all the assets necessary to operate. Lenders or creditors also contribute. What the owners supply at the outset, supplemented by earnings that are not withdrawn, is called the net worth or proprietorship; the creditors' contributions are termed liabilities. It is thus clear that the assets must exactly equal the liabilities plus the proprietorship. This relationship may be written:

$$Assets = Liabilities + Proprietorship$$

The balance sheet allows four elements of the firm's financial condition to be computed. These are the integrity of the investment made by the owners, the relation of earnings to investment (this requires additional information from the income statement), the ability of the firm to pay its debts, and the sum invested in plant and equipment to operate the business. To secure this information assets are divided into current (those that arise out of the productive activities of the firm), fixed (those invested in plant or machinery), and other (such as patents and goodwill). Liabilities are usually divided into current (debts due within one year) and long-term. The proprietorship is ordinarily divided into capital stock, that part of the contribution of the owners subject to withdrawal only in the event of liquidation of the business; capital surplus, the amount contributed by owners beyond the minimum legally required capital; and earned surplus, the undistributed profit left in the business. A two to one ratio of current assets to current liabilities is usually considered satisfactory evidence of the ability of a firm to pay its debts. Net working capital is the excess of current assets over current liabilities. Firms may use consolidated balance sheets to indicate the combined financial position, at any time, of two or more related companies, usually a parent and its subsidiaries. Many United States firms issue balance sheets on the last day of each calendar quarter.

A balance sheet for a large enterprise is shown in table 9-1.

The Income Statement.   The income statement deals with profit and loss. It shows the changes that have occurred over a given period of time, usually one year, in accounts that affect the profit. The profit-and-loss statement is in effect a summary of revenues and expenses. It links the balance sheet at the beginning of the period with the balance sheet at the end of the period.

The operating revenue (gross revenue), which is the gross sales less the returns and discounts, minus the cost of sales, which is the production costs of a manufacturer or the costs of the merchandise of a trading concern, is equal to the gross profit. Gross profit less selling, administrative, and general expenses and less depreciation is equal to net operating profit. When interest on debt and income taxes is deducted from net operating profit, net income (net profit) or net loss remains. The income statement generally shows amounts paid out as dividends on preferred stock, if any, and on common stock. The balance represents addition to earned surplus.

Obviously profit need not represent cash accumulation, since revenues and costs do not necessarily involve cash transactions. The only cash required by the firm is the amount that must be available for specific outlays such as wages of employees and dividends. Even reserves for depreciation are not ordinarily in cash form and appear as deductions from fixed assets.

Income statements are prepared in many different ways. The business firm whose balance sheet is given above might show the following income statement. Notice that the addition to reinvested savings

TABLE 9-1

BALANCE SHEET, DECEMBER 31, 1970

Assets		**Liabilities**	
Cash on hand and in banks	$ 300,000,000	Notes payable	$ 150,000,000
Marketable securities	350,000,000	Accounts payable	425,000,000
Accounts receivable	1,000,000,000	Dividends payable	75,000,000
Inventories	1,100,000,000	Taxes accrued	350,000,000
		Other costs	450,000,000
Current Assets	2,750,000,000	Current Liabilities	1,450,000,000
Investments	250,000,000	Long-term debt	400,000,000
Plant and equipment		Other liabilities and reserves	250,000,000
(2,400,000,000)		Total Liabilities	$2,100,000,000
less depreciation			
(1,350,000,000)	1,050,000,000	**Proprietorship**	
Other assets	200,000,000	Preferred stock	100,000,000
		Common stock	550,000,000
		Reinvested earnings	1,500,000,000
		Total Proprietorship	2,150,000,000
Total Assets	$4,250,000,000	Total Liabilities and Proprietorship	$4,250,000,000

becomes part of the total reinvested earnings and is incorporated into the balance sheet. Table 9-2 is an income statement.

View of the Economist. To adapt financial statements to economic analysis, economists must make revisions. Many of the concepts used by accountants are for their own convenience (a practice also followed by economists in defining terms) or are based upon the needs of the firm for tax or legal purposes. For example, accountants are ordinarily guided in determining depreciation figures by the maximum allowances permitted by law or on the basis of a rigid formula. In both cases, the result may be considered arbitrary in the sense that it has no necessary connection to the market value of the asset; and it is the latter figure that is most significant to economists. Furthermore, the accountant usually includes only outlays actually made as costs of the firm. Economists, however, wish to know the implicit costs, too. There are costs of operation that the owner of the business fails to count because he uses his own labor, capital, or other property. The economist must include as costs those sums which correspond to the largest return that this labor, capital, or property can earn in an alternative use.

TABLE 9-2

INCOME STATEMENT, 1975

Net sales of products and services to customers		$6,300,000,000
Cost of goods sold		4,300,000,000
Labor	2,250,000,000	
Materials	2,050,000,000	
Gross profit		2,000,000,000
Selling, administrative, and general expenses		1,100,000,000
Depreciation		200,000,000
Net operating profit		700,000,000
Other income		50,000,000
Interest on debt		18,000,000
Income taxes		350,000,000
Net income (net profit)		382,000,000
Dividends paid to preferred stockholders		7,000,000
Dividends paid to common stockholders		200,000,000
Addition to reinvested earnings		175,000,000
Reinvested earnings on January 1, 1975		1,325,000,000
Total reinvested earnings on December 31, 1975		$1,500,000,000

Failure by accountants to provide these adjustments in financial statements is responsible for the frequently expressed conclusion that the owner of the corner grocery store is operating at a profit when in fact he is not. The proprietor may be putting in a working day of twelve hours, six days a week, and using his own accumulated capital in the business. But he is not likely to pay himself the amount that he could earn for seventy-two hours of work in another store or allow for the interest or dividends his capital could earn elsewhere. As a result, profit in such enterprises computed by the accountant is unduly inflated in the economic sense.

Chapter 10
DEMAND AND SUPPLY

Where private enterprise prevails, the economic system revolves around prices. What, how, and for whom goods and services are produced is determined in the market by persons (households), businesses, and government units that have money to spend and that decide to spend more of it on certain items and less of it on other items. In a mixed economy some decisions regarding the nature of output are made by the government independent of price or cost considerations; they may be based on a principle that stresses the general welfare of the population, as when an anti-poverty program is instituted. But even in such a mixed economy the price mechanism is still the most important coordinating factor.

Thus far in considering how the income and output of an economy are determined we have dealt with general movements in price. i.e., inflation and deflation. The next few chapters establish how individual prices of goods and services are set and how they are related. These questions are closely linked to the price paid for factors of production—wages, rent, interest, and profit. The subject of factor payments constitutes the core of the study of income distribution.

Prices of goods and services are based on decisions of consumers and producers. These decisions coalesce in the market. The price mechanism is a basic feature of the economy because the scarcity of resources limits the volume of goods and services that can be produced.

MARKET PRICE

It is widely recognized that many economic problems lend themselves to effective analysis by the consideration of supply and demand. These concepts help us to understand the price mechanism, but they must be defined with great precision if they are to have the same meaning to all who use them. Demand and supply are terms that have pertinence not only in discussions concerning individuals (households) but also groups of individuals.

Markets. A market is rarely identified by a geographic locale or by physical location. Rather it represents a pattern of coherent relationships among sellers and buyers of a good or service. In some instances a market may be relatively isolated and involve few persons, as in the case of a shoeshine stand on a street corner. At other times it may extend around the world and involve very large numbers of persons, as exemplified by purchasers and sellers of gold. Generally price movements in any part of a market affect prices throughout the market.

Demand. Demand by an individual for a good or service indicates the quantity that he is willing to buy within a range of prices at any specified time. Such information provides a demand schedule, if put in tabular form, or a demand curve, if plotted on a graph. An individual demand schedule for a particular brand and quality of butter, for example, shows different quantities of butter that would be purchased by a person or household at various possible prices to meet needs during a specified period (for example, one month). The schedule might indicate how many pounds of butter would be purchased if the price ranged from $.40 to $1.40 per pound, rising by units of $.20. When plotted, it would be negatively sloped or downward sloping. This means that the lower the price of butter, all other prices remaining the same, the more butter an individual tends to buy, because (1) lower prices increase purchasing power and make possible additional purchases and (2) lower prices for butter encourage substitution of butter for other goods. (The notion of consumer satisfaction or utility, upon which these actions depend, is discussed in the next chapter.) Higher prices for butter lead to less demand for the opposite reasons.

Specifically, table 10-1 lists a series of prices in one column and the corresponding quantities purchased in a given period of time (or flow of the commodity) in a second column. The same information is obtained from a graph that plots quantity purchased on the horizontal axis and price on the vertical axis. The curve connecting the known points shows the approximate quantities a consumer will demand at alternative prices. It intersects the horizontal axis at the quantity the consumer wants if the butter is free and the vertical axis at the price at which no butter

TABLE 10-1

DEMAND SCHEDULE FOR BUTTER

Price per Pound	Quantity Purchased per Month (Pounds)
$1.40	0.25
1.20	0.50
1.00	1.00
0.80	1.60
0.60	2.25
0.40	4.00

will be purchased. Figure 10-1 is based upon the information available in table 10-1. In order to provide simplicity and clarity in a discussion, straight lines are often used to depict demand schedules.

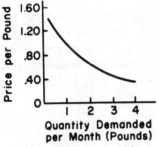

Fig. 10-1. Demand curve for butter

The market demand schedule combines the demand schedules of all individuals in the same market. It is derived by adding the individual quantities demanded at each price. As with the individual or the household demand schedule, it may be presented in a table or a graph. The market demand curve is also negatively sloped, not only because each individual tends to buy more at lower prices, but because purchasers not previously in the market tend to enter as the price falls. The market demand schedule reveals the quantity of goods demanded at different prices when prices of other goods and all incomes are fixed. In recent years considerable empirical work has been done in measuring market demand.

Supply. The supply schedule of an individual or firm shows the relation between the price and the quantity of a commodity or service that would be offered for sale in a given period of time (i.e., the flow of the commodity). The relationship between price and quantity is positive.

When the schedule is based upon the amount of the commodity available to the seller at a particular time, it refers to the market period. Less will be offered at lower prices, depending on how perishable the commodity is, because the seller will tend to wait for higher prices. More will be put on the market at higher prices because the prospects of still higher prices decline. But if the time period involved is increased so that the quantity that can be supplied varies, production costs must also be considered in the supply schedule. Usually two types of periods are analyzed under these circumstances. The short-run period is one in which the firm has committed itself to bear fixed costs—for example, because it owns factories or equipment or has rented them for a specific time. The long-run period is one in which all costs of the firm vary with output. It should be clear that the short run for some companies faced with fixed costs for an extended time may be longer than the long run for firms or types of businesses with no fixed cost commitments. Generally the supply curves of both periods are positively sloped or upward sloping because higher prices indicate greater profit and therefore would stimulate greater output. Furthermore, the unit cost of many commodities increases as more is produced. Rising cost per unit of output is illustrated by the principle of diminishing returns, which states that beyond a certain point of production additional units of input applied to a fixed quantity of another input yield a lesser amount of added output.

TABLE 10-2

SUPPLY SCHEDULE FOR BUTTER

Price per Pound	Quantity Offered per Month (Pounds)
$1.40	20,000
1.20	19,500
1.00	18,000
0.80	15,000
0.60	9,000
0.40	1,000

The individual supply schedule may be shown as a table (table 10-2) or a graph (figure 10-2). It relates the price to the quantity that would be offered in a particular period. These data are graphed on page 139. Again, straight lines are often used to show supply schedules.

The market supply schedule is the sum of the individual supply schedules in any market. It is positively sloped because individual schedules have that relation and also because new sellers enter the market at higher prices. This schedule shows the total quantity that sellers would offer at different prices.

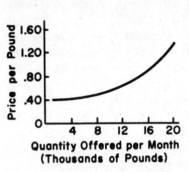

Fig. 10-2. Supply curve for butter

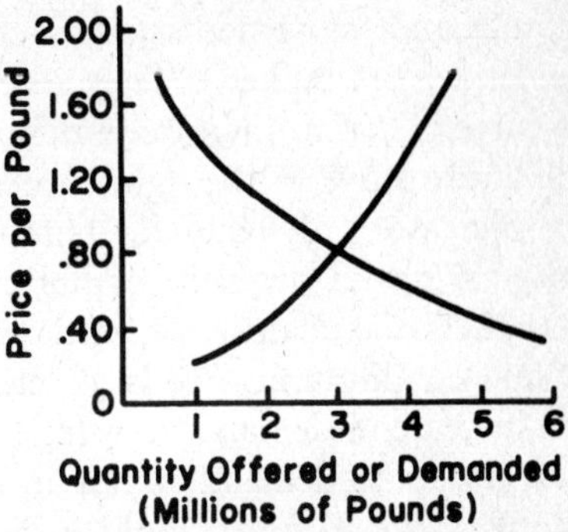

Fig. 10-3. Market equilibrium of price and quantity of butter

Price. The actual market price is determined from the relationship between the market demand schedule and the market supply schedule. It is the price at which all who are willing to pay that price or more will get the product or service and all who are willing to sell at that price or lower will find a buyer. The market price is an equilibrium price because there tends to be no movement away from it, other things being equal. Although all who are willing to buy or sell the good at the market price are able to do so, some buyers (those whose demand for the good is partially or wholly activated only at prices below the market) and some sellers (those willing to sell all or part of their supply of the good only at prices above the market) do not transact any business or as much business as they would at other prices. If the price is above equilibrium, the pressure of excess supply forces the market price down; if the price is below equilibrium, the pressure of unsatisfied demand forces the market price up.

The graph of market equilibrium shown in figure 10-3 combines the market demand and market supply schedules. It shows the equilibrium price as $.80 per pound of butter and the equilibrium quantity as 3,000,000 pounds.

The supply and demand curves indicate that at different prices quantities supplied or demanded vary. But changes in income, population, prices of other commodities, or tastes may shift the demand for a good or service; whereas changes in costs, prices of other commodities, technology, need for money, or objectives of a firm may shift the supply of a good or service. Such changes involve more than a movement along a curve (termed a change in quantity demanded or supplied). They necessitate a shift in the entire schedule or curve. Thus an increase in demand or an increase in supply moves the entire curve to the right. A decrease moves the curve to the left. An increase in demand for butter, for example, means that at any price, a greater quantity of butter is demanded than previously or that the same quantity of butter now is demanded at a higher price.

The equilibrium price is affected by shifts in supply or demand. An increase in demand or a decrease in supply raises the price while a decrease in demand or an increase in supply lowers the price. Should demand and supply increase (or decrease) simultaneously, the price may be higher or lower, depending on the relative movements involved in the two changes.

ELASTICITY

With respect to individual or market demand and supply schedules, a small percentage increase or decrease in the price of a good results in some percentage change in quantity. The relationship between these changes involves the concept of price elasticity.

Elasticity comparisons do not relate increases or decreases in price with corresponding changes in quantity but rather link the percentage movements in the two variables. For example, nothing is revealed about price elasticity of demand if it is known only that the price of butter has declined by one cent per pound and that the quantity demanded has gone up 200,000 pounds. But a statement that permits elasticity to be measured is one such as: If the price drops from $1.00 to $.99 a pound, then the quantity demanded rises from 10,000,000 to 10,200,000 pounds.

Price elasticity is the ratio of the percentage change in quantity to the percentage change in price, when a small change in price occurs. If the percentage changes are the same, the ratio is equal to one and unitary elasticity exists. If the percentage change in quantity exceeds the percentage change in price, the ratio is more than one (or less than minus one when price and quantity move in opposite directions) and demand is elastic. But if the percentage change in price is greater than the percentage change in quantity, the fraction is less than one (it is between zero and one or between zero and minus one) and demand is inelastic. The formula is:

$$Elasticity = \frac{Percentage\ Change\ in\ Quantity}{Percentage\ Change\ in\ Price} = \frac{\dfrac{Change\ in\ Quantity}{Quantity}}{\dfrac{Change\ in\ Price}{Price}}$$

Elasticity of Demand. The numerical illustration used above specifies that a 1 percent drop in the price of butter results in a 2 percent increase in quantity. The elasticity of demand at the price $1.00 is less than minus one; it is elastic. If the same market demand schedule for butter revealed that a decline in the price of a pound of butter from $.20 to $.19 would increase the quantity demanded from 100,000,000 to 100,200,000 pounds, it may be concluded that the demand for butter at $.20 a pound is inelastic. Here too price falls by one cent, and quantity rises by 200,000 pounds. A decline of 5 percent in price results in an increase of only one-fifth of 1 percent in the quantity demanded. It is thus possible and often the case that the same demand schedule is elastic at some prices (generally the higher ones) and inelastic at others (generally the lower ones). Elasticity of demand has a negative value ranging between zero and minus infinity.

The elasticity of demand may also be analyzed in terms of the impact of a change in the price of a good on the expenditure (price multiplied by quantity). If the price drops slightly and the expenditure increases or if the price rises slightly and the expenditure declines, demand is elastic. For example, a one-cent drop in the price of butter from $1.00 raises expenditure by $98,000. But if the price change and expenditure move in the same direction, then demand is inelastic. For example, a one-cent drop in the price of butter from $.20 lowers expenditures by $962,000. Should a small change in price have no effect on expenditure, unitary elasticity of demand exists. On a straight-line demand curve unitary elasticity represents the dividing point between the elastic and the inelastic portions.

The two extreme cases of elasticity are the perfectly elastic curve and the perfectly inelastic curve. A perfectly elastic curve (infinite elasticity) is one in which the quantity demanded does not depend upon price, i.e., an unlimited quantity is demanded at the prevailing price. Such a curve is a horizontal line and, as will be seen in chapter 12, is used to show that the demand for the product of a firm operating under conditions of pure competition is such that it can sell all it has to offer at the market price. A perfectly inelastic demand curve (zero elasticity) is one in which the same quantity is demanded at all prices. It is shown graphically by a vertical line. It might be used to illustrate the demand by an individual for a drug necessary to sustain his life.

Elasticity of Supply.   The concept of elasticity of supply is similar to the concept of elasticity of demand. Elasticity of supply relates percentage change in quantity offered for sale to percentage change in price; as the supply curve is positively sloped, the elasticity of supply is positive. If percentage change in quantity is the same as percentage change in price, unitary elasticity of supply exists. Such a curve would be a straight line passing through the origin at any angle. A straight line intersecting the vertical axis is elastic throughout (greater than one) whereas a line intersecting the horizontal axis is inelastic (less than one) along its entire length.

The extreme cases of elasticity of supply are those in which supply is perfectly elastic (infinite elasticity) or perfectly inelastic (zero elasticity). A perfectly elastic supply means that any quantity will be offered at a given price. Thus banks and the government are ready to supply any quantity of one-cent pieces for one cent each. On the other hand, a rare coin (indicated by a particular date and mint-mark) represents perfect inelasticity because a greater quantity is not available regardless of the price offered.

Income Elasticity.   Shifts in the demand curve may arise because of changes in income. An individual or a community whose income rises may greatly increase the demand for a product even if the price does not change, as in the case of entertainment outlays; it may only slightly increase demand, as for orange juice; leave demand unchanged, as for bread and rolls; or even decrease demand, as for goods (sometimes called inferior goods) such as baked beans or margarine, which might be replaced by meat or butter. These changes are measured by income elasticity of demand, which equals percentage change in quantity demanded when price remains unaltered, divided by percentage change in income. Although income elasticity values in actual experience are generally positive, the illustrations above indicate that they may also be zero or negative.

Cross-Elasticity. Another type of elasticity arises out of the inter-relations of demand among products. Thus, if a pound of coffee is purchased, there is a joint, cooperative, or complementary demand for sugar and a competitive, rival, or substitute demand for tea. The cross-elasticity of demand is the percentage change in the quantity purchased of one good divided by the corresponding percentage change in the price of another good. It may vary from plus infinity to minus infinity. Joint goods have negative cross-elasticities because a rise in the price of one leads to a fall in consumption of the other; competitive goods have positive cross-elasticities because a rise in the price of one leads to a rise in consumption of the other. Goods that have little relation to each other should have cross-elasticities close to zero.

APPLICATIONS OF DEMAND AND SUPPLY ANALYSIS

It should be clear that there are many forces working on supply and demand that influence price. For example, government legislation or trade union policy may affect supply and demand.

Taxes. Many business operations affected by government action may be better understood by demand and supply analysis. For example, does the buyer or seller bear the burden of an excise tax levied by the government? If the tax is levied on the seller, the supply curve is decreased because the seller offers the same quantity as before only at a price that now includes the tax he must pay. But if the tax is imposed on the buyer, the demand is lowered because the buyer is willing to pay the same amount as before, after subtracting the tax, for any specified quantity. In either case, however, the burden of the tax is shared by both sellers and buyers (unless demand is perfectly elastic or supply is perfectly inelastic in which case the tax burden falls on the seller; or demand is perfectly inelastic or supply is perfectly elastic in which case the tax burden falls on the buyer). A tax on the seller leads to an increase in equilibrium price that is less than the amount of tax the seller must pay; a tax on the buyer leads to a decrease in equilibrium price that is less than the amount of tax the buyer must pay. In estimating revenue to be derived from a tax, the government must allow for shrinkage in demand that accompanies a higher selling price.

Maximum Prices. Supply and demand schedules may be used to understand the difficulties involved in government price fixing. Efforts by the government to maintain price stability during the Second World War led to the imposition of price ceilings on many goods. For example, during the war, the United States experienced a decrease in the supply of sugar as a result of importation difficulties and an increase in demand because of the generally rising income of the population. Usually in either circumstance the price of sugar would have risen in a free market. But the government, having arbitrarily fixed the price at a previously prevailing equilibrium level, was intent on maintaining stability. As the fixed price brought about a situation in which the quantity demanded exceeded the quantity supplied, it became necessary to ration the supply available in some equitable way.

In such cases, a black market could develop in which some persons would buy quantities of the commodity from sellers who are not willing to sell at the established price but would sell at prices above the legally fixed ceiling prices. Many so-called shortages of a war economy occur as a result of price controls and price ceilings. In free markets only temporary shortages occur.

Minimum Prices. Supply and demand analysis makes possible not only the study of price ceilings but also the study of government efforts to maintain price floors. Attempts to maintain farm prices at the parity level or at a specified fraction of the parity level and to fix minimum wages above the rate that would otherwise prevail may be analyzed in terms of demand and supply. In agriculture, forcing the price up above the one prevailing in the free market means that there are sellers who would like to sell some quantity of a commodity for which there are no buyers. This quantity is then purchased by the government and is usually stored. Similarly, forcing the wage above the market rate by means of minimum wage legislation, reduces the demand for labor. Other things being equal, the result is unemployment for those who are willing to work below or at the legal minimum but can find no buyers for their labor.

AGRICULTURE

Analysis of the agricultural industry provides an understanding of the operation of a free market and the role government plays in influencing the forces that determine demand and supply. The index of agricultural output in the United States has moved in a consistent upward trend. Employment in agriculture, however, has been characterized not only by a declining proportion of the total labor force but during the past half century also by an actual decrease in the number of workers, as shown in table 10-3.

Technology. Technological advance in agriculture, including improved machinery and fertilizer, crop development, and soil analysis, has been responsible for the rising productivity of agricultural labor. The rate of increased efficiency in recent years has been substantially greater than that in the nonagricultural sector of the economy. Considerable advancement in agricultural knowledge has resulted from the work of public agencies: the U.S. Department of Agriculture, county extension services (supported in part by local governments), and land-grant universities engaged in agricultural research.

TABLE 10-3

DECREASE IN AGRICULTURAL WORK FORCE

Year	Agricultural Workers as Per Cent of Total Work Force	Number of Agricultural Workers
1820	72	2,070,000
1880	50	8,610,000
1910	31	11,340,000
1969	5	3,606,000

Source: *Historical Statistics of the United States, Colonial Times to 1957*, 1960, p. 74 and *Economic Report of the President*, February 1970, p. 202.

The rapidly rising output has been responsible for some of the major problems of American agriculture. Increased production of many agricultural commodities cannot readily be absorbed at prevailing prices in a domestic market where population increase is relatively slow and most consumers already are fairly well fed. There are few occasions in which new uses or promotional efforts lead to greater consumption. Nor can international markets be much expanded because rising foreign agricultural output and tariffs imposed abroad serve to limit exports.

Prices and Income. Food production has been rising, but the demand for food has not kept pace. Higher real incomes enjoyed by consumers have been responsible only for a relatively small increase in demand for agricultural commodities compared to nonagricultural goods. Generally rising incomes do little to increase consumption of goods, such as foodstuffs, which typically have a low income elasticity of demand. Relatively large increases in supply and relatively small increases in demand over the years have tended to bring about lower prices in agriculture. The attendant migration from the farms has been inadequate to reduce output sufficiently to maintain the level of prices.

The balance between supply and demand in the competitive agricultural market is often brought about by a decline in farm prices. But prices may have to drop sharply because, though consumers may alter the quantities of individual food purchases somewhat as prices change, the total volume consumed remains approximately the same. Furthermore, since farmers receive less than forty cents of the dollar that consumers spend on food, a fall of 5 percent in farm prices leads to a decline of only 2 percent in food prices.

Declining prices, however, do not generally discourage the farmer who wishes to remain in agriculture from using his fixed resources of land and family labor to capacity. Nor do they lead to any curtailment in the development and adoption of new and improved methods of farming. Lower prices may cause some farmers who are able to find jobs elsewhere to leave the land and may discourage other persons from entering agriculture. But the land remains available for use, and those who take over its cultivation are likely to produce as much as before. The main check on output is the financial inability of individuals to buy necessary inputs or replace equipment.

Because of the large number of producers of farm products, farmers are not in a position to affect prices by their individual actions in the market. Actually farmers normally produce as much as possible because they thus increase their total income (unless unit costs of production rise above price). But such action increases output, weakens price structure, and brings prices down. The relatively inelastic demand for farm products pushes farm prices down sharply.

Price, it appears, does not play a major role in affecting supply or demand. The relative inelastic demand for agricultural commodities and the large unplanned variations in supply associated with weather conditions have led to large fluctuations in price. Farm incomes vary sharply from year to year, and over a period of time the per capita income of farmers has been much lower than that of persons employed in the nonagricultural sector of the economy.

Government Intervention. Farmers have turned to the government for assistance. They have organized associations and lobbies because they recognize that their bargaining power is markedly stronger when acting collectively in selling to or buying from a few large firms. Farmers have felt that a purely competitive market does not enable them to deal effectively with rapidly rising productivity and slowly rising demand because under such circumstances the equilibrium price falls and results in reduced farm income. Nor have they been satisfied with the fluctuations in their income. Political pressure has been used effectively by farm lobbies to achieve results more favorable than those produced by a competitive market.

Parity. The policy of parity was formulated by the federal government to meet demands by farmers for an improved economic status involving higher real incomes and greater stability of income. The parity ratio measures the purchasing power of farm products in terms of goods purchased by farmers. This ratio was originally based on average prices prevailing during the five years between 1910 and 1914 (represented by 100) because Congress felt that nonfarm and farm prices were reasonably balanced at that time. But generally the base years have been moved forward. Thus parity identifies farm prices that enable farmers to buy as much now for a unit of output as they were able to buy in the base period. Empirically agricultural prices have been relatively highest during periods of war.

The federal price support program for farm products goes back to the Agricultural Adjustment Act of 1938, although there had been several unsuccessful attempts to help farmers as early as the 1920s. Under this law and its amendments support was mandatory for some crops and discretionary for other crops and for livestock. But the list of commodities eligible for support varied from time to time. The federal government stood ready to buy each of the designated crops at a specified fraction of its parity price. During the 1960s high production of many supported crops forced market prices down and greatly increased government outlays to farmers. Government efforts to alleviate the problem by imposing limits on the acreage used for agricultural production were not very successful.

Attempts by the government to support farm prices at levels above those that would prevail in competitive markets led to huge surpluses. Federal support policies subsidize farmers and therefore keep more workers in agriculture than would otherwise remain.

When a significant number of farmers do not participate in price support programs, market prices may drop below support levels. A variety of reasons may be responsible for the lack of participation. A farmer may disagree with the philosophy of the support program and stay out. Storage facilities adequate to meet government standards may not be available to the farmer. The quantity of the commodity owned by a farmer may be too small to induce him to take part in the program. The quality of the commodity may not be sufficiently high to meet eligibility. Paperwork and red tape involved in selling to the government may discourage some farmers. Market prices, of course, are also affected by sales of the supported commodities that are owned by nonproducers; only producers (landowners, tenants, and sharecroppers) have been eligible for support.

In the early 1970s substantial increases in U.S. agricultural exports as a result of rising world demand led to higher domestic food prices and reduced excess farm capacity. A new farm policy was adopted by Congress in 1973. The Agriculture and Consumer Protection Act encouraged greater farm production, established guaranteed minimum or target prices to replace the previous system of price supports, and limited total annual payments to any farmer for all commodities to $20,000.

Chapter 11
CONSUMER SATISFACTION
AND COST

The market price is determined by demand and supply. The demand schedule depends upon the satisfaction and the preference of consumers for goods and services; the supply schedule depends upon the cost of production.

MAXIMIZATION OF SATISFACTION BY THE CONSUMER

The demand schedule of an individual depends upon the satisfaction obtained from the units of a good or service consumed during any period of time. The total satisfaction, or total utility, derived from all units increases to a point as more units are consumed, but the added satisfaction of the last unit, or marginal utility, falls and eventually reaches zero. This is the principle of diminishing marginal utility. Thus during any specific period more units of a good than are ordinarily used will be demanded by the consumer if the price falls.

Substitution Effect and Income Effect. Further analysis of the demand curve is made possible by the concepts of the substitution effect and the income effect. The substitution effect indicates that if the price of any commodity declines while prices of other goods and income remain the same, the consumer can increase his satisfaction by purchasing more of the good which has fallen in price and less of the other goods. The consumer substitutes what has become cheaper for what has not. But in addition there is an income effect. The lower price enables the consumer to buy the same quantity as before with less income. The added real income will be used to increase the quantity of all goods purchased. Both the substitution effect and the income effect lead to an inverse or negative relationship between price and quantity demanded. These effects will also be considered later in relating wage rates, hours of labor, and leisure.

Maximizing Utility. The rational consumer is engaged in maximizing the total satisfaction or utility he can obtain from his income. The equilibrium position is attained if the last cent of expenditure (or addition of one cent to disposable income) yields the same satisfaction regardless of the item of consumption on which it is spent or, as an alternative, if it is saved. This is not to say that the last unit of each good gives the same satisfaction but rather that the marginal utility of each good in relation to the price of that good is equal. This condition describes a situation in which the consumer cannot increase utility by shifting consumption spending from one good to another. The rational consumer is not necessarily weighing each purchase with the utmost care. But each time he decides to make important changes in his consumption habits or spending pattern, he carefully considers the satisfaction to be derived from any purchase, relative to possible alternatives. Occasional departures from normal actions and impulsive decisions do not overshadow the basic importance of rational consumer behavior.

Graphical Presentation of Equilibrium. The equilibrium position of a consumer may be shown graphically by an indifference curve technique that uses equal-utility curves (contours) and consumption-possibility lines (budget lines). The indifference curve, or equal-utility curve, shows the various combinations of goods for which an individual has no preference, he is indifferent as to which combination to consume. In the simplest case two commodities are involved. These may be bread and wine (or specific units of food and clothing). The consumer may be equally satisfied with one loaf of bread and six glasses of wine, two loaves of bread and three glasses of wine, or three loaves of bread and two glasses of wine. These combinations represent three of the many possible points on an indifference curve. Naturally other combinations of these items may be more or less desirable to the consumer and therefore fall on other indifference curves.

The pattern of indifference curves for a consumer is plotted in figure 11-1. Each curve is concave to the origin because as either of the goods becomes scarcer its relative marginal utility increases; the consumer is therefore willing to give up less of this good for a particular amount of the other. The farther the nearest point of an indifference curve is from the origin, the greater the satisfaction of the consumer at any point along the path of that curve.

The consumption-possibility line shows the various combinations of the two commodities (at fixed prices) that may be purchased with a specified sum of money. This may be indicated by a straight line whose slope depends on the relative prices of the two goods. The more money available to purchase the consumption items, the farther to the right the line will be. See figure 11-2.

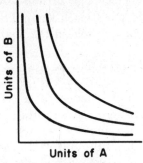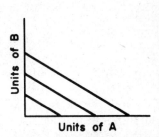

Fig. 11-1. Equal-utility curves

Fig. 11-2. Consumption-possibility lines

The consumer's equilibrium position identifies the quantities of each commodity that give maximum satisfaction for different expenditures. It can be found when one of these graphs is superimposed on the other (axes constructed to the same scale). Equilibrium is indicated by the point at which the consumption-possibility line (indicating the sum that the consumer is willing to spend on the two commodities) is tangent to an indifference curve. Any other point on this line will intersect a lower indifference curve and therefore will yield the consumer less satisfaction. Naturally if the consumer increases his expenditures (moves to a consumption-possibility line farther to the right), he can increase his satisfaction because the point of tangency will be with a higher indifference curve.

Consumer's Surplus. The concept of marginal utility is used to define the term *consumer's surplus.* The consumer, who gets less satisfaction from each additional unit of a good he buys in any period of time, pays a price for each unit equal to the satisfaction he gets from the last unit. But the utility of each unit other than the last is greater than the marginal utility. The total utility provided by the units less the marginal utility multiplied by the number of units is equal to the consumer's surplus.

Paradox of Value. Marginal utility may also be used to explain the paradox of value posed by Adam Smith in 1776. He inquired why water which is very useful to man is cheap while diamonds which are far less useful are dear. Smith was not able to answer the question clearly although he differentiated between value in use and value in exchange. But today the question is explained simply in terms of marginal utility. Although the total utility of water may exceed the total utility of diamonds, the last (marginal) unit of water sold in the market (which determines the price) has much less utility and costs less than does the last unit of diamonds sold in the market.

COST OF PRODUCTION

The supply schedule links price with the amount of a good or service offered in the market by a seller and it also relates price to the output of the industry. Though in the very short (market) period the output is taken as fixed so that the quantity available depends on inventories, the longer (short-run and long-run) period allows producers to adjust their stocks. Whether the quantity of goods on hand is increased depends on the possibilities of maximizing profits or minimizing losses rather than on the costs of production alone.

A firm decides whether or not to produce by comparing expected selling prices or revenues with expected production costs. In this manner it is able to anticipate a level of profit. Closer examination of possible alternative ways of producing an identical volume of output will be made later in connection with the discussion of production functions. It is sufficient to remark now that various combinations of inputs of productive factors are capable of yielding the same output and that alert producers will choose the least costly combination. In general the cost of output consists of payments for factors of production used.

Total Cost. The cost of production is dependent upon the amount of output. Nevertheless, the firm is usually obligated to make certain payments regardless of whether it has any output. As a rule the shorter the time period, the more numerous the obligations that cannot be avoided. Thus a firm signing a five-year lease on a factory building is contracting to make a rental payment each month, and a firm hiring a manager for a year is undertaking a definite salary commitment. In the longer period as commitments expire they need not be renewed. Costs that are independent of output are called fixed costs (FC). Costs that change with output (though not necessarily in proportion) are termed variable costs (VC) or out-ofpocket expenses. Fixed costs plus variable costs equal total costs (TC). Since variable costs rise as output increases, total costs must also rise as the firm produces more.

A firm has fixed costs only in the short run. In the long run all costs vary with changes in output because all contracts and obligations binding the firm eventually terminate. Each firm that produces goods or services requires a specific time period to eliminate fixed costs, and the long run for one firm may be shorter than the short run for another. For example, the fixed costs of a steel plant, which include in part the depreciation of equipment, normally must be borne by entrepreneurs for a much longer period than the fixed costs of a shoe store.

Figure 11-3 relates TC, VC, and FC.

Average Cost.   Frequently it is useful to deal with costs in terms of units of output. In such cases the relevant categories are average fixed costs (AFC), average variable costs (AVC), and average total costs (ATC) or, more simply, average costs (AC). Average fixed costs are computed by dividing FC by the number of units. As more units of output are produced, the fixed costs are allocated to a greater number of items so that AFC continues to diminish. Variable costs rise as output increases, but not necessarily at a uniform rate. Generally the cost of the first units of output is high, but as output increases, improved efficiency and specialization reduce the cost of additional units. Beyond a certain output (as the firm approaches or reaches capacity) the principle of diminishing returns becomes important. Crowded conditions, tired workers, and machines temporarily broken, among other conditions, may be responsible for a proportionally greater increase in the variable costs. Average variable cost, obtained by dividing VC by the number of units of output, thus takes the form of a U-shaped curve. It follows that average total cost, TC divided by the units of output or the sum of AFC and AVC, is also U-shaped. ATC falls when both its components decline. The downward movement continues even after AVC begins to rise until the increase more than overcomes the continuing decline in AFC. Then ATC begins to rise, too.

Generally a U-shaped ATC or AVC curve should reach its minimum or lowest point near the output capacity of the firm. In some industries average variable cost appears to be constant over an extensive range of outputs, rather than U-shaped. This means that the cost of each additional unit of output remains the same until the firm approaches its capacity level. At that point diminishing returns set in and a sharp rise in AVC occurs.

Marginal Cost. Another concept that is essential to understand the economist's view of costs involves the differences or changes in cost as output increases or decreases. The extra cost necessary to produce one more unit of output—the last unit—is called marginal cost (MC). It is simply the increase in TC or VC as output rises by one unit. In practice, of course, many types of output are produced in multiple units rather than by adding one unit at a time. Under such circumstances, the MC is measured by the change in TC divided by the change in the number of units produced.

The marginal cost curve passes through the minimum point of both the U-shaped AVC curve and the U-shaped ATC curve. This occurs because the average cost (total or variable) of the firm rises when an additional unit of output (marginal cost) costs more than the average of all the preceding units, and the average cost falls when an added unit costs less than the average. It is possible, however, for ATC (or AVC) to fall as MC rises, provided that MC is below ATC (or AVC). When MC is equal to ATC (or AVC), ATC (or AVC) is at its minimum.

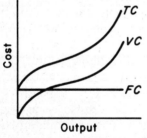

Fig. 11-3. Total cost, variable cost, and fixed cost

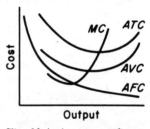

Fig. 11-4. Average total cost, average variable cost, average fixed cost, and marginal cost

The relationship between the average and the margin may be clarified by the following example. Assume that in a particular college course seven examinations scheduled during a semester will be the basis of determining the final grade. Students may wish to compute their average grade after each test score is returned to them, in order to measure their performance in the course to that point. Suppose one student has obtained an 80, 70, and 90 on the first three exams. His average therefore is 80. Consider the fourth exam as the marginal one or last one in the group of the first four. If he gets more than an 80 his average will go up, but if his score is below 80 then the average falls. That is, if the marginal score is above the average the average rises, but if it is below the average then the average falls. Once the average is computed for four tests the computational process may be repeated for the fifth one, which then represents the new margin.

The relationship between ATC, AVC, AFC, and MC is presented diagrammatically in figure 11-4. (See p. 154.)

The following hypothetical example in table 11-1 illustrates the interrelationships of some of the different kinds of cost.

TABLE 11-1

COST RELATIONSHIPS

Units of Output	Fixed Cost	Variable Cost	Total Cost	Marginal Cost	Average Fixed Cost	Average Variable Cost	Average Total Cost
1	$500	$1,000	$ 1,500	$1,000	$500	$1,000	$1,500
2	500	1,600	2,100	600	250	800	1,050
3	500	2,000	2,500	400	167	667	833
4	500	2,300	2,800	300	125	575	700
5	500	2,900	3,400	600	100	580	680
6	500	4,300	4,800	1,400	83	717	800
7	500	6,300	6,800	2,000	71	900	971
8	500	9,500	10,000	3,200	63	1,188	1,250

The minimum marginal cost is at four units of output, but the minimum average total cost is at five units.

Long-Run and Short-Run Costs. The long-run average cost curve of a firm shows the lowest possible cost of producing different amounts of output. Each output is produced by that combination of factors (allowing land, machinery, and labor to vary in any proportion) that results in the lowest cost. Thus moving along the curve involves changes in factor combinations, including plant. The shape of the long-run cost curve usually takes one of three possible forms. (1) Some firms may show rising costs or decreasing returns to scale. Greater production, even with all factors adjusted optimally, occurs only with higher average costs per unit of output. (2) Other firms may exhibit constant costs or constant returns to scale. The average cost per unit of output remains the same as the scale of production increases. (3) A third group of firms may operate under conditions of decreasing costs or increasing returns to scale. The unit cost of output falls as the scale of production gets larger.

In most industries long-run average costs tend to fall or remain constant over a wide range; few industries show a pattern of rising costs. The pattern of costs in any situation depends on the technology, including the machinery and equipment available, and the extent to which division of labor occurs. Whether an industry has firms operating at the lowest possible average cost depends on the size of the market and the extent to which profit maximization is the guiding principle.

The short-run average cost curve relates variations in cost with changes in output as one or more factors are held constant. It has already been indicated that the shape of this curve generally takes the form of a U. At the output at which the fixed factors of a firm are technologically geared to produce at the lowest possible cost, the short-run average cost curve is tangent to the long-run average cost curve. This means that the short-run average cost of the firm for any other output could be lower than it is if an appropriate change in technology were made. In no case, however, will the short-run curve fall below the long-run curve. These relationships are shown in figure 11-5.

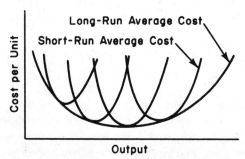

Fig. 11-5. Relation between long-run average cost and short-run average cost

It has been indicated that the market price is based upon the relationship between demand and supply. The supply schedule, however, may pertain to the market period, short-run period, or long-run period. Only in the long run must prices cover the average total cost of production; in the short run they need be no higher than the average variable cost and in the market period they are largely independent of cost. It is for these reasons that supply is sometimes considered the dominant factor influencing price in the long run, while demand is more important in the short-run and market periods.

Implicit, Opportunity, and Social Costs. When measuring and analyzing costs of production, economists are concerned with more than cash outlays for resources and factors. Three relevant and important concepts are implicit costs, opportunity costs, and social costs.

Implicit costs (or imputed costs) refer to factor payments of wages, interest, and rent when an entrepreneur employs his own labor, capital, or land. Frequently the entrepreneur calls his total revenue, less cash outlays for factors of production, the profit of the enterprise. He does not deduct implicit costs (i.e., the returns that should be paid to the factors he supplies himself).

Opportunity cost (or alternative cost) involves sacrificed possibilities or opportunities. It is the value of a resource or factor which is used in the best alternative way. Thus implicit costs of the entrepreneur are opportunity costs; their value equals the amount that the resources or factors can earn elsewhere. Generally, however, the opportunity costs of a firm are identical to the market prices of the goods or factors purchased. The actual price paid by a firm for a ton of steel ingots is also the opportunity cost because that is the price of steel ingots for any use. The opportunity cost of labor, to an individual receiving a wage (price of labor), is the best foregone alternative employment in which the same working time might be used (including, as a possibility, the value of leisure given up).

There are numerous occasions when social costs (costs to society) clearly differ from private costs (costs to the firm). For example, factories that fill the air with chemicals, smoke, and dirt or that deposit waste into the rivers are generally exempt from bearing the resultant costs to the community. Smog reduces the pleasantness of an environment, affects health adversely, and increases the need to clean and paint in the surrounding area; pollution of the waterways creates health hazards and destroys scenic beauty. Smog and pollution produce social costs; in the absence of government regulation, such costs have not been part of the private costs of industry. Similarly, private enterprise regards the cost of natural resources, such as timber standing in forests, in terms of the price it must pay for them. The needs and desires of the public for conservation, scenic beauty, and public parks are frequently ignored, often with subsequent high social costs.

Differences between social cost and private cost imply that the allocation of resources desired by society differs from the allocation that private enterprise finds most profitable. Generally the greater the gap between private and social cost, the stronger will be the incentive of society to take action through government to modify the behavior of private business; in some cases, society may undertake public ownership and control of the resource or productive activity. In general the difference between social cost and private cost is difficult to measure.

Sometimes social benefits exceed private benefits. For example, farmers who bear the cost of preventing soil erosion on their land reduce the prospects of flooding for the inhabitants of an entire region. But only the farmer pays the cost. Similarly, producers whose equipment becomes obsolete or workers who are displaced by technological advance sustain economic burdens, but society as a whole gains from improved machinery. Frequently the government must undertake the production of goods that provide satisfaction to people who might not be willing to pay for them. Public health activities, such as disease prevention, benefit all within a community. Private enterprise ordinarily will not undertake such work because it is not profitable, and the government must provide these necessary services through the tax system. Goods or services of this type are called collective consumption goods.

Equilibrium.   The cost data of a firm provide sufficient information to establish the supply schedule but are inadequate to determine the actual output. In order to know how much a firm will produce, the demand schedule for its product must also be known. For example, a firm will not produce anything, regardless of cost, if there is no demand for its output. Since the typical firm is organized to make and to maximize profit, it tends to produce that amount which will provide the widest margin between the revenue from the sale of its product and the cost of manufacturing the product. In some cases the firm is not able to make a profit, since cost exceeds revenue at all levels of output. Under such conditions the firm attempts to minimize its losses. It produces the quantity at which total revenue exceeds total variable cost by the greatest possible amount. Thus part of fixed cost is recovered. If, however, total revenue never exceeds the variable cost, then the firm shuts down entirely, limiting its losses to the fixed cost.

Revenue.   Revenue is the amount of money received by the firm from sales. Total revenue (TR) is that sum derived from sales at each output; average revenue (AR) is TR divided by the number of units sold. (Average revenue corresponds to price.) As in the case of cost, the marginal concept is important here also. Marginal revenue (MR) is the difference or change in revenue as sales increase or decrease by one unit. If the change in revenue of the firm reflects sales involving more than one unit, MR may be found by dividing the change in TR by the change in the number of units sold.

MARGINAL ANALYSIS

The solution to many output problems may be obtained through marginal analysis. Businessmen frequently maintain that they do not consider marginal cost and marginal revenue concepts in making their decisions but rather depend on the relationship between total costs and total revenue. There are nevertheless important reasons for studying marginal behavior and marginal technique. (1) Entrepreneurs who seek the highest possible profit level act as if they base their decisions on marginal relations. (2) Many firms must decide whether to take another order or produce another unit of output at a particular price. These questions are essentially of a marginal nature. (3) The most efficient allocation of resources, regardless of whether the economy is capitalistic or communistic, requires that the marginal cost of producing any good anywhere in the system be equal. If the MC of producing a good by one firm is lower than that of another firm, or if the marginal cost of output is lower when one resource is used instead of another resource, society may increase its efficiency by shifting from the higher MC to the lower MC firm or resource. (4) The supply curve of the firm in the short run, which indicates the amount of output that will be offered at various prices, is that portion of the marginal cost curve above the average variable cost curve. If average revenue is below AVC, it would pay the firm to shut down since total revenue is insufficient to allow recovery of variable cost. The supply curve in the long run is that part of the marginal cost curve which lies above the long-run average cost curve.

Chapter 12
COMPETITIVE AND
MONOPOLY MARKETS

A market is a difficult concept; in essence, it consists of a group of firms from which a group of buyers purchase a commodity or service. The extent of the market depends on many factors, including the type of goods, the distance separating participants, and the prevailing prices. Different market structures exist in the United States. The nature of the structure is determined by the number and size of firms, the number and size of buyers, the degree to which action by one firm influences other firms, the extent to which different firms are able to alter the demand for the goods they sell, the degree to which the commodity sold by different firms varies, the amount of information sellers and buyers have about transactions, and the freedom of firms to enter or to leave the industry.

The meaning of competition is not the same to the economist as to the layman. Competition to the general public implies sellers and producers who are vying with each other for customers and profits. Advertising, improving the quality of the product, and lowering the price are among the techniques used by each of the firms to increase the number of buyers and the quantities each buyer purchases. To the economist, however, such actions represent limitations on the extent or degree of competition.

The three main types of market structures are perfect competition, monopoly, and imperfect competition.

PERFECT COMPETITION

Perfect competition (or pure competition, although for advanced analytical purposes these terms are usually not interchangeable) operates under the following conditions: All firms or sellers in a market are able to sell as much of the product as they have at the market price without influencing the price to any extent whatsoever, and all buyers are able to purchase as much as they desire at the same price without affecting the price. These conditions imply the participation of a sufficiently large number of buyers and sellers in the market so that each has a role so small that his actions do not affect the price. (Thus price collusion is precluded among buyers and among sellers.) The product involved must be homogeneous, or identical, so that buyers are indifferent as to which sellers they purchase from. All buyers and sellers must have full information about prevailing price conditions, and new firms must be in a position to enter the market if they find it desirable to do so. Markets are removed from perfect competition to the extent that these conditions are absent.

A typical firm in a perfectly competitive market, like all profit seekers, attempts to maximize its profits (or minimize its losses). Since such a firm has no control over price, its revenue is directly proportional to sales. Total revenue (*TR*) is equal to price multiplied by the number of units sold; average revenue (*AR*) is equal to *TR* divided by the number of units sold (which is equal to price); and marginal revenue (*MR*) is equal to average revenue, as each additional unit sold adds to *TR* an amount equal to price. The *AR* and *MR* curves may be represented graphically by the same horizontal line. This line is the demand schedule facing the firm. It is perfectly elastic and implies that the firm may sell as much as it chooses at the prevailing price level.

Equilibrium. In any market structure maximization of profit for a firm occurs at that output where total revenue exceeds total cost (*TC*) by the greatest amount. Assuming that the average total cost and the marginal cost (*MC*) are rising (and they will beyond a certain output), then the firm will attain its largest profit when *MC* is equal to *MR*. (It is necessary for *AR* at that output to be no less than average total cost.) Profit maximization occurs because the cost of the next unit of production will be greater than the revenue derived from its sale; total profit therefore declines. Furthermore, producing and selling one unit less causes the firm to give up a greater amount of revenue than cost. It should be clear therefore that the output at which marginal cost is equal to marginal revenue is the output at which total revenue exceeds total cost by the largest amount. The equilibrium output is derived from the point where *MC* = *MR*. In a perfectly competitive market *MC* equals price, and *MR*, at equilibrium.

Yet it may be that revenue is inadequate to meet costs incurred by the firm, so that there is no output at which *TR* equals or exceeds *TC*. In this case, the intersection of *MR* and *MC* shows the output at which the firm minimizes losses, i.e., at which *TC* exceeds *TR* by the smallest amount. The firm produces as long as it is covering its variable cost, which means that *AR* is no less than average variable cost. It shuts down, however, if price falls below the minimum average variable cost because it is then losing more than its fixed cost.

The behavior of a firm in a perfectly competitive market depends upon the time period involved. In the short run, it is possible that profit above the amount necessary to keep a firm operating in the industry (excess profit) is present or that loss occurs. But such conditions cannot exist in the long run. If firms have freedom of entry into and exit out of the industry, excess profit attracts new producers or leads to expansion of existing firms and loss forces some firms from the industry. Additional firms increase the total supply of the industry and tend to force price down; simultaneously, they bid for more factors of input and thereby tend to raise the costs of each firm. Thus excess profit is squeezed out. On the other hand, a decline in the number of firms has the opposite effect. The market price tends to rise and the costs of each firm tend to fall so that loss disappears.

The long-run equilibrium of the firm in perfect competition is one where profit is just enough to keep it operating. There is no excess profit and no loss. Total cost, which includes the profit necessary to keep a firm in business (normal profit), is exactly equal to total revenue. More precisely, $AC = AR = MC = MR$ at the long-run equilibrium output of the firm. Furthermore, the industry is neither expanding nor contracting. This means that firms cannot lower their costs by expanding the scale of operations. The firm produces the output at which price is simultaneously equal to short-run average total cost and long-run average total cost. This output occurs only at the minimum point of the long-run average cost curve. Long-run equilibrium is not possible in a competitive industry in which decreasing costs prevail, because expansion of the firm lowers its cost and thereby increases its profit.

The three profit situations of short-run equilibrium are demonstrated graphically in figure 12-1. But only the normal profit case is possible in the long run.

At any time, of course, even under conditions of perfect competition, there is considerable diversity among firms. They vary in size and operate under different schedules of costs. But only the most efficient firms, earning higher profit rates, survive. New firms therefore are inclined to imitate the more efficient methods of production, and the inefficient firms are gradually forced out of the industry. In the long run the average costs of all firms in a perfectly competitive market are at the same level; this is also the minimum level that existing technology makes possible.

Producer Cooperatives. The equilibrium market price in a perfectly competitive industry may exist at a level where the demand curve is inelastic. Though an individual seller is in no position to do anything about the situation, a combination of sellers may attempt to reduce output or limit supply and thereby increase total revenue and profit. Such is the purpose of many producer cooperatives which are organized to market agricultural commodities. A higher price, of course, is of benefit to each member. But the tendency of some sellers to exceed the sales quota allotted to them leads many producer cooperatives to fail in their objective to restrict supply.

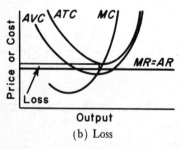

(a) Excess profit

(b) Loss

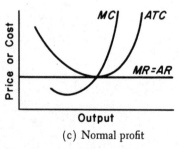

(c) Normal profit

Fig. 12-1. Short-run equilibrium in perfect competition

MONOPOLY

Monopoly exists where there is a market in which a single seller produces or controls the entire supply of a good or a service that has no adequate substitute; the firm is therefore able to influence the price considerably. Monopoly represents the extreme departure from perfect competition. Telephone and electric companies ordinarily constitute monopolistic enterprises in most communities (markets). Advertising may occur, but the emphasis is on attaining the goodwill of the public and on expanding the market rather than on puffing the superiority of its product over related products. Monopolistic firms, however, are relatively rare in the United States economy.

Demand. Although the cost curve of the monopolistic firm is based upon considerations similar to those affecting the cost curve of perfectly competitive firms, the demand for the output of the monopolist is quite different. The perfect competitor can sell all he wants without affecting price, but the monopolist has considerable control over price because he has a unique product. An increase in price, therefore, is accompanied by a decline in sales. Thus the demand for his product is negatively sloped. The demand curve facing the monopolist is the same as the market demand curve of a competitive industry. An objective of a monopolist is to make the demand for his product as inelastic as possible so that a higher price would not lead him to lose many customers. He also wishes to prevent other firms from entering the industry.

In the case of monopoly, unlike perfect competition, marginal revenue is below price (average revenue) for any unit of output (after the first) because of the negatively sloping demand schedule facing the seller. This means that as the price falls, marginal revenue, shown by the change in total revenue, declines by more than the price. Thus, if the tenth unit of a good can be sold only by reducing the price from $1.00 to $.99, MR falls more rapidly than price (and is less than price) because one cent of revenue is lost for each of the first nine units. Total revenue for the sale of nine units is $9.00, and total revenue for the sale of ten units is $9.90. MR is $.90, the price of the tenth unit less nine cents.

Equilibrium. If the object of a monopoly is to maximize profit, output is in equilibrium when $MC = MR$. At this point TR exceeds TC by the greatest possible amount. Generally, however, this situation represents equilibrium both in the short run and the long run because freedom of entry for new firms is not easy, nor are substitute goods readily available. Naturally the assumption that profit exists must be made (TR exceeds TC at some output), otherwise the monopolist would shut down completely if he were able to.

The diagrammatic representation of the equilibrium of a firm in a monopoly market is shown in figure 12-2.

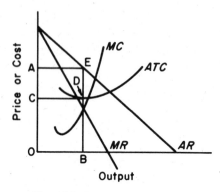

Fig. 12-2. Monopoly equilibrium

The equilibrium output of *OB* in the diagram is determined from the intersection of *MC* = *MR*. The price charged, however, is *OA*. It is read from the *AR* (price) line. Thus the excess profit of the firm is shown by the rectangle *ACDE*, which is equal to the difference between the price and the cost per unit multiplied by the number of units sold. Note that the equilibrium output of a monopolist must occur at an elastic point on the demand curve; otherwise revenue could be increased and cost reduced (thus raising profit) by curtailing output. It should also be clear that if the cost of production schedules of a monopoly and a competitive firm are similar, then price is higher and output lower under monopoly.

Unlike a perfect competitor, the monopolist has no supply curve. There is no unique relationship between price and output in monopoly. At the equilibrium output, where *MC* = *MR*, there may be several possible market prices depending on the shape and slope of the demand schedule. Similarly, at any monopoly price there may be more than one equilibrium output. Therefore, unlike perfect competition, an increase in demand need not cause both price and output to rise in the short run.

Monopoly Power. The amount of monopoly power exercised by a firm may be judged by the extent to which its demand schedule is affected by the actions of other firms. The greater the effect on the monopolist's demand curve, the smaller the amount of monopoly power. Measurements of monopoly power have depended upon a determination of the concentration ratio (discussed in chapter 13) and an examination of the rate of profit.

Price Discrimination. The existence of monopoly power may permit the seller to practice price discrimination. If it is possible to break up the market into distinct groups of buyers so that more than one price may be established, both total revenue and output increase. The monopolist will increase his profit if he charges higher prices to those whose demand is less elastic and lower prices to those whose demand is more elastic. Price discrimination assumes that different prices are charged for reasons other than differences in cost. It presupposes that the seller is able to prevent the resale of the product. Such separation of markets may be feasible in the area of international trade (the domestic market may be inelastic and the foreign market may be elastic because of competition), the sale of services (a doctor may charge his wealthier patients more), and the marketing of goods that require installation or servicing by the seller.

Restraints. The monopolist is subject to some serious restraints in attempting to fix prices and maximize profit. In the first place, setting high prices to maximize profit could lead buyers to purchase other products. For example, aluminum might be substituted for steel or tea for coffee. Second, undue profit might induce the government to investigate the industry. This possibility often discourages firms from charging the highest price the market will bear. Third, high profit provides an unusually strong incentive for new firms to seek entry into the industry. Fourth, in some cases the monopolist faces legal enactments and administrative regulations that may limit his actions. The government may prevent him from withdrawing his resources from the business even if he is losing money. Thus, despite losses sustained by the Penn Central Company, no freight or passenger services could be eliminated without the approval of the appropriate governmental authorities.

IMPERFECT COMPETITION

Firms generally try to move out of markets that are more competitive and into those that are less competitive. They do this in part by attempting to differentiate the product they sell. For this reason many firms try to popularize brand names. Demand for a particular brand tends to move the good out of a perfectly competitive market and allows the producer to exert some influence on price. But limitations are imposed on the ability of sellers to influence price and increase profit by the possibility that consumers may substitute other brands. Similarly, when only a few firms produce a good, even if it is homogeneous (for example, rubber bands or nails where brand name is unimportant), some control over price may be exercised by producers. However, the influence here is limited by the likelihood that other products will be purchased by the consumer to meet his needs or that new firms will enter the industry.

Industry in the United States typically operates in markets that fall between perfect competition and monopoly. Imperfect competition (or monopolistic competition) involves markets in which firms are able to affect the price of the products by their actions. It occurs when one of the following three conditions is present: There are many sellers of a product that is differentiated or nonhomogeneous, regardless of whether the differences are real or are imagined by buyers; the number of firms is small, but the product is homogeneous; the number of firms is small, and the product is differentiated. The last two cases describe oligopoly.

Imperfect competition therefore is usually analyzed under two subdivisions: (1) many firms selling a differentiated product and (2) oligopoly. It is generally assumed that considerably greater relative ease of entry into the industry exists in the first case than in the second case.

Many Sellers of Differentiated Products.   In this type of market, each firm sells a product that varies somewhat from that sold by its rivals. The demand curve facing the firm therefore is no longer perfectly elastic but rather negatively sloped. It shows the demand for the product at different prices on the assumption that other firms do not change their prices. A more differentiated product tends to have a less elastic demand curve. The cost curve again is assumed to be U-shaped.

In the short run excess profit may prevail. Maximization of profit for the firm occurs where total revenue exceeds total cost by the widest margin. This is, of course, at the intersection of *MC* and *MR*. If it should happen that demand lies below cost at all levels, then the firm minimizes losses where *MC* equals *MR*. The fact that new firms can enter and existing firms can leave the industry if conditions warrant, or that one firm can closely imitate the operations of another, leads to a long-term situation in which excess profit or loss is eliminated. Firms are in equilibrium when total cost (including normal profit) equals total revenue. This means that average total cost equals average revenue and that marginal cost equals marginal revenue at the equilibrium output. The price curve (AR) is tangent to the ATC curve at that output.

Figure 12-3 (p. 170) represents the three types of short-run equilibrium in a market that has many sellers of differentiated products. In the long run, however, only the normal profit is obtainable. The equilibrium price is above the minimum average total cost; and the equilibrium output is below the output that is produced at the minimum average total cost (the firm operates with excess capacity).

The imperfect competitor engages in nonprice competition and thus has more control over price. The product actually may be somewhat different in design, composition, or quality; the service rendered at the time of sale may vary; the convenience of obtaining the product may induce the purchase; or, as a result of advertising, customers may unjustifiably assume that the product is different. The perfectly competitive firm has no need for nonprice competition, as it is able to sell all that it has.

Oligopoly. Oligopoly describes a market in which there are only a few firms (duopoly is used if there are only two). The product may or may not be differentiated.

The demand curve facing the oligopolist is negatively sloped, and the cost curve assumes the usual U shape. Each of the sellers is able to supply a relatively large proportion of the market demand for the product. The price may be established at any level, ranging between the price that would exist under monopoly and the price that would be determined under conditions of perfect competition. Corresponding variations in quantity occur. If the product is homogeneous, all the firms must charge the same price; but if there is differentiation they need not do so.

Oligopolistic firms clearly realize that any action on their part will normally lead to a reaction by their rivals. Rigid prices therefore are not uncommon in these industries. Nevertheless, in order to avoid losing customers, oligopolies are more likely to match price cuts than price increases.

Oligopolists do not necessarily impose the monopoly price even though it is most profitable for them to do so. Limitations on their freedom arise from differences among them in evaluating business conditions and in the strategy to follow; illegality of price collusion;

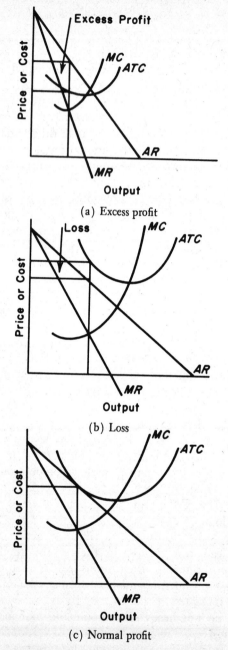

(a) Excess profit

(b) Loss

(c) Normal profit

Fig. 12-3. Short-run equilibrium in imperfect competition

tactics used by large buyers to divide sellers; unwillingness of small producers of the product to follow the lead of larger firms; and possibilities that price increases will bring new firms into the industry.

Firms in oligopoly markets characteristically exert influence on the price, devote attention to the quality of the good, and depend on advertising. But economic waste tends to arise because of the heavy selling outlays and the existence of a considerable amount of unused capacity.

It is generally recognized that resources are not allocated in the same way under conditions of imperfect competition and monopoly as they are under perfect competition. The price charged by the seller is above marginal cost at the equilibrium output. Furthermore, the firm does not produce and sell at the lowest possible average total cost. Monopolists and imperfect competitors receive a higher price and produce less than do perfect competitors having the same cost curves. These departures from a perfectly competitive market (in which consumer satisfaction is maximized) lead to apparent distortions in what is produced and in who receives factor payments. The interest of the public is not protected automatically by the "invisible hand" that functions under conditions of perfect competition. Nevertheless, it is true that consumer preferences do play a part in establishing prices in the imperfectly competitive market. However, the monopolist appears to have greater incentive to innovate, and thereby reduce the ATC curve, than the firm in the perfectly competitive or imperfectly competitive market because the monopolist is in a better position to retain the gains of his efforts in the long run. Imitators are likely to eliminate the advantages of other firms after a short time. Sufficient empirical evidence is not yet available to enable economists to assess the relative performance of firms under conditions of perfect competition, imperfect competition, and monopoly.

Market Power of Buyers. Some cases of imperfect competition are associated with the market power of buyers rather than sellers. For example, the government may be the sole purchaser of satellites or rockets; only a few firms may purchase certain agricultural produce or hire some types of specialized labor. In such cases buyers may exercise some control over price. A market that has one buyer is called monopsonistic; if there are only a few buyers it is termed oligopsonistic (duopsony refers to two buyers).

ALTERNATIVES TO SHORT-RUN PROFIT MAXIMIZATION BY THE FIRM

Much of current economic analysis revolves around the assumption that business firms attempt to maximize profit in the short run. It has been suggested that in reality a firm may have a completely different goal or it may have more than one motive. (1) The maximization of profit in the long run may be the purpose of the enterprise. This requires that consideration be given to future growth and public goodwill at the cost of greater immediate profit. (2) Average-cost pricing (or full-cost pricing) is used. The firm computes the unit cost of its product (including the fixed cost) based on current or estimated future production and then adds a certain percentage, called *markup*, to establish the price. Demand or revenue factors therefore are not given consideration unless the markup is varied in response to business conditions. (3) The maximization of sales has been suggested as the basic policy and driving force of many firms. These companies are operated by executives (rather than owners) who seek larger salaries, greater fringe benefits, more prestige, and increased power. Growth in the size of the firm rather than in profit may satisfy these executive ambitions as long as the stockholder does not complain about his return. (4) The principle of *satisficing* has been proposed as an explanation of the objective of the firm. This means that the firm attempts to achieve a particular minimum level of profit and hold a certain fraction of the market. If this is accomplished, it makes no further effort to improve its position.

IV Distribution

Chapter 13
GOVERNMENT REGULATION AND CONTROL OF BUSINESS

Almost all proponents of laissez-faire recognize the need for some government regulation of business. The successful operation of the United States economy is generally considered to require public action to maintain competition and enforce contracts. The past hundred years have shown that consumer interests suffered as industry developed, formed combinations, and became concentrated. It has been a major task of the federal government to prevent business firms from gaining and exerting monopoly power over output, prices, and profit. This has been done in three ways: antitrust legislation, regulation of public utilities, and government ownership and operation of business.

Public criticism or political motivation often brings about government action against business firms that are characterized by huge aggregations of capital, enormous volumes of sales, and great numbers of employees. Firms that dominate particular markets or impede competition are also subject to government scrutiny. But intervention ordinarily occurs only if large-scale economic activity is involved.

There has been prolonged debate as to the merits of big business. Persons who favor big businesss maintain that: (1) Huge enterprises possess certain operating advantages that bring about lower prices, superior quality of products, new types of products, and better service. (2) Economies of scale and lower costs per unit arise in connection with management efficiency as well as in raising capital, buying raw materials, and selling finished products. (3) Potential competition leads to the use of the most advanced technology and to vast research projects that hasten technical progress in order to raise productivity. (4) Output may be diversified to reduce risk and consolidate the successive stages of production. (5) Larger firms are better able to service government contracts.

Objections to big business are expressed mainly in terms of (1) the detrimental effects of restraint of trade—for example, adverse impacts on prices, capital investment, and small competitors. Furthermore, it has been suggested that: (2) Higher education is under financial pressure to adapt its curriculum to the job requirements set by big business. (3) Vast advertising expenditures force particular products on a reluctant public. (4) Evidence is lacking to establish conclusively that large firms produce at lower unit cost or finance much significant research.

Not all monopolies and large enterprises have been subject to dissolution or regulation. Indeed, there are cases in which the government has permitted and encouraged combinations and certain restraint of trade practices. Furthermore, relatively small businesses in local markets are not generally disturbed, regardless of how much monopolistic control they exercise. Such situations may be especially common in rural areas.

COMBINATIONS AND CONCENTRATION

In the past century various types of business combinations have emerged in the United States. Some of these combinations have been associated primarily with restraint of trade or monopolization of industry, but others have served the public interest. The method of combination chosen has depended upon the objectives of the businessmen involved.

Types of Combination.   The main forms of combination include: (1) trusts, organizations in which separate corporations hand over voting rights of their stock to a board of trustees that is then able to control all the participating companies (the term *trust* today may refer to any large company regardless of its type of control; (2) pools, organizations based on agreements between two or more companies to fix prices, divide marketing territory, reduce output, or share profit (on an international scale such organizations are called cartels); (3) mergers, organizations in which one company acquires the stock or assets of another and then dissolves it (amalgamations or consolidations refer to a new corporation set up to take over two or more established corporations); (4) holding companies, organizations in which a corporation holds enough stock of another corporation to be able to control it. The holding company, exemplified by the American Telephone and Telegraph Company and by the General Motors Corporation, is a popular combination device today. One holding company may control several other holding companies (which in turn may control others), thus establishing a pyramid structure. The holding company, or parent corporation, may or may not be an operating company (i.e., engaged in actual production), but the subsidiary ordinarily is.

Combinations are also classified as horizontal or vertical. Horizontal combinations are those in which firms or plants producing the same goods or engaged in the same business (normally competing with each other) are brought under the same management. Vertical combinations are formed when plants and firms engaged in all or several of the various stages of production from the extraction of raw materials to fabrication of the final product are brought together under one management. Safeway Stores and Ford Motor Company are examples of horizontal combinations, and the Aluminum Company of America is an example of a vertical combination. Very often both these types of combination are evident in structural changes made by a company.

Extent of Concentration.   A complex set of forces determines the degree of concentration or market dominance of business firms in different sectors of the United States economy at any time as well as the rate at which concentration changes. Ordinarily concentration is a situation associated with sellers of goods, but it does arise occasionally among buyers. For example, there are only a small number of buyers of leaf tobacco, fluid milk, and crude petroleum.

Some factors in the economy tend to increase the extent of concentration, but others serve as deterrents. Firms attempt to grow to a more efficient size by taking advantage of technology to achieve the economies of large-scale production or marketing of output. Greater output often results in more efficient sales promotion. Furthermore, enterprises attempt to reduce competitive forces by eliminating rivals; entry of new firms is prevented through such techniques as controlling patents or sources of supply. Outside financial interests with a stake in the profits of a firm also tend to encourage concentration through mergers. Similar pressures for expansion exist in firms that have substantial sums of undistributed liquid profits. Tendencies toward concentration are discouraged by the legal enactments dealing with antitrust, the reluctance of some entrepreneurs and managements in control of a business to form a merger or combination that requires yielding some or all of their powers to others, and the growth of the economy and markets which increases demand and tends to reduce the proportion of output produced by any one firm.

The concentration ratio measures the extent to which the number of firms involved in the production or marketing of any one product is limited. The ratio takes various forms but generally it is an expression of the percentage of employment provided or value of goods shipped (sales, value added, assets, or output also may be used) by a small number of the largest firms in an industry. Frequently, but not necessarily, four firms are used to measure concentration.

Concentration ratios in manufacturing based on percentages of employment, payroll, value of shipments, and new capital expenditures are given in tables 13-1 and 13-2.

TABLE 13-1

PERCENT SHARE OF LARGEST MANUFACTURING COMPANIES, 1967

Size	Employees	Payroll	Value of shipments	New capital spending
50 largest	20	25	25	28
51–100 largest	6	7	8	13
101–150 largest	4	5	6	6
151–200 largest	4	3	4	4
Total	34	40	43	51

Source: *Statistical Abstract of the United States*, 1974, p. 720.

The figures available do not show whether the concentration of industry has been increasing or decreasing in the United States. In the first place, any conclusion will depend upon the measurement used. Second, some industries have tended to greater concentration, others to less concentration, and a few indicate no significant change over time. Third, many large firms are so diversified that they cannot readily be classified in a particular industry or associated with a specific product. Fourth, low concentration ratios for an industry on a nationwide basis may occur with high concentration patterns on a local level. Fifth, the extent of tacit, though illegal, collusion between firms is unknown; thus effective concentration may be greater than any measurement indicates. Sixth, considerable competition may exist between products even though the concentration ratio of any one of them is high; for example, steel and aluminum, or cigars and cigarettes, are interchangeable in many cases.

TABLE 13-2

NUMBER OF COMPANIES AND PERCENT OF THE VALUE OF TOTAL
SHIPMENTS MADE BY THE FOUR LARGEST IN 1970
(MANUFACTURING INDUSTRIES HAVING THE
GREATEST VALUE OF SHIPMENTS)

Industry	*Number of Companies*	*Percent*
Motor vehicles	107	91
Petroleum refining	276	33
Blast furnaces and steel mills	200	47
Meat packing plants	2,529	23
Motor vehicle parts	1,424	58
Aircraft	91	65
Radio, TV communication equipment	1,111	19
Fluid milk	2,988	20
Plastic products	4,495	8
Newspapers	7,589	16
Metal stampings	2,564	40
Pharmaceutical preparations	791	26
Papermills	203	26
Bread and related products	3,445	29
Aircraft engines	205	68
Construction machinery	578	42
Bottled and canned soft drinks	3,057	13

Source: *Statistical Abstract of the United States*, 1974, pp. 720–721. Number of companies in 1967.

Multinational Companies. The substantial outflow of U.S. capital to many parts of the world after the Second World War led to rapid expansion of multinational companies. A multinational corporation is defined as a company that operates in at least six countries, has annual sales above $100 million, and has foreign subsidiaries accounting for at least 20 percent of its assets. It operates under one overall management but is separately chartered in each country. These firms serve to transfer management skills, capital, and technology among nations.

It has been contended that multinational corporations reduce international trade barriers, increase world economic development, promote local growth among suppliers, and create more purchasing power and sources of tax revenue. On the other hand, it is alleged that they gain unfair tax advantages over domestic firms, exercise undue economic and political power, and export jobs from their own countries. The leading U.S. multinational companies are General Motors, Exxon, Ford Motor, General Electric, and International Business Machines. Important multinational companies also operate from the Netherlands, Great Britain, West Germany, Canada, Switzerland, Sweden, Italy, and Japan.

ANTITRUST ACTION

During the nineteenth century, state courts in the United States subjected contracts between firms involving restraint of trade to the rules of common law that prohibited trade conspiracies. These contracts therefore were unenforceable. It was not until the late 1870s that improved means of transportation and new techniques of production made it more profitable to operate larger units and to serve more extensive markets. In a number of industries, expansion of manufacturing and concentration of output in the hands of a few large companies made the problems of monopolies, trusts, and combinations a major economic issue. Industries such as oil, sugar, and whiskey were involved. Firms adopted a variety of ill-fated techniques to increase profit. The adverse effects on consumers of divided markets, fixed prices, and limited output became noticeable as prices rose sharply. The Sherman Antitrust Act of 1890 was passed by Congress to eliminate some undesirable practices. This act forbade contracts, combinations, and conspiracies in restraint of trade and prohibited monopolization and attempts to monopolize.

Statutory Enforcement.   Enforcement of the statute by government was at first not vigorous. Indeed, the greatest merger movement in U.S. history took place between 1898 and 1902. But the antitrust campaign was intensified by Presidents Theodore Roosevelt and William H. Taft early in the twentieth century. In 1904 the first dissolution order was handed down by the U.S. Supreme Court in the Northern Securities case involving the Great Northern and Northern Pacific railroad combination. This was followed in 1911 by decisions of the Supreme Court requiring both the Standard Oil Company and the American Tobacco Company to be broken up. President Woodrow Wilson continued the campaign against monopolies, and in 1914 Congress passed the Federal Trade Commission Act and the Clayton Antitrust Act. The Federal Trade Commission Act set up an administrative agency to prevent unfair competition and to prohibit practices that excluded competitors, that led to monopoly, that were deceptive, or that were unethical. The Clayton Act made several specific monopolistic practices illegal.

In the next twenty years there was relatively less activity in the antitrust field. In 1920 the Supreme Court decided that the United States Steel Corporation, the largest industrial combination in the country, did not violate the law because it was not abusing its power to eliminate competitors. Under the "rule of reason" only unreasonable restraint of trade was illegal. Subsequently, there were very few important antitrust decisions until 1935 when the Supreme Court held that the National Industrial Recovery Act (NIRA) was unconstitutional. This statute, which had been enacted in 1933, contained many varied provisions; among other things it suspended the antitrust laws in those industries adopting codes of fair competition approved by the president. The object of this aspect of the NIRA was to terminate the unrestricted competition that some government officials and economists felt was intensifying the Great Depression.

More rigid enforcement of the antitrust statutes began in 1935. The Robinson-Patman Act of 1936 clarified the meaning of price discrimination and closed some loopholes that had permitted unusually big price advantages to those firms purchasing large quantities of goods. The Wheeler-Lea Act of 1938 increased the enforcement powers of the Federal Trade Commission. The number of antitrust actions brought by the government increased greatly after 1938. Some of the major court decisions of subsequent years limited previously established rights of patent holders (Hartford-Empire case of 1945), declared control of more than 90 percent of a market illegal although smaller proportions may not be (Aluminum Company case of 1945), limited the possibilities of oligopolistic industries (American Tobacco Company case of 1946 and Paramount Pictures case of 1948), and abolished the basing point system of pricing (Cement Institute case of 1948). Decisions of the Supreme Court have oscillated between the proposition that monopoly power *per se* is illegal and that it is the abuse of monopoly power which is unlawful. In 1950 Congress strengthened the antitrust laws by enacting the Celler-Kefauver amendment to the Clayton Antitrust Act. The amendment prohibits mergers lessening competition when brought about by the purchase of assets of another company; previously only mergers resulting from the purchase of stock had been considered unlawful.

Almost all states have antitrust laws that prohibit combinations in restraint of trade. Such laws, however, have had minimal enforcement and limited effectiveness in connection with local combinations and associations. Antitrust laws, however, are peculiar to the United States. Very few other countries have legislation of this type; instead they use a variety of other means to regulate industry and prevent practices deemed objectionable.

The main object of the antitrust statutes in the United States is to protect consumers against monopoly practices and collusion by sellers that reduce competition. But although competition is recognized by Congress as the best way of protecting the public, there have been a number of legislative enactments, in addition to the NIRA, that provide exemptions from the basic antitrust policies of the federal government. The most important of these are the Miller-Tydings Act of 1937 and the McGuire Act of 1952. They permit resale price maintenance contracts between manufacturers and distributors at the retail level if state fair trade statutes are in effect. The Clayton Act itself specified that labor unions should not be considered unlawful combinations. Congress has also exempted from antitrust laws agricultural cooperatives, firms combining for the purpose of exporting goods, insurance companies, and railroad traffic rate-setting associations. Furthermore, some industries have been allowed to establish monopolies subject to strict governmental control. These special industries include the public utilities (see p. 185).

Antitrust enforcement is vested in both the Department of Justice and the Federal Trade Commission, but duplication of action and effort by these government units is unusual. Private persons injured by antitrust violations may sue for triple damages. This provision serves to check questionable practices by corporations. Furthermore, companies are willing to settle cases with the government rather than go to trial and risk an adverse court decision, as the latter result provides the evidence (showing violation of the law) needed by those who sue for damages.

Questionable Practices. The antitrust laws apply both to the form of business and to the nature of specific business practices.

They deal with the establishment of a monopoly by a firm and the elimination of competition among rival concerns. Some illegal action may be taken by firms acting alone, but other unlawful conduct is carried on in concert.

The prices of many manufactured goods and some agricultural commodities differ from prices determined by supply and demand in a competitive market. Instead they are "administered" or "quoted" by the sellers. The extent of discretion available to the seller in fixing and maintaining administered prices depends on the degree of monopoly present in the market. Generally in oligopolistic industries firms use a variety of pricing practices. These are (1) price stability, which requires large changes in demand or cost of production to bring about alterations in the price of a product; (2) price uniformity, which may indicate collusion among firms (but which may also only indicate that products are so similar and standardized that higher prices by any firm result in a loss of customers and that lower prices are met at once by rival firms); and (3) price leadership, which means that one or more firms set the pace and the other firms follow (but which does not necessarily mean that restraint of trade exists).

Some competition between firms using administered prices is in a nonprice form. It may involve product differentiation and frequent style changes; or it may consist of extensive advertising and other selling efforts to influence purchasers. These types of competition do not necessarily indicate that restraint of trade exists.

Monopoly power is weakened by interindustry competition. Such competition has increased as a result of the growth of advertising which attempts (1) to get a larger portion of the consumers' purchasing power for established products and (2) to create a demand for new products. For example, yachts compete with homes, one type of food with another, and automobiles with furniture. Furthermore, firms producing different materials, such as aluminum and lumber, have tried to influence the tastes of consumers who buy household furniture. Nevertheless, interindustry competition does not necessarily eliminate market domination by a firm.

It is unlawful for individual firms to engage in many practices that restrain trade and reduce competition. Such prohibited practices include preventing competitors from getting supplies and equipment or credit by arranging exclusive buying contracts, keeping rivals out of markets by requiring buyers of a product to agree to purchase one or more other items on an exclusive basis, charging different prices to each buyer on a basis not reflected by cost factors, obtaining unjustified price concessions, squeezing profit margins on nonintegrated competitors by manipulating prices at those stages of production where competing companies buy and sell in the market, and quoting delivered prices to the customer that include phantom or arbitrary freight charges. Generally court action has eliminated many of these practices. Of course, such practices are also illegal when employed by a group of firms.

Interlocking directorates is a technique that tends to reduce competition since the same group of persons serves on the board of directors of a number of companies. Common attitudes and policies harmful to competitors may thus develop.

Questions of unlawful actions arise in connection with trade associations established to promote the common interest of sellers of similar products. In 1776 Adam Smith wrote in *The Wealth of Nations*: "People of the same trade seldom meet together, even for merriment and diversion, but the conversation ends in a conspiracy against the public, or in some contrivance to raise prices." This comment is still pertinent today. Nevertheless, a number of activities of trade associations, such as industrial research, joint advertising, and collective bargaining are not antitrust law violations. Others, including standardization of products and uniform selling terms, may be illegal.

Outlawing predatory business practices may be incidental to government policy prohibiting restraint of trade. The antitrust laws are designed primarily to maintain a competitive market rather than prevent actions by firms that adversely affect competing firms. However, it must be expected that the competitive process will lead to the elimination of some firms.

Patents present a special problem of monopoly and restraint of trade. Under federal law holders of patents have the exclusive right for a period of seventeen years to do as they choose with new goods or productive processes invented. Not only may they produce monopolistically, but they may license others to use the invention or refuse to allow its use. The object of patent grants is to stimulate invention and permit inventors to benefit financially from their work. The U.S. Supreme Court, however, has prohibited interfirm licensing schemes and patent pools that are used to perpetuate or establish illegal monopolies. There are not enough data to predict that research and development would be curtailed significantly if economic privileges currently associated with patents were reduced or eliminated.

PUBLIC UTILITY REGULATION

An entirely different approach has been taken by the government in connection with a group of industries, called public utilities (or natural monopolies), in which competition leads to inefficient and wasteful operation. The philosophy of the government in these cases is to permit monopolies but to impose regulations that lead to price, output, and profit that approximate those that would prevail under competition.

Characteristics of Public Utilities. Firms in public utility industries generally have huge fixed costs and relatively low variable costs. Normally, therefore, they are functioning at a level where average total unit costs decline as business expands. Furthermore, they operate with unused capacity much of the time because their facilities must be adequate to meet peak loads. If more than one firm exists, competition among the firms is continuous and intense. Price wars or cutthroat competition for customers leads first to very heavy losses and eventually to the elimination of firms until only one remains or to agreements to stabilize prices at a level that maximizes profit. During the struggle, however, price may fall substantially if a firm is willing to operate as long as variable costs are covered.

Examples of public utilities are found in the transportation field, including railroads and local transit; in the communication industries, including telephone and telegraph; and in companies supplying gas, electricity, and water. In all these cases, duplication of facilities necessary to provide services or goods is uneconomical and often inconvenient for the public; more than one telephone company in an area is a good example. Public utilities have several other characteristics that link them to government in a special way. They are considered to be industries affected by the public interest, they use public streets and need franchises or certificates to operate, and they sometimes require help from the government to buy private property for business use.

Statutes. In 1887 Congress decided that individual railroad companies should be permitted to monopolize specified passenger and freight transportation services subject to regulation by a government administrative agency. It passed the Interstate Commerce Act, under which the Interstate Commerce Commission (ICC) was created. The ICC has power to approve railroad rates and quantity and quality of service. The federal government also regulates firms engaged in motor transportation, air transport, inland waterways shipping, and maritime activities. In fields other than transportation, price and service controls have been established over communication media including the telephone, telegraph, radio, and television industries, and over interstate electric power and natural gas operations. A variety of independent agencies exercises authority in each of these areas.

State regulation of public utilities antedates federal intervention. Today state agencies set or approve rate schedules and service standards of local electric, gas, and water companies. There has been some overlapping authority between the two levels of government in connection with railroad and telephone companies, but any difficulties have not proved serious. Federal law often provides minimum standards for state agencies.

Enforcement.   The regulation of the level of rates charged for service raises complicated questions concerning the fair return on capital utilized by the public utility. Firms must be able to pay rates of return to investors sufficiently high to attract the necessary investment capital. The problem is twofold. First, how is the value of the capital used for the benefit of the public to be measured? Second, what is a fair rate of return? The amount invested by the company (rate base) may be determined on the basis of the original cost of the facilities less depreciation, the current reproduction cost of the facilities, or the current cost of the facilities necessary to replace the service being rendered. It is obvious that widely different rate base values might be obtained, depending on the method of computation used, since the cost of equipment changes over a period of time and the most appropriate types of facilities for rendering service change with technological advance.

Different attitudes are held by utilities, consumers, and regulatory commissions regarding the appropriate rate base. When prices are rising, utilities favor a reproduction cost base but consumers favor an original cost base. The reverse is true when the price level is declining. Regulatory agencies are usually disposed to support the consumers' view. Generally the courts have held that any method may be used to establish the value of the property of the company provided that the result is reasonable. This means that the firm receives a fair return on a fair value of the property.

It should be clear that the value of the invested capital of a public utility cannot be determined by the method used for establishing the value of ordinary business property. The value of a business is usually estimated by capitalizing its expected earnings over time. That is, the present value of the anticipated total future profit is the expected net earnings of the firm adjusted by the interest rate currently prevalent for investment returns of comparable risk. The expected earnings of public utilities, however, depend on the rate base and the rate of return fixed by the regulatory agency; therefore expected earnings cannot be used to determine the rate base and rate of return.

The rate of return permitted on the value of the capital of the public utility takes into account the fact that the business is a monopoly and has relative stability of income. Regulatory commissions historically considered 6 percent to be a reasonable return, although there is much variation in returns in the United States. Furthermore, it must be determined in conjunction with the rate base. Obviously, if prices are rising, 6 percent on a reproduction cost base yields higher earnings than if applied to an original cost base.

In dealing with charges imposed by public utilities for service, the regulatory agencies must consider not only the problems involved in determining the levels of rates but also the appropriateness of the patterns of rates. Patterns relate to the different rates paid by different customers. The task of the regulatory commission is to set or approve rates somewhere between the cost of the service, which represents the minimum reasonable charge in most cases, and the value of the services (or what the traffic will bear), which represents the maximum possible charge.

Public utilities ordinarily have periods of peak loads. They are anxious to attract additional users during periods when capacity is not fully utilized because such business adds relatively little to total cost but may greatly increase total revenue. They also have different classes of customers, namely, household consumers, commercial or business firms, and industrial plants. The public utility may be tempted to impose higher rates on those groups of customers whose demand is more inelastic. Differential rates may be justified if they lead to extra business. For example, the telephone company lowers rates at night and on weekends, when business firms are not

using the service; electric companies usually supply current to industrial users in off-peak hours at lower rates to lessen the likelihood
that this group might buy generators and make their own power
(leading to even higher rates for residential consumers). Additional
usage may also be encouraged by reducing rates to customers who
purchase larger quantities of service.

The quantity and quality of service is also subject to regulation.
Railroads, for example, may be inclined to curtail the number of
night passenger trains if few travelers make use of the service or to
eliminate branch lines to particular localities if that part of the
operation is not showing a profit. But such action requires approval
of the regulatory body, and approval may not be granted if suspension of service would impose undue hardships on certain groups of
persons. Though utilities have been reluctant to extend service to
isolated regions or in some cases to improve their service, they may
be compelled to do so. In these instances losses incurred in one part
of the business may be recovered by the imposition of higher rates
elsewhere.

Although cutthroat competition and deterioration of service on
railroads made them the first public utility subject to federal regulation, the lapse of time has significantly altered the situation. The
growth of alternative means of transportation, including buses, trucks,
pipelines, and air carriers, has brought vigorous competition to the
business of moving passengers and freight and has led a number of
economists to express the opinion that regulation of this industry
may no longer be necessary.

GOVERNMENT OWNERSHIP

A method of preventing restraint of trade other than antitrust
laws and public regulation of business enterprise is government ownership and operation. This technique has been widely used at the
municipal level in connection with the supply of water, electricity,
and gas, and the operation of local transit facilities; private ownership
of these businesses is also quite common. Government ownership of
public utilities is justified on the grounds that successful regulation is
too complex and that some public operation is desirable as a yardstick against which private performance may be measured. Government ownership occurs when utilities are not profitable, as in the
case of many local transportation systems, or when profits may not

be immediately realized, though current investments are necessary, as in the case of waterworks in growing communities.

Federal ownership of public utilities prevails mainly in the area of hydroelectric power development. Here the supply of electricity is usually only one phase of a project. Potentials of several rivers are being used for the purposes of controlling floods, supplying water, improving navigation, providing irrigation facilities, helping to conserve soil, and producing electricity. Private enterprise could not be expected to undertake the various nonprofitable but extremely desirable operations involved. The federal government owns and operates facilities for the generation of electric power. The best known of these projects include the Tennessee Valley Authority (TVA), the Hoover Dam in Nevada, the Bonneville Dam and the Grand Coulee Dam in the Pacific Northwest, and the Shasta Dam in California.

The government engages in a variety of other activities, where costs are met from tax receipts. It provides such services as education, fire protection, health protection, garbage collection, and mail delivery. Although these functions might be profitably performed by private enterprise, the public apparently favors spreading the cost of the services to the entire population and eliminating profit incentives. Thus all wealth and income classes have relatively equal access to such services.

Chapter 14
PUBLIC FINANCE

Government activities satisfy human wants, affect output levels, and redistribute income. Some aspects of these activities may be considered within the framework of public finance, a subject that deals with government expenditure and revenue. More specifically, public finance is a study of the spending pattern of federal, state, and local governments, the ways in which governments obtain funds, and how the money is budgeted, controlled, and conserved. It includes the problem of borrowing money and handling a public debt which arises when expenditures exceed revenues. Government financial operations are intended to provide for the general welfare and therefore do not ordinarily yield profit. Furthermore, unlike private business, the public may be compelled by the government to render financial support and to accept some of the services provided (for example, education of children).

GOVERNMENT EXPENDITURES

Before the end of the nineteenth century outlays by all levels of government in the United States were only about one billion dollars, of which somewhat over half were made by localities. During the past eighty years public expenditures have risen substantially.

Reasons for Growth. Government expenditures have been growing as a proportion of gross national product, particularly during periods of war. But more than military and defense needs have been responsible for the increase in government spending. (1) The government has expanded output of the type of goods *purchased* by producers and consumers. At the federal level this has particularly involved the production of electric power and atomic energy. (2) There has been an increased expenditure for goods that are consumed by society as a whole. These goods, which include highways,

191

hospitals, and parks, are not purchased directly by individuals. Though much of the construction and maintenance of public goods is done by private enterprise, production is paid for by the government. (3) Increasing control and regulation of business enterprise to protect the public have added to the costs of operating the government. (4) The expansion of public welfare services and payments has been enormous. Many of these activities have been concerned with redistribution of income and reduction of poverty. But in addition the public has pressed for higher standards of consumption, health, and economic security. (5) In recent years, government spending has been associated with fiscal policies intended to maintain high levels of output and employment to achieve economic stability, and to moderate business fluctuations. (This role is described in detail in chapter 6.) (6) Higher expenditure has been necessitated by the growth of population. (7) Part of the larger outlays has been caused by higher price levels.

There is considerable disagreement in the United States today as to whether the functions and expenditures of government should be increased or decreased. This is not a matter to be decided solely by economists. Certainly as the gross national product rises it becomes more feasible for the government to undertake additional activities and to produce a greater quantity of public goods. But the public attitude concerning the type of economy it wishes to have must be the decisive factor. Though the nature of public activity is decided by representatives elected on the basis of one vote for each citizen, private production and resource allocation are determined by the dollar expenditures of individuals, so that persons with greater income and wealth have a greater voice in decisions.

Types of Expenditure. Government expenditures were more than $432 billion in fiscal 1973, of which 52 percent originated in outlays made by the federal government, 23 percent by the states, and 25 percent by local government. After allowing for intergovernmental transactions during the year, i.e., grants made among the different levels of government, the distribution of expenditures changes. Federal spending remains at 52 percent, state expenditures fall to 18 percent, and outlays of local governments increase to 30 percent. Direct expenditures are made for current operations, which include public payrolls and purchase of goods and services to perform various government functions; capital outlays, which involve construction projects and purchase of land and equipment; assistance and subsidies to individuals and businesses; interest on debt; and insurance benefits and repayments. Table 14-1 lists the types of direct expenditure of the different government levels. The largest government expenditure by function or purpose is for national defense and international relations. This is followed in order of magnitude by outlays for education, social insurance payments, public welfare, interest on the debt, highways, health and hospitals, and conservation of natural resources. Functional expenditure is shown in table 14-2.

Each level of government concentrates on different types of expenditures. Two-fifths of the federal expenditures is for national defense and international relations. The largest amounts spent by state governments are for education, public welfare, highways, and health and hospitals. More than three-sevenths of local spending is for education; other substantial outlays are for highways, public welfare, and health and hospitals. Per capita expenditures for particular functions vary greatly in the fifty states and among local governments.

TABLE 14-1

GOVERNMENT EXPENDITURE BY PERCENTAGES, FISCAL 1973

	All Governments	Federal	State	Local
Intergovernmental	—	15.5	34.4	0.6
Current operation	56.7	39.4	37.7	73.5
Capital outlay	12.8	7.5	12.4	16.1
Assistance and subsidies	7.1	6.9	5.8	4.1
Interest on debt	6.0	6.8	2.0	4.2
Insurance benefits	17.4	23.9	7.7	1.5
Total	100.0	100.0	100.0	100.0

Source: United States Department of Commerce, *Governmental Finances in 1972–73*, p. 5.

Cost-Benefit Analysis. In recent years cost-benefit analysis has come into prominence as a technique for determining the desirability or timing of government inventment projects. Costs and benefits are valued over time to decide whether a project should be undertaken and public expenditure made. Such analysis has been used most frequently to study projects involving water use (for example, irri-

TABLE 14-2

GOVERNMENT EXPENDITURE BY FUNCTION, FISCAL 1973

	Amount (Millions of Dollars)	Percent
National defense and international relations	79,624	18.5
Education	75,690	17.5
Insurance trust expenditure	75,326	17.4
Public welfare	26,967	6.2
Interest on general debt	25,117	5.8
Highways	19,173	4.4
Health and hospitals	18,669	4.3
Natural resources	16,372	3.8
Utility expenditure	11,204	2.6
Postal service	9,572	2.2
Veterans service	7,351	1.7
Police protection	7,331	1.7
Sanitation	5,322	1.2
Local fire protection	2,770	0.6
Liquor store expenditure	1,831	0.4
Other functions	50,275	11.7
Total	432,594	100.0

Source: United States Department of Commerce, *Governmental Finances in 1972–73*, p. 7.

gation, flood control, navigation, and hydroelectric power), transportation(for example, roads, railways, and inland waterways), and land usage (for example, urban renewal, recreation, and land reclamation).

GOVERNMENT REVENUES

The government receives funds from several sources. These are (1) taxation; (2) receipts such as special assessments, fees, and fines, from various types of administrative functions; (3) income from government business enterprises; (4) grants from other government units; and (5) public borrowing.

Role of Taxes. Taxes constitute the main source of government revenue. In fiscal 1973 the different units of government in the

United States collected $286,595,000,000 in taxes. This sum is equivalent to per capita payments by the population of $1,366, of which about $789 went to the federal government, $324 to the state governments, and $252 to the various local governments. The types of taxes that are imposed and the tax structure need to be analyzed carefully before the impact of taxes on production, consumption, investment, and employment may be made and the soundness and equity of the tax system evaluated.

Historically most government revenue was received from sales and leases of the public domain and from taxes imposed on domestic consumption and foreign trade. Generally taxes were levied on the underprivileged classes, frequently to support the upper classes. Taxes as a form of financial imposition on all citizens and residents of a country is a modern phenomenon.

Several objectives have been suggested as the basis for imposing taxes, including ability to pay, benefit received, ease of administration, adequacy of revenue, and consistency with economic goals. However, the usual standard for determining which taxes are to be imposed has been the ability to pay and the desire to minimize the sacrifice of the payer. This standard meets the generally accepted definition that a *tax* is a compulsory contribution from a person to the government to defray the expenses incurred in the common interests of all. The benefit-received principle is linked more closely with *special assessments* (which usually are single payments made to defray the costs of specific improvements to property levied according to the benefit accruing) and with *fees* (which are recurring charges for services that yield advantages to those making the payment). In a few cases taxes are related to benefits; for example, gasoline taxes are sometimes set aside by government for highway construction and improvements. But special assessments and fees are not generally considered taxes; rather they are direct charges for specific services or benefits.

Tax provisions and schedules should be easy to understand and payments due should be simple to compute, although it may not always be possible to effect these conditions. For example, excess profits tax laws may be expected to contain more complicated provisions than statutes dealing with personal income taxes. The government should strive to make tax payment procedures convenient for taxpayers. It is mainly for this reason that income taxes, which formerly were paid at one time on earnings of the preceding year (for example, in March 1939 on the income of 1938) and in some cases thereby imposed a hardship, were put on a pay-as-you-go basis by the federal government early in the 1940s. (Income tax deductions from paychecks gave rise to the take-home-pay concept.) The cost of collecting and administering a tax should be reasonable in terms of yield to both the taxpayers and the government. The amount and time of payment should be fixed with certainty. Compliance must be enforced. Illegal evasions should be made difficult and legal avoidance through loopholes and subterfuges should be discouraged.

Until the 1930s government revenues were considered adequate if they were sufficient to balance the budget, either on an annual basis or over the period of a business cycle; but since then many economists have suggested that deficit financing, in which expenditures exceed revenues, is justified and desirable if it leads to sufficient total spending to maintain full employment. Adequacy of revenues is related to policy objectives in this formulation of purpose. This concept, however, which involves a counteraction to instability of spending in the private sector of the economy, applies only to the federal government. Generally state and local governments are not geared to pursue fiscal policies intended to stabilize the economy. They are still primarily revenue-raising units whose function is to maintain balanced budgets averaged over the period of a business cycle. States and localities must impose taxes carefully so as not to put residents and local businessmen at a competitive disadvantage with a neighboring geographical region.

Economic activity may be influenced by the nature of the tax. For example, some taxes bear more heavily on consumption while others are aimed at saving. The government sometimes tries to discourage the consumption of specific goods by imposing high taxes on them, as in the case of liquor and cigarettes. On the other hand, taxes on retained earnings of corporations tend to discourage saving and investment. Heavy personal income taxes may reduce incentives to work harder or longer. Other efforts by government may be geared in the direction of encouraging economic growth, discouraging layoffs, or reducing the severity of business cycles. The government can use the tax structure as an important tool to implement its economic policies.

The impact of a tax is on the person who makes the payment to the government, but the burden may be shifted to another. Usually the tax is passed forward. This is possible, for example, if the tax can be considered part of the cost of production and included in whole or in part in the price of the goods produced or services rendered. In the case of an import duty, on the other hand, the tax might be shifted to the foreign seller in certain instances. The *incidence* or burden of a tax therefore brings about changes in the pattern of the distribution of real national income. The effect of a tax is considered to be the alteration in the level of national income caused by the influence of the tax on consumption, investment, and government purchases. Both incidence and effect of various taxes are difficult to isolate and determine. But it has already been seen that price analysis is a useful tool with which to examine the shift in and incidence of taxation.

Classification of Taxes. There are several ways in which taxes may be classified. (1) Direct and indirect taxes. The distinction between direct and indirect taxes depends on whether or not the levy can be shifted. A direct tax is borne by the person upon whom it is imposed; an indirect tax may be paid by one person and then shifted forward or backward to another. Taxes on personal income, wealth, land, or estates are usually considered direct. Sometimes a direct tax is considered to be one levied directly on persons and an indirect tax one levied on goods and services.

(2) Progressive, proportional, and regressive taxes. In each of these cases, the tax category is determined by the relationship of the amount of tax paid to the income (or wealth) of the person. If the proportion of tax paid is higher as income rises, the tax is said to be progressive; if the tax takes the same percentage regardless of income, then it is proportional; and if the ratio of tax falls as income increases, the tax is regressive. Generally taxes on personal incomes, estates, and gifts are progressive. Many taxes, however, are difficult to categorize. For example, a sales tax levied at a uniform rate on all purchases of consumer goods is regressive because consumption constitutes a smaller fraction of personal income as income rises. But if the sales tax excludes the purchases of food items, rent, and local transit it is no longer readily evident whether the tax is regressive, proportional, or progressive. This classification may be applied to the tax system as a whole. Studies of the percentage of income paid by family units as taxes in the United States do not clearly reveal whether or not the overall tax structure in this country is progressive.

(3) Specific and ad valorem taxes. The distinction between specific and ad valorem taxes is made primarily in connection with custom

duties. A specific tax is an amount placed on a quantity or physical measure of a good imported or exported. An ad valorem duty is a rate placed on the value of a good. In the United States export duties are prohibited by the federal Constitution.

Sources of Revenue.   Almost three-fifths of federal revenues (and about five-sixths of federal taxes) are obtained from personal and corporate income taxes, with the balance derived mainly from insurance trust revenues (social security taxes), excise taxes, and current charges for goods and services. The personal income tax, of course, is a progressive tax, but exemptions and deductions permitted by law tend to counteract much of the steepness of rate increases on higher incomes. Revenues derived by the federal government from individual income taxes are nearly three times those obtained from levies on corporation incomes. Sources of tax revenues are given in table 14-3.

Much of the revenue of government comes from the sales of commodities and services. The federal government collects over $22.0 billion (about a tenth of its revenues) from such operations, most of which comes from sale of natural resources, payment by foreign governments for military and other supplies, sale of property, and rent receipts from housing projects. Over two billion dollars of interest earnings on loans are received by the federal government. State governments derive about $12.4 billion from sales of goods and services, primarily as tuition and other charges at institutions of higher learning, from liquor stores, and as interest earned on loans. Local governments receive just over $17.5 billion, mainly from utility revenue, school lunch sales, hospitals, sewerage charges, housing and urban renewal, special assessments, and earned interest. Insurance trust revenues, normally not considered tax receipts, are derived from various government social insurance programs, contributory retirement systems for public employees, and life insurance programs sponsored by government. They amounted to $76.7 billion in fiscal 1973, of which $60.2 billion were collected by the federal government, $14.7 billion by the states, and a little over $1.8 billion by local governments.

In recent years more state and local revenues have come from the federal government in the form of grants-in-aid. During 1973 the federal government sharply increased such payments. It provided states with an average per capita revenue of $145.81 and local governments with an average of $52.74 per person. Payments, however,

TABLE 14-3

TAX REVENUES BY PERCENTAGES, FISCAL 1973

	All Governments	Federal	State	Local
Income	56.8	84.2	30.9	4.5
Individual	42.3	62.4	22.9	4.5
Corporation	14.5	21.8	8.0	—
Property	15.8	—	1.9	82.9
Sales, excises, and customs	21.6	11.9	54.5	9.3
Sales	8.0	—	29.1	6.0
Excises	12.4	10.0	25.5	3.3
Customs	1.1	1.9	—	—
Other	5.8	3.9	12.7	3.3

Source: United States Department of Commerce, *Governmental Finances in 1972–73*, p. 4.

show wide variations both among the states and localities of the United States.

States are barred only from levying taxes on interstate commerce. Consequently, they use every major form of taxation available to the federal government excluding customs duties. The local units of government, which operate on the basis of tax powers delegated to them by the states, are dependent on property taxes for about five-sixths of their revenue. Property taxes, however, bring in a very small

TABLE 14-4

GOVERNMENT REVENUES, FISCAL 1973
(MILLIONS OF DOLLARS)

	All Governments	Federal	State	Local
Revenue from all sources	426,172*	247,849	129,800	129,082
Intergovernmental revenue	—	—	32,692	47,866
Taxes	286,595	165,494	68,069	53,032
Charges and general revenue	62,837	22,120	14,348	26,369
Insurance and trust revenue	76,740	60,236	14,690	1,814

Source: United States Department of Commerce, *Governmental Finances in 1972–73*, p. 1.
* Net of intergovernmental transactions, to avoid duplication

fraction of state income and are not used at all by the federal government. They are levied almost entirely on real estate because of the
difficulty of administering them when imposed on personal property.
Frequently, they are unfairly assessed in relation to the value of the
property (i.e., the property is not evaluated at its true market price
by the assessors). But primarily the weakness of the property tax is
its relative inelasticity or its inability to increase proportionately
during periods of rising prices because of the reluctance of cities to
raise assessments or tax rates for fear of driving out business and
industry and discouraging new enterprise. As a result, localities have
become increasingly dependent on grants from the states and federal
government to balance their budgets.

State revenue comes mainly from the sales tax (levied on the
purchase price of a good or service) and the excise tax (levied on
the specific commodity). Almost all of the state excise tax revenue
is derived from levies on gasoline, liquor, and tobacco. In recent years
state income taxes have increased in importance as a major source
of revenue. States too have been faced with the problem of additional
revenue required to meet expanding functions. To some extent
federal grants are becoming an important part of state budgets.
Though the financial operations of states and municipalities have
thus far been concerned only with customary revenues and services
and have therefore failed to affect stabilization efforts, federal grants
for state activities may bring greater flexibility and permit consideration of the state of the economy in the formulation of budgets.

PUBLIC DEBT

If tax revenues are insufficient to meet the requirements of public
expenditures, governments resort to borrowing. For a long time the
prevailing notion was that except under emergency or extraordinary
conditions, such as wars or severe depressions, public budgets should
be balanced. Such policy, it was contended, maintains a strong credit
position for the government and prevents inflationary pressures from
emerging. Indeed, the federal debt limit is set by an act of Congress
(although it has been changed from time to time); some state debt
limits are fixed by state constitutions or state legislation; and local
debt limits are subject to state authority.

The Burden of the Debt.   It has generally been recognized that
government obligations and securities should be relatively riskless,

that the debt should be held widely among the population, and that debt management should attempt to minimize inflationary and deflationary effects. But most recently attitudes of economists have emphasized that the public debt should be used to bring about increased growth in the gross national product and prevent unemployment. They recognize that despite the increase in the federal debt from only $1.2 billion just before the entry of the United States into the First World War to more than $500 billion in 1975, the larger burden can be carried without too much difficulty. In the first place, for the past thirty years, the debt has been declining relatively rapidly in relation to GNP, thereby increasing the ease with which it can be supported by the growing volume of tax revenues. Second, the ability to service the debt (i.e., pay interest charges) depends on the interest rate the government contracts to pay. Third, a debt held internally, rather than by foreign governments or individuals living abroad, is easier to support, since it does not drain dollars from the country. But even when the debt is held domestically, income is redistributed from those persons paying taxes, who are a large group, to those persons owning the debt, who are a smaller group.

It is basically incorrect to say that public borrowing today places a burden on future generations. Real costs consist of resources and capital used up. The methods by which current operations of government are financed—whether by taxation, borrowing, or printing new currency—need not affect the output of subsequent generations. The volume of resources and capital passed on to them is important. Only as the money debt affects the redistribution of income at some later date may production and employment be influenced. As long as the debt is held domestically and does not lead holders to increase consumption at the expense of capital accumulation there is relatively little effect on the volume of production.

The credit standing of the United States is very high. There is little likelihood or danger that the government will become bankrupt. Demand for its securities is strong, and the rate of interest it must pay is below that charged to other borrowers. It is also unlikely that the size of the public debt has had adverse psychological effects on businessmen and thus discouraged private investment. Although a growing public debt may tend both to expand and to contract private investment incentives, businessmen are more concerned with profit expectations and the general economic climate than with the size of the public debt. Actually it is more important for firms to know that private debt incurred by individuals and corporations has increased much more rapidly than the public debt during the past few decades. There is however the possibility that waste and inflation may become more prevalent if the public becomes accustomed to a policy of deficit financing.

The Growth of the Debt. The total debt of all levels of government in 1973 was $646.6 billion, of which $458.1 billion had been borrowed by the federal government, $59.4 billion by the states, and $129.1 billion by localities. In all cases the trend of indebtedness has been rising. U.S. government agencies, including those supervising insurance trust funds, have been assuming a larger proportion of the federal debt. Nearly 92 percent of state and local debt represents long-term obligations, of which 40 percent is nonguaranteed (i.e., obligations payable only from specific earnings or special assessments) and 60 percent is based on the full faith and credit of the issuing authority. The per capita debt outstanding for state and local governments varied from $219 in South Dakota to $2,272 in the state of Alaska.

About three-fifths of the federal debt is marketable, which means that it can be readily bought and sold. It is classified according to the period of maturity into bills (up to eighteen months), certificates of indebtedness (usually between nine months and one year), notes (one year to five years), and bonds (five years or more). Most of the remainder, which is nonmarketable, is divided mainly between savings bonds and special issues held by government agencies that are compelled by law to invest their funds in this way. The division is shown in table 14-5.

More than 28 percent of the federal debt is held by U.S. government agencies and trust funds, 16 percent by the Federal Reserve Banks, and the balance by the public. The largest groups of public holders are individuals, commercial banks, and foreign governments and nationals. The latter group has 12 percent of the debt in its possession. Holders of the federal debt are shown in table 14-6.

Reduction of the Debt. The size of the public debt may be reduced if government revenues exceed government expenditures. Such a development must be carefully supervised, however, to avoid a contraction of effective demand in the economy which might induce a recession. It is also possible to pay off obligations and reduce the federal debt with funds that become available when the government

TABLE 14-5

GROSS FEDERAL DEBT BY TYPE OF SECURITY, MARCH 1975

	Amount (Billions of Dollars)	
Marketable	300.0	
Bills		124.0
Notes		141.9
Bonds		34.1
Nonmarketable	209.7	
Savings		64.8
Convertible		2.3
Special issues		116.0
Foreign issues		24.0
Other		2.6
Total	509.7	

Source: *Federal Reserve Bulletin*, April 1975, p. A 34.

TABLE 14-6

GROSS FEDERAL DEBT BY OWNER, JANUARY 1975

	Amount (Billions of Dollars)	
United States government agencies and trust funds	139.0	
Federal Reserve Banks	81.3	
Public	273.8	
Commercial banks		54.5
Mutual savings banks		2.6
Insurance companies		6.2
Other corporations		11.5
State and local governments		30.6
Individuals		86.3
Foreign and international		61.5
Other		20.6
Total	494.1	

Source: *Federal Reserve Bulletin*, April 1975, p. A 34.

opens new bank accounts or creates new currency. This process is called monetizing the debt. But if the rate of growth of the economy is insufficient to permit the ready absorption of the expanded money supply, inflationary effects would be evident. Of course, inflation reduces the burden but not the size of the public debt.

Local Financing Problems. Local fiscal difficulties have grown rapidly during the past decade because of the rising inability of cities to finance public services. While many middle- and upper-income families have gradually been migrating to the suburbs and thereby reducing the municipal tax base, the increased proportion of poor remaining in urban centers has required more welfare benefits, sanitation services, police and fire protection, health facilities, and education expenses. It is becoming more difficult and costly for cities to borrow from private investors and banks to finance their budget deficits.

Various proposals have been made to alleviate the financial burdens of the cities. They include increasing the amounts of federal revenue sharing; shifting the burdens of certain local obligations, such as welfare and education, from local to federal and state governments; revising the basis of property taxes; and consolidating central cities with the suburbs as political units in order to widen the tax base.

Chapter 15
RENT, INTEREST, AND PROFIT

Distribution theory is the study of the allocation or apportionment of income. Functional income distribution deals with the division of income among the factors of production in the form of rent, interest, profit, and wages; it explains why particular amounts of money or rates of return are paid for the use of land and capital and for entrepreneurship and labor. Personal income distribution concerns the income received by persons who supply the factor services. An individual, of course, may supply more than one factor. In this chapter distribution theory and rent, interest, and profit are discussed. In subsequent chapters wages and personal distribution of income are considered.

The statistics of functional distribution show that the share of national income going to labor as wages and salaries during the past century has remained close to four-fifths of the total, although there has been a slight upward trend over the past forty years. The remainder of the income, approximately one-fifth of the total, has been received by property factors. This portion shows a correspondingly slight downward trend. During depression periods the absolute amount received by all factors declines, although the proportional share of labor may rise. Indeed, at the lowest point of the depression of the 1930s total corporate profit was negative. Advancing technology and increased skill have raised the productivity of both capital and labor. Though the amount of capital has been growing more rapidly than the supply of labor, the return to each unit of capital has not declined. The effects of diminishing returns have not been felt because technological progress has offset the tendency for the payment to each unit to fall.

FUNCTIONAL DISTRIBUTION

Both distribution theory and price theory are part of microeconomic analysis. They are concerned with the efforts of the firm to maximize profit. Distribution deals with the pricing of input, i.e., the factors of production used by business enterprise, while price theory emphasizes the pricing of output. The relationships between the costs of input and the prices of output determine profit. These relationships are examined in the theory of production.

Production Theory. Production theory analyzes the various ways in which entrepreneurs may combine the different factors of production as they seek to maximize profit. The relationship between input and output for a particular state of technology is given by the production function. One objective of the entrepreneur producing a commodity or service is to find the least-cost or minimum-cost combination of inputs. This combination depends upon the marginal productivity of additional units of each of the factor inputs, as all other factors are held constant.

Marginal productivity is a concept that may be analyzed in terms of physical product added or revenue added. It depends essentially on the fact that the principle of diminishing returns is applicable in the process of production. Beyond a point, each unit of input of a productive factor adds less to the total output than did its predecessor unit. The additional output resulting from another unit of input is called the marginal physical product (MPP). The revenue added by this output, i.e., the difference in the total revenue of the firm, is the marginal physical product multiplied by the marginal revenue (MR is equal to price only under conditions of perfect competition). It is known as the marginal revenue product (MRP) or the marginal value product.

The least cost of producing any output is the one in which the last (or marginal) dollar spent on each input factor adds the same marginal physical product. Otherwise a greater total output would be obtained for the same cost by shifting input from the factor yielding less MPP for a dollar of expenditure to the one yielding more. In effect, this means that the least-cost equilibrium is one in which the MPP of each factor is proportional to its price. This relationship may be expressed mathematically as:

$$\frac{MPP \text{ of } A}{MPP \text{ of } B} = \frac{price \text{ of } A}{price \text{ of } B}$$

or

$$\frac{MPP \text{ of } A}{price \text{ of } A} = \frac{MPP \text{ of } B}{price \text{ of } B} = \frac{MPP \text{ of } C}{price \text{ of } C}$$

The least-cost combination may be obtained for any level of output. If the object of the firm is to maximize its profit (or minimize its loss) it produces at that least-cost combination at which additional expenditures for any factor equal the revenues derived from the sale of the extra product. This is another way of saying that production expands until the marginal cost of each factor unit of input equals the marginal revenue product or the marginal cost of a unit of output equals the marginal revenue. No great profit can be earned by transferring factors or adding units of input.

A change in the price of a factor of production will affect its use. A smaller amount of any input will be used if the price rises because the difference between the revenue derived from the *MPP* and the cost of the *MPP* has declined relative to other inputs. However, somewhat more of the other inputs will be purchased by the producer. The reverse analysis is applicable if the price of any input falls. The modification in the input mix resulting from a change in any factor price is known as the substitution effect or substitution principle. Changes in the prices of inputs not only lead to substitution of factors but also affect output because of the new relationships of costs of production to revenue.

Graphic Presentation. The equilibrium or maximization position of a firm may be shown graphically by using an analysis similar to the indifference curve procedure employed in connection with the measurement of demand. This requires the use of equal-product curves (also known as production-indifference curves or isoquants) shown in figure 15-1 and equal-cost lines represented in figure 15-2. Equal product curves indicate the various combinations of inputs of factors of production that yield the same output. An appropriate illustration would show the different combinations of labor and capital that are necessary to provide the same output. The figures for such a graph would be based on the production function. Combining more labor with less capital or less labor with more capital will yield the same product. Equal-cost lines show the various combinations of factors that have the same total costs. If it is assumed that a firm is able to buy as much of any factor as it wishes at constant prices, the lines are straight and parallel. The slope depends upon the relative prices of a unit of each factor.

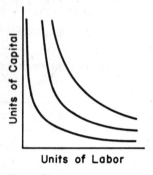

Fig. 15-1. Equal-product curves (in physical terms)

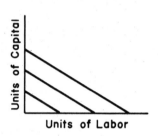

Fig. 15-2. Equal-cost lines (in money terms)

The combination of factors that results in the lowest cost for any selected output is indicated when one graph is superimposed on the other (axes constructed to the same scale). This is shown by the point at which the equal-product curve is tangent to an equal-cost line because that output requires a higher cost for all other input combinations. The particular output selected by the firm is the one at which the marginal cost of production is equal to the marginal revenue.

Prices of Input. The demand for output is a direct demand by consumers. The demand for factors of production by entrepreneurs is a derived demand, which is based on the ultimate demand for consumer goods. The price of the factor therefore depends in part on the price of the final good; but since the factor price is also part of the cost of production, it affects the price of the final good. Thus prices of output and of input are closely interrelated.

The price of each factor is determined by demand and supply. Although in the long run the price tends to equal the marginal revenue product, in the shorter period divergences may occur because of competitive imperfections in the purchase and sale of factors (including obstacles to mobility), changes in technology, changes in income and taste of consumers, and the virtual impossibility, in many instances, of separating inputs to determine their respective marginal physical products.

Property income arises from the ownership of physical assets or from claims to the earnings of these assets. Such receipts include rent, interest, and profit.

RENT

Rent is an intricate concept in economics. Considerable historical controversy has been generated by the earnings of land.

Rent for Property. Rent is the price paid for the use of physical assets such as land, farms, commercial buildings, machinery, equipment, and houses. If the user is also the owner of the asset, an implicit or imputed rent may be appropriately computed, equal to the amount that the asset would earn if leased to another person. A contract that provides for the leasing of physical assets may be negotiated for a very long period of time, but the rental payment is determined by the interaction of supply and demand. The same mechanism that determines the price of all goods and services is used.

The demand for productive property is similar to the demand for labor in that each of these demands is derived from the demand for the final product that the property or the labor helps produce. Rental payment is limited to an amount no greater than the marginal revenue product of an asset and is equal to the *MRP* if perfect competition prevails among those seeking to obtain the use of an asset. The owner leases the property to the person willing to pay the highest rent, who in turn employs it in that use where the marginal revenue product is greatest. To the extent that competition is limited or nonexistent among those wishing to use the asset, the amount of rent depends upon the respective bargaining abilities of the owner and renter but is less than the marginal revenue product.

Economic Rent. Economic rent (also termed economic surplus and pure rent) is a surplus; it identifies that part of the payment above the amount necessary to keep the factor from shifting to another use. Since land has many uses, all payments for its rental cannot be considered economic rent. Land that has several equally productive uses requires rental payment when leased but yields no economic rent. The whole payment is necessary to prevent the factor from shifting elsewhere. But economic rent may be paid for factors other than land. This is the surplus above the amount required to keep the factor in its present use. Individuals receiving very high salaries (for example, some entertainers) may be getting economic rent for providing a special talent of which the supply is fixed. The economic rent is that portion of the wage that is in excess of the amount that can be received by these persons in alternative work (see p. 211).

All payments made (other than those to cover maintenance or depreciation) for an asset whose supply is perfectly inelastic (i.e., has only one use and is fixed in supply) and available without any cost of production are economic rent. Such rent most generally occurs in connection with certain kinds of land. The supply of resources that yield economic rent is represented graphically by a vertical or perpendicular line. Economic rent therefore is determined by demand alone, rising as demand increases. Land on which lemons may be grown successfully in the United States or store space in the area around Times Square in New York City yields what approximates economic rent because the factor cannot be increased significantly in quantity regardless of the price offered, nor are the best alternative uses likely to bring any substantially comparable price.

Resources yield economic rent in relation to the extent that they are both productive and scarce. For example, the growth of population in a region makes land in the heart of the area relatively more scarce and therefore leads to higher economic rent. Although economic rent is one of the costs of production that the individual producer must meet, it is not a cost that determines the price paid by the members of society. The amount of economic rent does not enter into the price. Wages and interest are costs that must be paid to produce goods, but economic rent is a return derived from revenue. The owner of a store that is well situated receives a high rental from the person who leases it because the sales revenues in that neighborhood are high. If the location is less favorable the rent will be lower.

Quasi Rent. Assets or other goods that are not readily reproducible, such as an atomic energy plant that takes a long time to build or a patented product controlled exclusively by the patent holder for a fixed number of years, yield economic rent, generally called quasi rent, if sold during the period of time when similar goods are not available. Royalties, a special kind of rent, relate the payment for an asset with the extent to which the asset is used. When oil or mineral lands are rented, the amount of payment is usually tied to the amount extracted. Royalties of this kind are more suitable if depletion of a resource is involved in its use.

Historical Features. Economists have long regarded land as a peculiar factor of production because it is an inexhaustible gift of nature and a nonreproducible resource. The physiocrats, a group of eighteenth-century French economists, believed that land produces a net product but that labor and capital do not, and they argued that rent results from the bountifulness of nature. David Ricardo, on the other hand, one of the early classical economists, contended that land is scarce and rent results from the niggardliness of nature.

Much controversy has been generated by the question of whether those who own land that increases in value simply because of population growth deserve or are entitled to the higher economic rent they receive. One of the best known movements concerned with these "unearned" land increments was headed by Henry George, who in 1879 in his book *Progress and Poverty* proposed that society should utilize a single tax to raise revenue. This tax would be imposed on the economic rent of land. A tax upon any factor of fixed supply would have to be absorbed entirely by the owner. He could not shift any part of it forward to those who use the factor or to the ultimate consumers. It should be clear that a tax on economic rent would not affect the allocation of resources among potential uses. Criticism of this approach suggested that owners of land had purchased the resource at a particular price that may have already included some part or all of the economic rent and that their property should not be expropriated by any tax. Furthermore, as economic rent is also received by others than owners of land, equity of treatment would require similar taxes to be imposed in those cases. In general the appropriateness and equity of a single tax on economic land rent is subject to much doubt.

INTEREST

Interest is the price paid for the use of money borrowed from others. (Lenders of money or property receive interest as income.) Borrowers must not only return the funds or items that have been loaned to them at the time or times specified in their agreement, but they must also pay interest. The amount of interest is ordinarily expressed as a rate of return and may be paid in a variety of ways.

For example, if $1,000 is borrowed for a year, the borrower may obtain $1,000 on January 1 of one year and pay back $1,050 on January 1 of the next year. In this transaction simple interest of 5 percent per year is paid. As an alternative the lender may deduct a $50 interest charge immediately, giving the borrower only $950; such a loan has been made at a discount. One year later the borrower repays $1,000. In this case the true rate of interest exceeds 5 percent. It is $50 on $950 or just over 5.26 percent. Other arrangements may require the principal to be repaid in monthly or quarterly sums. Thus the true rate again exceeds 5 percent if $50 is paid as interest because the borrower does not have the entire amount of the loan for the full year.

Basis of Interest. Until modern times the payment of interest for loanable funds was generally condemned by society and by many religious authorities. This attitude was an outgrowth of the fact that money was ordinarily borrowed by persons in need for the purpose of increasing consumption. Although usury is still frowned upon, the development of modern economics in which the use of more capital enables an entrepreneur to increase his product and profit has made interest payments justifiable and more palatable. Interest has been explained in different ways. It is a payment (1) for the productivity of capital (the use of money to increase output), (2) for abstinence from or waiting for consumption (the convenience of earlier availability), (3) for the time preference of present over possible future consumption (the certainty of consumption), or (4) for giving up liquidity of money.

Functions of Interest. The interest rate has two main tasks: (1) It allocates the supply of funds for capital goods to those uses where the net productivities are greatest. (Net productivity may be computed as the annual percentage yield on the total cost of the investment.) Those capital goods are produced that are expected to provide the largest return. Production stops at the point where the rate of yield is equal to the rate of interest on investments of comparable quality. (2) It influences the rate of capital growth and accumulation by altering current consumption. Nevertheless, there is some question whether higher interest rates in the narrow customary range prevailing in advanced economics have much overall effect on increasing the volume of saving and whether changes in saving have much effect on interest rates. It seems more likely that a rising income level increases both the demand for loanable funds and their supply.

Capitalization. The interest rate is also the basis of determining the present value of an income stream or expected future returns. In effect, the interest rate is used to capitalize (determine the price of) an asset because assets are valued in terms of their earning expectations. For example, what is the current value of an annuity of $1,000 to be paid in perpetuity? Or stated in another way, how much should a person pay now for an agreement under which he and his heirs receive $1,000 forever? The answer is based upon the market rate of interest for that kind of risk. If the rate is 6 percent, then the annuity has a value of $16,667. A sum of $16,667 put aside at the annual rate of 6 percent will yield $1,000 a year. The following formula may be used:

$$Present\ Capitalized\ (Discounted)\ Value = \frac{Annual\ Return}{Interest\ Rate}$$

Suppose, however, the $1,000 return is not permanent but is to be received for a period of ten years. Obviously, such an arrangement is worth less. It must be priced at the sum of the present values of $1,000 in each of the next ten years. This is equivalent to the amount that must be set aside now in order to receive $1,000 in each of the next ten years. At 6 percent compound interest, $943 will be worth $1,000 a year from now. However, $890 is enough to reach $1,000 in two years, and $839 will grow to $1,000 in three years. The current total value of amounts necessary to pay $1,000 for a period of ten years is $7,357. The present capitalized value of money to be received for any number of years may be derived from the formula:

$$Present\ Capitalized\ Value = \frac{Amount\ of\ Return}{(1 + Interest\ Rate)^{Number\ of\ Years}}$$

The present value of a sum of money decreases the more distant the date that it will be received or the higher the present rate of interest.

This method of computation is also used to determine the present discounted value of capital assets or other property-producing income (such as stocks and bonds). If the rent or return derived from the asset during each year of its life is known (it need not be the same each year) and the market interest rate appropriate to the risk involved is given, then the value may be established. Of course, the numerator or the amount of return must be given as a net figure. Maintenance costs and tax payments must be deducted from the gross amount received. In general, however, the value of a capital good tends to be related to its cost of production. This is true because new capital goods will be produced if the capitalized value is greater. In the process the marginal revenue product, the rent, and the price of the good will fall. If the capitalized value of an asset is below the cost of production, new assets of that type will not be produced, and the price will tend to rise as old units wear out. If depreciation is taken into account, new and existing assets should yield the same return.

Variations in Interest. The rate of interest varies from time to time and from place to place. Different rates prevail in each borrowing market depending, among other things, on the type of borrower (including the financial history of the businessman, consumer, or government requesting the loan), the collateral put up for the loan, the degree of risk taken by the lender (including the region in which and the length of time for which the loan is made), the charge for processing and supervising the loan, and the size of the loan. All these factors underlie the supply and demand for money.

If the term *interest rate* is not further qualified, it often refers to the pure rate of interest, which is the rate of a relatively riskless long-term loan. (This rate is frequently considered to approximate the rate paid by the U.S. government on its long-term bonds.) The risk taken by the lender depends on the possibility that the borrower may default and on the prospect that at the time the loan matures a rising price level may have reduced the purchasing power of the principal below what it was when the loan was made. The increased degree of risk associated with money loaned for longer periods is responsible for the higher rates of interest on long-term loans. Table 15-1 indicates some of the different types of interest rates.

Demand and Supply. The interest rate for money is determined by demand and supply. Demand for funds is motivated by three factors: (1) the necessity for conducting transactions, (2) the need for precautionary action to meet unforeseen outlays, and (3) the speculation that prices will fall. Demand comes from business firms, consumers, and the government. Business enterprise wants money if profit expectations from investments are sufficiently greater than the costs of the funds borrowed. Obviously, other things being equal,

TABLE 15-1

INTEREST RATES, FEBRUARY 1975

	Percent per Annum
Prime commercial paper (4 to 6 months)	6.33
Finance company paper (3 to 6 months)	6.24
Prime bankers' acceptance (90 days)	6.35
U.S. government (6-month bills)	5.62
U.S. government (long-term)	6.61
State and local government (Aaa)	5.96
Corporate bonds (Aaa)	8.62
Corporate bonds (Baa)	10.43
Common stocks (dividend/price ratio)	4.61
Conventional first mortgages	8.88
Short-term business loans by banks ($1,000 to $10,000)	10.94
Short-term business loans by banks ($1,000,000 and over)	9.73

Source: *Federal Reserve Bulletin*, April 1975, pp. A 26–A 28.

more is likely to be borrowed at lower interest rates. Lower rates also encourage consumers to borrow more because they increase the preference for current consumption over future consumption. Furthermore, anticipation of higher prices serves as an incentive to borrow more when money costs less. Although consumer loans ordinarily are not related to the marginal productivity of capital, the purpose of the loan sometimes does affect the ability of a consumer to repay. For example, a person who borrows money to advance his education or training may be expected to increase his potential earning power and therefore be able to repay the loan more readily. There are many occasions when the government undertakes to borrow money. Generally there is a greater inducement for government, especially states and municipalities, to borrow at times when interest rates are lower.

The supply of funds depends on a variety of factors. Money is saved by individuals, business, and various levels of governments. Personal saving is undertaken for many reasons, but most of it is accumulated by the higher income groups. The largest part of business saving consists of funds reinvested by firms in their own enterprises; relatively little becomes available to others as loans. In general saving is converted into loanable funds through the action of banks, savings and loan associations, insurance companies, or other financial institutions. The supply of money, however, does not only depend on the amount saved. Commercial banks are in a position to extend credit if they have excess reserves. Similarly, funds become available if individuals and businesses, for whatever motive, are ready to reduce their cash balances. The government influences the supply of money mainly through changes in tax rates and in expenditures and through operations of the Federal Reserve System (see p. 61). As a rule, investment can come about only by abstaining from consumption; that is, it is an alternative use of resources.

PROFIT

Private enterprise in a capitalistic economy is primarily motivated by the search for profit. Profit ordinarily is considered to be the return to the entrepreneurial factor of production and is generally understood to be a form of property income. Profit includes payment for the ability and the willingness to undertake the production of goods and services.

Profit expectation is the incentive that encourages private business enterprise. Even an economic system dominated by huge corporations that hire managers who are paid fixed salaries to run business enterprises depends heavily on profit. Although management personnel may be concerned not only with the financial success of the business but with the attainment of social prestige, achievement of high standards of product quality, maintenance of high standards of employment, and enjoyment of the pleasant experiences of risking other people's money, they are usually paid bonuses based on the profit level of the firm. Furthermore, the job of the hired corporation official or manager ultimately depends on the satisfaction of stockholders, a group of persons primarily concerned with profit.

The General Meaning.   The concept of profit as a factor payment is elusive. The practical identification of profit receipts is extremely difficult because the term is commonly used in many different and arbitrary ways. The layman understands profit in the framework established by the accountant; but an accountant uses the word in three distinct ways. Gross profit is the difference between net sales and the cost of manufacturing the goods sold; net operating profit is the gross profit less selling and general expenses; and net profit is what remains after corporate income taxes and nonoperating expenses are deducted from the net operating profit. Thus in the case of a corporation net profit includes dividends paid to stockholders (both common and preferred) and retained earnings, and the net profit of a sole proprietorship includes implicit compensation for the labor of the owner. These definitions of net profit involve payments to more than one factor of production and are not very useful to the economist. Similarly, the meaning of profit for tax purposes is based upon the definition set up by the government. Furthermore, the profit position of a firm may be modified by altering the accounting procedures or changing the method by which depreciation is calculated.

Profit is the only return to a factor of production that may be negative. It is ordinarily considered to be the residual sum after all costs, including payments to other factors, have been paid out of revenues. Whenever costs exceed revenues, negative profit (loss) to the entrepreneur results.

The rate of profit may be expressed in a number of ways. It is ordinarily most meaningful to present profit as a fraction of the equity of the firm. It is sometimes given as a percentage of capital (which includes the funds borrowed by the business) or as a fraction of sales. In the latter two cases the profit rate is ordinarily much smaller. For the economy as a whole, profit may be expressed as a proportion of national income.

Profit Insurance. Insurance by businessmen against losses is possible only for hazards such as theft, fire, or flood. In these instances a group of persons agree to spread the risk among themselves by paying sufficient insurance premiums to cover potential losses in connection with a particular category of risk. It is a way of converting a loss that may possibly be large into one that is certain but small (the insurance fee). Protection against losses due to unfavorable business conditions, changes in tastes of customers, unemployment, or crop failures is not available from private insurance companies, however, because such insurance is not actuarially sound.

The government, however, may undertake to insure risks whose costs cannot be estimated accurately and may even assure a positive profit to the producer. For example, the federal government has guaranteed a profit to manufacturers during war periods in order to bring about rapid expansion of production of specific goods. Cost-plus contracts are awarded, under which an agreed percentage is added to the costs incurred in producing the goods.

The Economic Concept. The economic notion of profit involves the amount of revenues remaining after the opportunity costs, or the returns foregone by not using the productive resources in the best alternative, are fully met by the business enterprise. Thus the sole proprietor who works in his own establishment and uses his own savings must consider the payments that his labor and capital would earn if employed elsewhere. Before being able to determine profit, the proprietor must subtract the implicit wages and interest from his revenue. The net profit of a corporation is also higher than profit as defined by economists because it includes an amount equal to the interest that the funds of the stockholders could earn elsewhere. Economic profit is derived only after allowances have been made for all explicit and implicit costs.

Typically a firm must earn a minimum or normal profit in order to stay in business. The minimum profit necessary to prevent shutting down the business depends in part on the profit the entrepreneur can earn by producing another good, but it also depends on the industry involved. Customary earnings and expectations vary among industries. Within an industry the minimum profit necessary to continue production depends on the personality of the particular entrepreneur. Some individuals want to operate their own business regardless of the profit rate in order to have independence of action, protection against discharge, and the social prestige of ownership. Others require rather high rewards before assuming the burdens and responsibilities of entrepreneurship. Over the span of several years, total profit (as identified by the economist) must be equal to or greater than minimum profit to keep a business in operation. The difference between total profit and minimum profit is called *pure profit* or *excess profit*.

Pure Profit. The sources of pure profit are explained in many ways. (1) Profit is a return for undertaking and for bearing the risks and uncertainties of economic activity, fluctuating income, and business failure. Uncertainties arise from changing policies of government regarding fiscal matters or regulation, international events, actions of competitors, and many other considerations. (2) Profit is a return for innovation to a firm that introduces new inventions, techniques of production, or products. Profit may be increased to the extent that an entrepreneur is able to reduce costs below the level of his competitors. Such production advantages, however, are ordinarily temporary. (3) Monopoly may serve to protect the market of a firm and enable it to maintain a higher profit level. If a firm has a monopsonistic influence in the purchase of labor or other factors of production, it may pay less for these factors than the value of the marginal revenue product and thus increase its profit. (4) Profit arises through chance factors. Prices may increase suddenly and unexpectedly; competitors may be ruined by fire or flood; or tastes of consumers may change. Such situations create what may be termed *windfall profit*.

The word *profit* has had many unhappy connotations for the public, and politicians and lobbyists have sometimes attempted to curry favor by espousing higher taxes on profit. Yet there are many reasons why careful thought must be given to such taxes. Taxes on profit must not discourage capital investment or reduce incentives for innovation. On the contrary, venture capital often needs to be encouraged. Furthermore, although there might be a good deal of justification for taxing the pure profit of monopolies (providing it is not feasible as an alternative to enforce competition or regulate the earnings of the enterprise), it should be clear that in some cases pure profit in one year may serve only to offset losses in other years.

Measurement. Profit figures derived from national income tabulations compiled by the government consist of corporate profit plus that portion of the earnings of unincorporated enterprises that remains after the difficult and arbitrary task of removing implicit wages and implicit interest has been accomplished. The profit of corporations is divided into dividends, corporate taxes, and retained earnings. The portion of profit that the company keeps in the business provides a direct source of investment funds and is an important internal means of expanding capital. Additional investment funds come from dividend payments and profit earned by unincorporated business establishments.

Profit, as defined by economists, is the return to the entrepreneurial function, but its actual measurement is extremely difficult and complex. National income components do not disclose the opportunity costs of the funds invested by the owners of corporations; that is, an adjustment is not made for the interest that would have been earned if the money of the stockholders had been loaned to other businesses. Nor do national income statistics show pure profit. For many practical purposes, therefore, it is desirable simply to differentiate between income from labor and income from property without trying to break down property returns into rent, interest, and profit.

Chapter 16
LABOR AND WAGES

Labor is a special factor of production because it is performed by human beings. Persons who supply labor are concerned not only with pecuniary payments but also with the many tangible and intangible nonmonetary characteristics of a job environment. The market exerts a decisive influence in determining wages and working conditions and the extent of unemployment. Laborers have attempted to meet some of the problems associated with wages and working conditions by establishing trade unions and bargaining collectively with employers. Three-quarters of all workers in the United States, however, are not members of unions. Some other controls over the market and protection for workers are provided by legislation.

DEVELOPMENT OF UNIONS

The importance of labor unions in the United States arises not only from the economic power they wield but from the political influence they exert in the formulation of government policy. The current attitudes of organized labor are in large part an outgrowth of the evolution and development of the union movement.

Early History.   Labor unions, or trade unions, are associations of wage earners that attempt to protect and improve the conditions of work and advance the economic interests of workers. Although trade unions appeared in Great Britain around the mid-seventeenth century, it was not until the 1790s that they were formed in the United States. Unions in this country were very weak at first and tended to disintegrate after a few years of existence. Generally, organization was limited to groups of highly skilled workers—particularly shoemakers, printers, carpenters, bakers, and tailors—in Philadelphia, New York, Baltimore, Boston, and a few other cities. Unions did not organize on a national basis because the means of transportation were poor and markets were essentially local.

The strike was the main weapon used by unions to pressure employers for better working conditions, but state courts almost invariably supported the contention of employers that such action was illegal because it constituted a conspiracy. It was not until 1842, when the supreme court of Massachusetts ruled that strikes were not necessarily unlawful, that the courts began to broaden the scope of legitimate union activity, permitting unions to exert their economic strength.

National unions were established about the mid-nineteenth century. The development of a good network of transportation facilities led to the growth of national markets. Competition among products manufactured in different regions, and a greater mobility of craftsmen and other workers resulted. Unions felt the need to equalize the labor costs of production and regulate the movement of migrants to protect local employment opportunities. They therefore set up national organizations.

But labor espoused many conflicting objectives. A small section of the union movement was radical and militant and not always averse to violence. It was strongly motivated by class consciousness and desired the establishment of some form of socialism. The International Working Peoples Association (Black International) and later the Industrial Workers of the World typified this approach. Another, larger group of unionists was controlled by reform elements seeking to reorganize and improve society in order to achieve greater equality among classes. The Knights of Labor, the largest union of the 1880s, which sought to combine all workers in one organization, represented this approach. A third category of unions ultimately came to dominate the labor movement. These unions supported the philosophy that membership in each union should be limited to workers organized mainly along craft lines (i.e., by skills necessary for a particular type of job). They believed that the labor organization should work for higher wages, shorter hours, and improved working conditions; these goals are called *business unionism* or *bread-and-butter unionism*. The American Federation of Labor (AFL) formed in 1886 (as an outgrowth of an organization set up five years earlier) was the parent body of most unions inclined to this approach. Since 1890, with the exception of the years between 1938 and 1955 when it shared the stage with its offshoot and rival the Congress of Industrial Organizations (CIO), the AFL has been the most effective voice of the labor movement.

Modern Unionism. The AFL was a federation of national unions. Although even at the beginning of its existence some industrial unions (i.e., unions accepting all workers employed in an industry) were included, craft unions played the dominant role. In the early 1930s, however, some young and vigorous leaders in the labor movement questioned the success of the AFL. They felt that the labor movement should undertake to organize more industries and enroll more workers. By 1933 total union membership in the United States was under three million persons (slightly more than two million of whom were in the AFL), concentrated mainly in the building trades, printing, railroads, coal mining, clothing manufacture, and entertainment.

In 1933, at the depth of the depression, the advent of the New Deal under the administration of President Franklin D. Roosevelt provided a propitious period for the expansion of the labor movement. The attitude of the federal government immediately prior to that time had been neutral in labor-management disputes, but thereafter it was modified to encourage and assist the organizational efforts of labor. The internal struggle in the AFL between those favoring the continuation of craft union domination and those supporting the expansion of industrial unionism, particularly into the mass production industries, lasted for several years. In 1938 the expulsion of those unions in favor of industrial unionism led to the formation of the CIO as a second federation.

In order to meet the challenge posed to its leadership by the CIO, the AFL slowly modified its objections and resistance to industrial unionism. It also abandoned its former hostility to the intervention of government in the area of labor relations and followed the lead of the CIO in pressing for legislation that supported demands of labor. Active participation in politics was undertaken. Candidates were endorsed and political campaigns were conducted. During the 1940s and 1950s political lobbying became a major function of the labor movement. In many ways political pressure was as important as collective bargaining with employers. In 1955 the AFL and the CIO merged under the name of American Federation of Labor and Congress of Industrial Organizations (AFL-CIO). Labor hoped that this merger would increase its economic and political strength, even though the dispute between craft and industrial unionism had not yet been resolved. Indeed, many new jurisdictional questions and competing national organizations had developed during the years when the two federations had been rivals.

Recent Problems. By the 1960s the labor movement had spread geographically and industrially and was influential in the highest government circles. Although some labor leaders have gained much prestige and public respect and unions now have considerable strength, a number of difficulties are apparent. The union membership of about 20,000,000 persons (of whom almost 15,000,000 are in the AFL-CIO) has grown at a slow rate during the past decade. This means that less than a quarter of the labor force participants is organized (a much smaller percentage than in Great Britain); and as the labor force has expanded, a fixed union membership has become a smaller proportion of those subject to organization. Just under half of union membership is concentrated in five states—New York, California, Pennsylvania, Illinois, and Ohio.

The prospects of the labor movement for membership growth and expansion of bargaining power are not very bright. Many labor leaders are old and tired. They are more interested in maintaining the status quo than in undertaking new organizational projects. The growth of automation has weakened the ability of labor to strike successfully. Expansion of the service industries, where labor is weakest, and the relative decline of manufacturing, where it is strongest, have been trends that are disadvantageous to growth. On the whole, the labor movement has not been successful in organizing white-collar workers or in gaining many members in the poorly organized South. But some recent successes have been achieved, mainly among government employees.

STRUCTURE OF THE LABOR MOVEMENT

The labor movement is made up of many groups with divergent views and policies. The AFL-CIO, or parent body, is not centralized. It is essentially a loose federation of about one hundred and fifteen autonomous national unions (many called internationals because they also have members in Canada), each of which determines its own policies and selects its own officials. The largest national unions are the United Steelworkers, the International Association of Machinists, the Laborers International, the International Brotherhood of Electrical Workers, and the United Brotherhood of Carpenters.

There are more than forty national unions that have over one hundred thousand members.

It is quite possible for the public position taken by a national union on any issue to differ sharply from that assumed by the AFL-CIO acting as the spokesman for labor. For example, individual unions supported Republicans Dwight D. Eisenhower in 1956 and Richard M. Nixon in 1960 for president when the federation as a body backed their Democratic opponents. Only when problems of organizational jurisdiction, racketeering, and Communist domination arise does the AFL-CIO intervene in the internal affairs of its affiliates. The harshest penalty for refusing to accept a ruling of the AFL-CIO is expulsion. The AFL-CIO does not participate in the collective bargaining negotiations or strike activities of its national members. It receives financial support almost entirely from the per capita dues paid by its affiliates.

More than fifty national unions are independent of the AFL-CIO. Some of the more important of these are the International Brotherhood of Teamsters, the United Automobile Workers, the National Education Association, the United Mine Workers, several railroad unions, and a few unions that had been expelled from the CIO for being under Communist influence. Various links exist between some affiliated and independent unions (and, of course, among affiliated unions), and joint action is sometimes undertaken. In addition to the independent nationals nearly a half million workers are members of unaffiliated local unions and company unions (single-employer unions).

National unions have affiliated branches (varying in number from one to several thousand) called local unions; there are about 75,000 local unions in the United States. A worker joins the local that has jurisdiction over the work that he does. Membership dues are paid to the local, the amount usually being based on earnings. The local passes on a predetermined part of the dues to the parent national. Although nationals have much more control over locals than the AFL-CIO has over its affiliates, the division of power between the local and its parent varies among the unions. It generally depends on the nature of the industry, the structure of the product market, and the extent of competition. Thus the steelworkers union represents a centralized organization with most of the authority lodged at the national level. The carpenters union and the bricklayers union, however, place most of the responsibility for collective bargaining negotiations in the hands of the locals. The trend has been for the nationals to take over more control as mass production has increased and markets have expanded. The national ordinarily controls strike funds, administers health and welfare funds, exercises final disciplinary authority, holds veto power over local bylaws, and maintains general supervisory authority over local affairs.

COLLECTIVE BARGAINING

The bargaining position of an individual worker in modern industry is considerably weaker than that of the employer. Ordinarily the worker is not able to turn down employment over an extended period, is not adept at negotiating, and is less familiar with the labor market than is the employer. Collective bargaining has been supported by labor as a means of (1) equalizing the bargaining power of employers and employees, (2) establishing equality of working conditions throughout the market in order that employers may not take advantage of competition to lower wages and reduce standards, (3) enabling workers to share in the benefits of rising productivity of industry, and (4) providing increased purchasing power so that a stable economy is maintained.

Contracts. The union improves working conditions and increases the security of workers by negotiating collective bargaining agreements with an employer or group of employers (employer association). Although the figure for coverage is about the same as union membership, some union members are not covered by contracts (as in the case of many government employees) and some nonmembers are subject to the terms of an agreement (as in the case of an open-shop contract covering all workers).

Subject Matter. The major matters covered by agreements concern recognition of the union, wages, hours, working conditions, welfare benefits, adjustment of disputes, and the duration of the contract. Unions are interested not only in increasing real wages but in providing greater security of employment and job tenure, protecting employees against the hazards of retirement and unemployment, and raising the morale and self-respect of workers. Specific items of importance under the category of working conditions include provisions and rules governing seniority, apprenticeship, technological change, vacations, and holidays.

Union Security. The union is concerned with the degree of recognition granted it by employers; such recognition provides security for the organization. Ordinarily unions strive to obtain the strongest possible type of security. In the United States forms of union security range from a type of shop in which employers are required to hire only union members (closed shop) to a type of shop in which employers hire only nonunion workers. Generally both these arrangements are possible only if interstate commerce is not involved, as federal law prohibits discrimination against employees for union or nonunion membership. Most workers covered by contract are under a union shop, in which a firm may hire anyone, but those not members of the union must join after a probationary period of about thirty days. Other kinds of union security include open shop, where both union and nonunion workers are employed; agency shop, in which workers need not join the union but must pay the union a sum equal to the union dues so they are not "free riders"; and maintenance-of-membership shop, where those in the union at the time the agreement is signed must remain in good standing for the duration of the contract.

Wages. Unions have given special attention to the subject of wages because remuneration is the most important element in collective bargaining negotiations. Wages of unionized and nonunionized workers will be considered in a separate section below.

Hours. The matter of working time has undergone very important changes in recent years. Until the 1940s employees and unions were mainly concerned with the number of working hours per day. Indeed, some state laws specified the maximum number of hours a worker was permitted to perform in certain industries and occupations where overwork might injure his health or endanger the public. Employers therefore did not give much thought to the needs of workers beyond the actual working day. But the recent and widespread introduction of overtime payments, paid vacations, paid holidays, coffee breaks and rest periods with pay, paid sabbatical leaves, health and welfare benefits, and retirement plans have changed the nature of the employer-employee relationship. Employers now have a greater stake in the total working life of their employees and are more inclined to act accordingly.

Workers have chosen to take some of the benefits of the growth in per capita output in the form of added leisure rather than increases in income. It is estimated that since 1909 the average annual hours of employment per worker have declined about 25 percent because of shorter hours, longer vacations, and more frequent holidays. Moreover, between 1900 and 1975 male life expectancy rose by a considerably greater number of years than the expected number of male working years during the same period, mainly because entry into the labor force is later (as a result of an increase in the average number of years of schooling) and retirement is earlier. Thus output per man hour has risen much more than per capita output during the first three-quarters of this century. The reduction in working hours may be expected to continue in the future because of the general preference of workers for increased leisure, but modern production techniques and scheduling requirements impose some limitations on the choices open to workers.

Other Policies. Unions emphasize different and contradictory objectives and formulate their policies accordingly. They may seek to maximize the wages paid to those already employed or increase the volume of employment at the cost of lower hourly pay per worker. At times when contraction is necessary unions may try to protect the employment opportunities of older workers through rigid seniority clauses, or they may favor sharing available work among all those employed. Various attitudes have been expressed toward technological advance and automation. These range from encouragement, as exemplified by coal miners and lithographers, to resistance, as is sometimes the case in the building trades. Featherbedding (requiring more workers, work, and time than necessary) and make-work policies are followed occasionally in order to provide work and income for members. But these practices are not as extensive as is often claimed, being limited almost entirely to certain occupations in transportation, construction, printing, and entertainment.

Union policies have been oriented in the direction of restricting the supply of labor and improving its skill. Unions have generally opposed immigration, favored reduction in working hours, supported regulation of the labor of children and women, encouraged early retirement, and objected to work rules calling for greater expenditure of effort by workers. They have favored the expansion of educational opportunities and the improvement of vocational guidance techniques.

Grievances. The process of bargaining includes negotiation of grievances arising from the administration and the interpretation of the contract and from the day-to-day operation of the plant. Unions have made it possible for workers to get a fair review of their complaints. Previously the foreman or some other representative of the employer had the task of making unilateral and final decisions.

Other Functions of Unions. The main task of the labor movement today is to improve wages, hours, and working conditions through collective bargaining and political action. But locals, nationals, and the AFL-CIO engage in many other activities. These include supervising insurance funds; operating credit unions, banks, producer cooperatives, consumer cooperatives, and cooperative housing projects; running educational study and trade training programs; conducting recreational, social work, and publicity programs; and supporting or opposing some government policies that may not bear directly on labor matters.

WAGES

Workers supply labor in order to receive wages. The wages of union and nonunion members are established in the market. Most workers in the United States are paid for the time they work, although a minority are paid according to their output or on a combined time and piece rate basis.

Wage Rates. A wage rate (price of labor), like any other price, is determined by demand and supply. The abundance of natural resources, the quality of capital equipment available, the educational attainment of workers, the level of skills, and the entrepreneurial abilities all affect the wage level. These characteristics of the economy determine the marginal productivity of labor. The United States has the highest level of real wages in the world because it has the highest marginal product of labor.

Demand for Labor. The past three decades have brought about vast changes in the demand for labor and employment. Great transformations have taken place in different geographical regions, occupations, and industries. Employment has generally risen in all the states and regions of the United States but at significantly different rates. Higher employment levels have been particularly marked in Nevada, Arizona, Florida, and California. Occupations have also shown sharp changes. Employment has declined, for example, among farm workers, fishermen, telegraph operators, and textile weavers and spinners and increased among engineers and draftsmen, teachers, and nurses. Professional work provides a larger fraction of total employment, whereas unskilled work provides a smaller fraction. Goods-producing industries, such as manufacturing, mining, and construction, account for a smaller proportion of employment opportunities today, but government and service industries now offer an increasing proportion of jobs.

The shift in job patterns has affected a large number of workers, and many of them have found it difficult to adjust to the resulting change in their life. The problems they face involve finding new jobs when information about alternative jobs is inadequate, gaining marketable skills, and bearing the costs (monetary and emotional) of displacement. But many workers in the United States are highly mobile, although mobility declines with age. Millions of employees change their jobs each year, moving across state and county lines or shifting to another major occupation or to a new industry group. More training and retraining programs as well as improved education have made adjustment easier.

The demand for labor, as for other factors, is a derived demand because it depends on the demand for consumer goods and services that labor produces. The elasticity of demand for a particular type of labor affects the ability of the union to succeed in its wage demands. The demand for labor is more elastic if (1) the price of the consumer good or service produced is more elastic, (2) the ability to substitute other labor or other factors in the productive process is greater, and (3) the proportion of total cost of production going to labor is larger. If the demand for labor is elastic, higher wages reduce employment, while lower wages lead to more employment. But if the demand for labor is inelastic, higher wages tend to reduce employment relatively little, whereas lower wages do not tend to bring about employment of relatively much more labor.

Supply of Labor. Labor supply identifies the quantity of labor that will be offered at different wage rates. In general the relationship is positive. This means that at higher wage rates more labor is offered because work is more attractive. (See figure 16-1.) Some individuals will supply more labor and others who were not in the labor market may decide to enter. Wages in this context represent a composite of many different features to workers, including not only the rate of pay but fringe benefits, physical environment of the plant, opportunities for advancement, and residential facilities in the community.

Changes in the wage rates paid to labor bring about a substitution effect and an income effect. The substitution effect measures the impact of wage rate changes on the amount of labor offered by individuals. The income effect measures the impact of income changes on the amount of labor offered by individuals. At higher wage rates most workers tend to substitute some work for leisure; but as higher wages also raise incomes, some workers are inclined to replace some work by leisure. The effects of substitution and income interact when wage rates change; this interaction generally leads to a greater quantity of labor offered when rates rise, but sometimes a lesser quantity is supplied. For example, workers wishing to earn a particular income will offer less work as wages rise or second workers in a family unit may drop out of the labor force if the wages of the main earner rise. Figure 16-2 shows a case in which the income effect of changes in wage rates is greater on the individual or in the market than the substitution effect and that the supply curve of labor therefore bends backward.

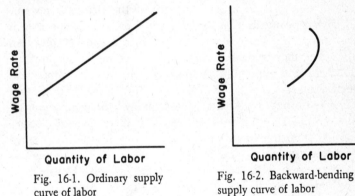

Fig. 16-1. Ordinary supply curve of labor

Fig. 16-2. Backward-bending supply curve of labor

The total labor supply of the nation depends upon the number of residents available for work, the foreign labor available, the hours labor is willing to work, and the quantity of work and quality of skill and energy going into each hour of labor. These factors are affected not only by wage rates but also by customs, laws, the group work requirements of modern production methods, and the prevailing levels of training and education. Generally the elasticity of supply depends upon the degree of labor mobility possible. It is therefore greater for the firm than for the industry, and it is greater for the industry than for the economy. Furthermore, the supply of labor is less elastic in the short run than in the long run.

The Labor Market. Labor market situations can be classified as markets in which (1) there are many buyers and many sellers, (2) there is one buyer (or a few buyers) and many sellers. (3) there are many buyers and one seller (or a few sellers), and (4) there is one buyer and one seller.

(1) In a purely competitive labor market with many buyers and many sellers, employers will hire additional workers at any particular wage as long as the marginal revenue product (incremental dollar market value of the total product) resulting from the labor of each new worker is at least equal to his wage. (The demand for labor is equal to its marginal revenue product.) Of course, insofar as some factors of production can be substituted for others, the entrepreneur uses the one that yields the greatest output per unit of cost. Wage rates are kept uniform throughout the market by the element of competition. Employers desiring to pay less than the value of the marginal product will find that their employees move to other firms. It is true that in most cases an estimate of the marginal revenue product cannot be made with any degree of precision, especially if the firm is large and the operations are intricate and complex. An estimate is even more difficult in much of the employment provided by government and charitable organizations, because no product is sold. But employers nevertheless make the effort to decide if another worker is *worth* hiring. If the industry is monopolistic or oligopolistic in the product market (but competitive in the factor market), wages remain equal to marginal revenue product. But in this case, since product prices are higher and output smaller than in the case of perfect competition with similar cost levels, fewer workers will be employed and wages will be lower because the demand for labor is smaller.

(2) If the employer has a monopsonistic position because he is the only purchaser in a particular region, as in a mining town, or the only purchaser of a special type of labor, as in the case of skilled telephone repairmen, wages are likely to fall below the marginal revenue product. The monopsonist will hire workers only until the last worker hired increases costs, shown by the marginal cost of labor (MCL), as much as he increases revenues, shown by the marginal revenue product or demand for labor. The actual wage set by the monopsonist is likely to be the minimum wage that the worker is willing to take, shown by the supply curve of labor. Figure 16-3 illustrates that the

wage (OZ) and employment (OB) are lower than in the competitive
case (OW and OC, respectively). The extra cost to the monopsonist
of hiring another worker is greater than the wage of that worker
because a higher wage must be paid to all employees.

(3) If there are many buyers of labor but if the supply is monop-
olized because a union has control, then, at the cost of lower employment, wages may be higher than in the competitive case. The union
accomplishes this by restricting the quantity of labor to the point
where the last worker hired increases the wage bill of the employer,
shown by the marginal demand for labor, by an amount equal to
the cost of supplying him, shown by the supply curve of labor. The
actual wage set by the monopolist, which in this case is the union,
is likely to be the maximum the employer is willing to pay, shown
by the marginal revenue product or demand for labor. Figure 16-4
illustrates that the wage (OZ) is higher and employment (OB) is
lower than in the competitive case (OW and OC, respectively). The
union is able to increase total wage receipts only by taking a lower
wage rate.

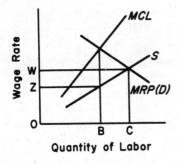

Fig. 16-3. Labor market monopsony

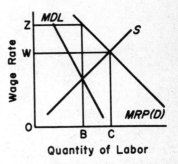

Fig. 16-4. Union monopoly

There are several techniques that unions use to secure higher wages.
When they control entrance to the trade and can decrease the supply
of labor, wages may be raised above the equilibrium level that would
have been determined by the original supply and demand for labor
(though at the expense of a smaller volume of employment). Unions
have been able to increase wages by raising the derived demand for
labor. One way of doing this, for example, is by encouraging con-

sumers to purchase products bearing the union label. Unions have also been able to raise demand by bringing about higher productivity of labor. This has sometimes come about from the higher morale of workers following negotiated contractual improvements in working conditions and increased job security or through union-sponsored training.

There are four factors basic to wage bargaining between employers and unions. These are: (*a*) changes in the productivity of labor, (*b*) ability of the employer to pay, (*c*) comparable wage rates in the area or in the industry, and (*d*) changes in the cost of living. Economic conditions prevailing at the time of bargaining determine the factor that each party emphasizes.

(4) If the union has monopoly power and the employer has monopsony power in the labor market (a situation termed bilateral monopoly), the wage rate is indeterminate in economic theory. It may be as high as the marginal revenue product or as low as the wage rate labor is willing to take. It depends, in practice, on the relative economic strength and bargaining ingenuity of the two sides and on the attitude of the public.

Union Achievements. There has been disagreement over whether unions have significantly raised real wages. (Of course, money wage increases do not necessarily represent real wage increases.) Logically it appears that unions have been responsible for higher wages, but careful examination of the facts does not clearly support this conclusion. Currently, unionized industries frequently pay higher wages than nonunionized industries, but they did so even before they became unionized because they generally have been dominated by large firms that use highly skilled workers. Furthermore, nonunionized sectors of the labor force, such as agricultural and domestic workers, have shown greater relative increases in wages than unionized groups in recent years. It has been argued that unions have been able to get increases for workers only when the demand for labor rises or productivity increases and that these wage gains would have been achieved by the workers in any case; on the other hand, it has been suggested that employers granted higher wages to nonunionized workers matching the gains of unionists in order to reduce the likelihood of union success in organizing their plants. Over the past half century, the share of national income going to wage earners has not risen substantially despite the vast increase in unionism during the same period. The best available evidence seems to show that unions have raised the wages of their members about 10 percent above what they would be if there were no union present.

Generally wage increases can come only from higher productivity that expands total output. Union pressure for raises beyond this level, averaging about 3 percent each year, only inflates prices. Historically the increase in real earnings of workers has been closely related to advances in the productivity of labor. Since 1900, for example, total real hourly earnings of production workers in manufacturing have increased at about the same average rate as the average hourly productivity of manufacturing labor.

Differentials. Many of the rate differences in the wage structure are explained easily enough. Different jobs pay varied rates because of the characteristics associated with the job, which Adam Smith listed as the agreeableness of the work, the training and skill required, the steadiness of employment, the responsibility lodged in the job holder, and the prospects for promotion. But there are external factors that influence wage rates and that often lead to different rates for those doing the same job. These include the geographical location of the work, the cost of living, the ability of the employer to pay, the wages paid by competitors, the power of the union, the legal requirements, the discrimination because of color or sex, and the ignorance of the job seeker.

Another way of looking at wage differences is in terms of equalizing and nonequalizing differentials. Equalizing differentials are of two kinds. They may be paid to compensate for the nonpecuniary disadvantages of a job, such as the size or location of a firm, the personality of the employer or fellow workers, and the nature of the work. They may also arise from certain characteristics of the worker not related to work skills, including pleasantness, cooperation, proper grooming, and good looks. Equalizing wage differentials induce some workers to take jobs in inferior working environments or lead to employment opportunities for some inferior workers. There is a certain amount of public disagreement, however, on the justification of wage differentials based on differences in personal characteristics.

Nonequalizing wage differentials arise from differences in the quality of labor. The noncompeting groups in the labor market may not be substituted easily for each other because the education and training required for jobs vary markedly or because some unusual or special talent is possessed by an individual. Noncompeting groups are exemplified by lawyers and carnival barkers or by surgeons and butchers. Special talent characterizes a top-ranking golf or tennis star capable of earning large sums in tournament play. To the extent that mobility is possible between occupations wage differentials may decline over time. But when a special talent or ability is present, the worker obtains compensation above what he is able to obtain elsewhere; this extra compensation is called *pure economic rent* (because it is comparable to the payment made for the use of a fixed supply of land).

Since 1900 women have constituted an ever-increasing fraction of the civilian labor force, and a greater percentage of working-age women have been joining the work force. However, the income of women employed full-time is only a fraction of the earnings of men. The differential is due to discrimination, occupational segregation, and women's higher job turnover and absenteeism rates.

UNEMPLOYMENT

Although cyclical unemployment has receded into the background as an important factor of economic disruption since the Great Depression of 1929 to 1933, much concern has been manifested regarding structural unemployment (i.e., the mismatching in the economy of available workers and available jobs) and its component, technological unemployment. The structurally unemployed are those displaced as a result of technological change, lack of skill, illiteracy, discrimination, and the processes that create distressed areas. The evidence is not clear that structural unemployment is rising. Although technological advance and automation have led to displacement of labor, most of this unemployment is temporary because these workers shift from one job to another in the expanding economy. Government and industry try to provide job information, improve mobility and transfer possibilities, offer retraining opportunities, and maintain aggregate demand to minimize the adversities of technological change. Nevertheless, the economy must provide several million new jobs each year to take care of displaced workers and those persons, mostly youths, who are entering the labor force. Government incentives for reducing unemployment have been tempered by the fear of intensifying price increases. In the mid-1970s, however, the government has no clear policy as it is faced with continuing inflation and high unemployment.

LABOR LEGISLATION

Before the 1930s the federal government did not regulate or participate in labor relations, except with regard to its own employees and the railroad industry. Some state statutes dealt with wage payments, the length of the standard working day, and child labor.

Early Legislation. At first, laws concerning government workers related to wage rates and hours of work, but more recently they have dealt with the rights and privileges of government employees to engage in collective bargaining. Although the federal government and many states specifically forbid their employees to strike, the process of negotiation, especially in connection with grievances, has gradually gained widespread acceptance. Today about 18 percent of the total labor force works for federal, state, and local governments.

Congress has frequently treated railroad workers with special favor because the railroads occupied a strategic position in the economy, because the industry was one of the few clearly defined by the courts in the nineteenth century to be engaged in interstate commerce, and because the railroad labor unions were among the first to achieve considerable economic and political strength. Federal intervention in the labor affairs of the railroad industry began in 1888, long before other industries were subject to such legislation. But the basic provisions dealing with labor relations were set forth in the Railway Labor Act of 1926 and the important amendments added in 1934. This law recognized the desirability of collective bargaining and implemented the process for the railroad industry (and, since 1936, for the airline industry). It created the National Mediation Board (1934) to determine the appropriate bargaining units on carriers, to mediate disputes regarding the formulation of new agreements, and to enforce fair collective bargaining procedures. The National Railroad Adjustment Board was established to settle grievances and interpret contract provisions. The closed shop is prohibited, but the union shop has been legal since 1951.

Effective regulation of collective bargaining in industry generally began in 1935. Government policy foreshadowing the encouragement and protection of collective bargaining became evident with the passage of the Norris-La Guardia Act in 1932, which made it extremely difficult to obtain injunctions in labor disputes in the federal courts, and the short-lived National Industrial Recovery Act of 1933, which encouraged workers to join unions. It was the National Labor Relations Act (Wagner-Connery Act) of 1935 that laid the groundwork for present-day labor relations. The law gave employees the right to be represented in collective bargaining by unions of their own choosing, and it prohibited employers from committing unfair labor practices. These unfair practices may be classified as interfering in the organizational efforts of workers, discriminating against employees or applicants for employment because of union activity, and refusing to bargain collectively. The National Labor Relations Board (NLRB) was created to implement the provisions of the law. Congress had decided to force both sides to the bargaining table, but it did not require either party to come to terms or to make concessions.

The Taft-Hartley Act. The Wagner-Connery Act, which helped labor strengthen its position, was subject to much criticism because it imposed duties and obligations on employers but none on unions. In 1947 the Labor Management Relations Act (Taft-Hartley Act) was passed, amending and extending the National Labor Relations Act. It shifted the government to a more neutral position. Employees were given the option of organizing or refraining from joining a union. Certain practices by unions were called unfair and were prohibited. It became illegal for unions to coerce workers to join, to refuse to bargain collectively, to engage in sympathy or jurisdictional strikes, and to carry on many different kinds of secondary boycotts. The statute also prohibited the closed shop in interstate commerce, established the Federal Mediation and Conciliation Service as an independent agency, and permitted court injunctions to be issued in national emergency disputes upon the application of the government to provide cooling-off periods of up to eighty days. The law restricted political contributions by unions, outlawed strikes by government employees, and provided procedures for law suits by and against labor unions. The statute defined collective bargaining and specified the meaning of good-faith negotiations.

Other Legislation. The Labor-Management Reporting and Disclosure Act (Landrum-Griffin Act) was passed in 1959 as a result of criticism concerning the lack of democracy in, and the improper administration and procedures followed by, some labor unions. The law established the right of members to participate in union affairs, required a variety of reports from unions and their officials, regulated the establishment of trusteeships, attempted to prevent racketeering and dictatorial practices by labor leaders, and provided for bonding officials who handle union funds. The law was the first effort by the government to police the internal affairs of unions and legislate democracy in a private organization. Congress also made certain amendments to the Taft-Hartley Act. Bans on secondary boycotts and organizational picketing were tightened and provisions giving special advantages to the building and construction industry unions included.

Beginning in 1938 with the Fair Labor Standards Act (Black-Connery Act or Wage and Hour Act) and thereafter through a series of amendments that followed, the federal government undertook to improve labor standards. The law provided that covered workers in interstate commerce be paid a designated minimum hourly wage and overtime at one and one-half times the regular rate for work beyond forty hours a week. In 1976 the minimum wage was $2.30 per hour. The statute also prohibited child labor. Other legislation had already set minimum wage and overtime rates for those employed on government contracts.

Recent labor legislation by the federal government has dealt with discrimination in private employment. Title VII of the Civil Rights Act of 1964, known as the Equal Employment Opportunity Act, attempts to eliminate discrimination based on race, color, religion, national origin, and sex in hiring workers and in setting conditions of employment in industries engaged in interstate commerce. It applies mainly to employers but also imposes obligations on unions and employment agencies. The task of enforcement is given to the Equal Employment Opportunity Commission. In 1967 a law was enacted prohibiting discrimination against older workers.

The government also participates in the settlement of labor disputes, generally through mediation machinery. Government mediators, both federal and state, are called upon for assistance by disputants or proffer their services when controversies arise. Mediators provide suggestions and advice to prevent strikes from occurring or bring to an end those that have begun. Much of the success of mediation efforts depends upon the confidence that the parties have in the mediator. Arbitration involves rendering decisions that are binding on parties having a dispute. It rarely is undertaken or regulated by the government, except in the railroad industry. Labor and management, however, generally agree to use this technique to settle controversies arising from the interpretation of contracts.

Federal laws cover many aspects of labor, including labor relations, wages and hours, discrimination in employment, and social security (discussed in the next chapter). In many states equivalent and supplementary statutes have been enacted in these fields to deal with those workers engaged in intrastate commerce or to raise federal standards.

Chapter 17
INEQUALITY OF INCOME

Traditionally, distribution theory has been used to analyze the proportion of national income that is earned by each factor of production. This analysis, called *functional distribution*, proved useful in the eighteenth and nineteenth centuries to describe personal distribution of income because during that era payments for land, labor, and capital were made to relatively distinct social-political classes—landowners, workers, and capitalists. But the diffusion of factor ownership among the population and the greater complexity of the concept of capital in the twentieth century have sharply reduced the usefulness of factor distribution as a measure of personal distribution.

During the twentieth century much sentiment has been expressed in favor of achieving a greater equality of income and wealth to permit all members of democratic societies to enjoy approximately equal amounts of satisfaction from the goods they consume and to prevent the concentration of economic power. It is generally felt that it is desirable for high-income recipients or wealthy persons to give up some resources so that the purchasing power of low-income recipients or poor persons may be increased. This attitude has prevailed in spite of the impossibility of making interpersonal comparisons of satisfaction.

Yet there are sound reasons for allowing inequality to continue, subject to the control of its degree and extent. Inequality generally provides the incentives necessary to induce greater ingenuity, effort, and output from many persons who otherwise might contribute no more than a routine performance. The economy, which gains much from the work of these people, must reward them suitably under the present realities of life. Furthermore, the high incomes associated with inequality provide the source of much of the investment funds in the economy. A very large proportion of personal saving is undertaken by persons in the upper income groups.

DISTRIBUTION OF PERSONAL INCOME

Some of the most important economic questions revolve around the relative amount of income received by individuals. For example, demands by labor for more wages, by business entrepreneurs for higher prices, and by farmers for more government price support raise recurrent problems. Solutions require an analysis of the means by which the total income of the economy may be increased so that more is available for division among the recipients and also an analysis of whether any given total income is properly apportioned. Despite the fact that the United States is the wealthiest country in the world and boasts the largest national income, the average income in 1974 (if the total is divided equally among the population) was about $5,400. Such a sum is hardly conducive to luxurious standards.

Distribution of personal income, which is that received by individuals and family units, shows a very wide range. Some persons supplying factors of production sustain heavy losses during the year, and others earn several hundred million dollars. A graphic representation, shown in figure 17-1, is skewed sharply to the right, indicating that most earners are concentrated near the lower end of the scale but that a small number of earners receive very large sums. These huge incomes, however, are derived by property owners who contribute capital and land to the productive process. The return to labor, shown in figure 17-2, constitutes a fraction of the total income. It is related much more closely to personal ability and, although skewed, extends over a much narrower range. Labor income—wages and salaries—usually varies between one million dollars and nothing each year. (Inequality in the remuneration of labor is increased if expense accounts of business executives are considered part of personal income.) There are many reasons for the differences in labor income of individuals, including variations in ability, mental alertness, and physical energy of workers and voluntary withdrawal of some persons from the labor force for part of the year. Other reasons for income differences were discussed in chapter 16 under the topic of wage differentials.

The real income of consumer units in the economy, of which about four-fifths are families and one-fifth unattached individuals, has continued to rise. Table 17-1 shows the distribution of families according to real income.

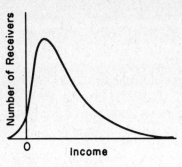

Fig. 17-1. Distribution of income

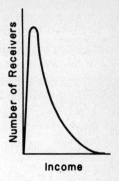

Fig. 17-2. Labor income

TABLE 17-1

PERCENT DISTRIBUTION OF FAMILIES BY REAL INCOME LEVEL, 1947–1972

(IN 1973 DOLLARS)

Family Personal Income	1947	1960	1972
Under 3,000	19	13	6
3,000–4,999	20	13	9
5,000–6,999	22	14	9
7,000–9,999	20	24	15
10,000–14,999	19	23	25
15,000 and over		13	36

Source: United States Department of Commerce, *Current Population Reports, Series P-60, No. 97, 1975, p. 27.*

The degree of inequality in the distribution of income is an interesting and perplexing question. Government studies show that the relative distribution of income by amount received has remained virtually unchanged since the end of the Second World War, although inequalities have been considerably reduced over the past forty-five years. The decline at the beginning of the period occurred in part because dividends, which are paid mainly to upper-income groups, declined as a fraction of personal income, while transfer payments (for example, relief checks), which are received only by lower-income groups, increased as a fraction of personal income.

Geographical. Personal income varies geographically. Cities, rather than rural areas, generally have more people with higher incomes because cities have a greater concentration of occupations paying higher wages and salaries. Nevertheless, the tendency has been for the per capita income of most states to converge toward the national average and for greater equality of income to prevail among the states. The regional distribution is given in table 17-2.

TABLE 17-2

PER CAPITA PERSONAL INCOME IN 1973 BY REGION

Region	Per Capita Personal Income (Dollars)
New England	5,164
Middle Atlantic	5,438
East North Central	5,254
West North Central	4,820
South Atlantic	4,547
East South Central	3,807
West South Central	4,156
Mountain	4,549
Pacific	5,320

Source: *Statistical Abstract of the United States,* 1974, p. 380.

Wages and Salaries. Most personal income is derived from wages and salaries. Table 17-3 shows the sources of such income, including the amounts flowing from different industries.

The Lorenz Curve. One of the most useful ways of depicting inequality is by the Lorenz curve. This graphic representation plots the cumulated frequencies against the cumulated values of a variable arranged in ascending or descending order. Perfect equality means that any percentage of the cumulated value of the variable being measured is received or held by an equal proportion of individuals. The greater the divergences in percentages, the more unequal is the distribution.

Thus the percentage of family units may be contrasted with the percentage of income received or percentage of wealth held and the degree of inequality established. In the former case a chart is constructed that relates the cumulative percentage of family units against the percentage of income received and, in the latter case, against the wealth owned. Perfect equality is shown by a diagonal. The area between the curve and the diagonal indicates the extent of the inequality. The Lorenz curve lies above the diagonal when the individuals are ranked and cumulated from highest to lowest income and below the diagonal when the cumulation is in the opposite direction.

TABLE 17-3

PERSONAL INCOME BY MAJOR SOURCES, 1973

		Billions of Dollars
Wage and salary disbursements	691.5	
Farms		4.3
Mining		7.4
Contract construction		42.1
Manufacturing		196.8
Wholesale and retail trade		112.9
Finance, insurance, and real estate		35.1
Transportation		30.8
Communication and public utilities		21.4
Services		93.9
Government		145.4
Other		1.4
Other labor income	44.9	
Proprietors' income	84.2	
Rental income of persons	25.1	
Dividends	27.8	
Personal interest income	87.5	
Transfer payments		117.5
Less: personal contributions for social insurance		43.1
	74.4	
	1035.4	

Source: *Statistical Abstract of the United States*, 1974, p. 378.

The Lorenz curve permits many interesting comparisons; the inequality of income or wealth in any country may be examined over a period of time and trends can be observed readily. Inequalities between countries or in different sections of a country may be plotted against one another. In addition, the degree of inequality of income and the degree of inequality of wealth may be contrasted by plotting them on the same scale. Similarly, income inequalities of different occupations, age groups, or races may be set up one against the other.

Table 17-4, which shows the distribution of families by personal income, may be used to illustrate the procedure. It reveals inequality by relating the percentage of income before tax to the percentage of families. The distribution of income after taxes would show a curve between the one plotted and the diagonal and would represent slightly less inequality. Of course, if the distribution of earnings had been cumulated from the lowest income quintile to all recipients of income, the degree of inequality would be the same, but the curve would lie below the diagonal. The Lorenz curve is plotted in figure 17-3.

TABLE 17-4

DISTRIBUTION OF FAMILIES BY PERSONAL INCOME, 1972
(BEFORE INCOME TAXES)

Percent of Families	Percent of Income
Upper 20	41
Upper 40	65
Upper 60	82
Upper 80	95
All	100

Source: *Statistical Abstract of the United States*, 1974, p. 384.

INEQUALITY OF WEALTH

Accumulating wealth is a long and difficult process. At any time, most of the wealth of the United States belongs to individuals who have inherited it. Only infrequently do people become wealthy suddenly. For example, the value of a business may increase sharply because of a patent or a government order, oil may be discovered on a piece of property, or land values may rise if a city expands. But the painstaking process of accumulating vast amounts of saving is the usual method, and this can almost never be accomplished from labor income alone. As a result, the composition and size of the very wealthy class change very slowly.

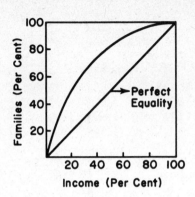

Fig. 17-3. The Lorenz curve

There are certain factors that tend to reduce concentration of wealth. Today the preservation of inherited fortunes requires more business ability than was the case formerly, when ownership of land was the main source of wealth. Estate and inheritance taxes also diminish the size of many fortunes. On the other hand, capital gains on property (i.e., the increase in the value of assets such as land or stocks) operate in the other direction. There is, however, no important historical or current evidence to support the thesis of Karl Marx, that the rich get richer and the poor get poorer, and that capitalists exploit wage earners.

Studies have shown that the ownership of wealth in the United States is even more heavily concentrated than income. (Unfortunately, comprehensive current data on wealth are not available.) About 28 percent of all spending units had negative net worth or had assets under $1,000 at the beginning of 1963; 23 percent had net worth between $10,000 and $25,000; and 17 percent possessed more than $25,000. About one-fifth of the spending units had no liquid assets (currency excluded); five-sixths had no corporate stock; and three-sevenths had no equity in their homes. Approximately 20 percent of the total wealth of the United States is owned by the public (the government). The net worth of consumer units is shown in table 17-5. The composition of national wealth is shown in table 17-6.

Although there has been some decline in the inequality of wealth in the United States during the past half century, the change has been smaller than the reduction in the inequality of income. The wealthiest 1 percent (adults) own about a quarter of the country's total wealth. During the 1920s the wealthiest 1 percent owned about a third of the total wealth. The decline would be somewhat smaller, however, if wealth were measured in relation to family units rather than in relation to individuals because married women represent an increasing fraction of the wealthiest group. At the beginning of 1963

TABLE 17-5

NET WORTH OF CONSUMER UNITS IN THE UNITED STATES

1962 Incomes (Dollars)	Average Net Worth	Median Net Worth
0 to 2,999	$8,875	$2,760
3,000 to 4,999	10,914	3,320
5,000 to 7,499	15,112	7,450
7,500 to 9,999	21,243	13,450
10,000 to 14,999	30,389	20,500
15,000 to 24,999	74,329	42,750
25,000 to 49,999	267,996	160,000
50,000 to 99,999	789,582	470,000
100,000 or more	1,554,152	875,000

Age of Family Head	Average Net Worth	Median Net Worth
Under 25	$762	$270
25 to 34	7,661	2,080
35 to 44	19,442	8,000
45 to 54	25,459	11,950
55 to 64	34,781	14,950
65 or more	30,718	10,450

Region	Average Net Worth	Median Net Worth
Northeast	$23,980	$8,600
North Central	23,632	10,150
South	18,318	4,460
West	26,192	7,650

Source: *Federal Reserve Bulletin*, March 1964, p. 291.

the average (mean) net worth of all families in the United States was $22,588 and the median was $9,550. Table 17-7 shows 16 percent of all families having negative or zero net worth, which means that their debts exceed or are equal to their assets. Inequality of wealth is much greater in Great Britain than in the United States, but inequality of income is somewhat less.

TABLE 17-6

NATIONAL WEALTH, 1968

Type of Asset		Amount (Billions of Dollars)	
Structures		1,537.0	
Nonfarm:	Public nonresidential		459.8
	Institutional		55.7
	Other private nonresidential		288.7
	Residential		682.8
Farm			50.0
Equipment:	Producer durable	377.0	
	Consumer durable	233.8	
Inventories:	Private farm	29.5	
	Private nonfarm	172.7	
	Public	14.0	
Land:	Private farm	152.6	
	Private nonfarm	418.6	
	Public	144.2	
Total		3,079.4	

Source: *Statistical Abstract of the United States,* 1974, p. 400.

TABLE 17-7

DISTRIBUTION OF FAMILIES IN THE UNITED STATES
BY NET WORTH, DECEMBER 31, 1962

Amount (Dollars)	Families (Percent)
Negative	11
Zero	5
1–999	12
1,000–4,999	17
5,000–9,999	15
10,000–24,999	23
25,000–49,999	10
50,000–99,999	4
100,000–199,999	1
200,000–499,999	1
500,000–999,999	(*)
1,000,000 and over	(*)

Source: Board of Governors of the Federal Reserve System, *Survey of Financial Characteristics of Consumers,* August, 1966, p. 96.
* Less than one-half of 1 percent.

STANDARD OF LIVING

Income bears heavily on the standard of living. Generally speaking, more income makes possible a higher standard of living while less income generally implies that the standard is lower. The *standard of living* measures the volume of goods and services consumed by a family unit over a relatively long period of time. It deals with actual consumption, not with what the purchaser could afford. In a broader context standard of living may refer to the consumption level of an entire nation or a regional subdivision of a country.

Measurement. Earnings and wealth are not the only factors that determine the standard of living. The standard of a family depends upon (1) the amount of money spent on consumer goods and services, (2) the purchasing power of money at the time and place the purchases are made, (3) the number of persons in the family unit, (4) the quantity and quality of durable consumer goods owned at the beginning of the period, (5) the value of goods and services provided by the government without charge, (6) the amount of free goods available, and (7) the amount of leisure. A family may improve its standard of living by shifting money expenditures to places where prices are lower, such as to discount stores, or by spending money that has been borrowed, received as a gift, or withdrawn from accumulated savings rather than currently earned. Although the value of goods provided by the government and the amount of leisure time are important elements in judging the standard of living, these items ordinarily are not included in the measurement because of the practical difficulties involved in doing so.

Annual income figures have certain shortcomings as a measure of the economic status of a family. Age, net worth, and investment in education and training of the labor force participant or income recipient may be used to estimate his expected lifetime income. Such data (other than age), however, are inadequate and many economists therefore are inclined to use consumption as the best measure of personal or family welfare. Typically, patterns for individuals show periods of net saving (i.e., earnings exceed consumption) and dissaving during different stages of life. The years prior to marriage may involve net saving for the young worker. Dissaving occurs in the early years of married life to meet current expenses, to buy durable consumer goods, and sometimes to purchase a home. When the children are grown and leave the family another period of net saving takes place. After retirement dissaving once again sets in.

Leisure. Leisure is recognized as desirable, but increasing amounts of it may bring about important problems. In 1931, John M. Keynes already foresaw some difficulties connected with growing amounts of leisure. In *Essays in Persuasion,* he wrote: "To those who sweat for their daily bread leisure is a longed-for sweet—until they get it."

Modern industrial society does not adequately prepare its members for the expansion of leisure that comes from gradually decreasing hours of work or the greater number of retirement years being experienced. Children and adults will require continual education to explore the possibilities that leisure provides.

REDISTRIBUTION OF PERSONAL INCOME

In the past hundred years the growth of an urban and industrial society in the United States has provided much impetus to the development of programs for the redistribution of income and wealth. Strong family ties were common in rural areas and small towns, and persons in need for whatever reasons were able to fall back on other members of their family. This was particularly true when the economy was dominated by farming. But modern life has sharply reduced family ability and obligations to care for needy relations. Furthermore, severe depressions have increased economic insecurity. Society therefore has undertaken to provide a degree of security through government action. This has been accomplished in part by forcing people to save some income to meet future needs, in part by using tax revenues collected from the general public, and in part by increasing the money supply available to the government.

Government participation in economic activities, to some extent, redistributes income from persons in the upper-income brackets to persons in the lower-income brackets and redistributes wealth from the rich to the poor. These government activities include poverty programs, payments made in connection with social security, and taxes on personal income and estates. Yet there are cases of government intervention in which the impact on the redistribution patterns is by no means clear, as when expenditures are made for public parks, municipal fire departments, tuition-free college education, public libraries, and subsidies for the arts. The farm parity program and government-imposed restrictions on entry into certain markets, as when entrepreneurs seek to start a bank or operate a radio station, are other illustrations. The nature of the effect of minimum wage laws on redistribution of income is doubtful because these laws may cause some unemployment.

Emphasis has been placed in recent years on the possibilities of improving the economic position of the poor by increasing the personal resources available to them. This process, called *investment in human capital*, includes formal education, on-the-job training, better medical care, and encouragement to migrate. It is intended to augment the future money earnings of individuals, but it yields psychic income (satisfactions other than material ones) by increasing skills, adding knowledge, and improving health.

It is clear that the more educated and the more skilled persons usually earn larger incomes than do those with less education and skill. Furthermore, unemployment is ordinarily inversely related to the level of education. Sometimes, however, investment in human capital does not affect personal income because the benefits are gained by the firms or governments that pay the costs.

Characteristics of Poverty. Though there had been much discussion relating to poverty during the depression years of the 1930s and many government programs were undertaken to alleviate the distress, the entry of the United States into the Second World War in 1941 coincided with improved economic conditions and terminated all special efforts to help the poor. On January 8, 1964, President Lyndon B. Johnson renewed the war on poverty in America in his state of the union message to Congress. Johnson said: ". . . this Administration today, here and now, declares unconditional war on poverty in America . . . . It will not be a short or easy struggle, no single weapon or strategy will suffice . . . . Very often a lack of jobs and money is not the cause of poverty but the symptom."

Describing the meaning of poverty in 1964, the Council of Economic Advisors wrote: "The poor inhabit a world scarcely recognizable, and rarely recognized by the majority of their fellow Americans. It is a world apart, whose inhabitants are isolated from the mainstream of American life and alienated from its values. It is a world where Americans are literally concerned with day-to-day survival—a roof over their heads, where the next meal is coming from. It is a world where a minor illness is a major tragedy, where pride and privacy must be sacrificed to get help, where honesty can become a luxury and ambition a myth. Worst of all, the poverty of fathers is visited upon the children."

Under the social standards prevalent in the United States today most people in the world are poor; and similarly most inhabitants of this country a century ago were poor. The standards that define the economic need of a representative family in the United States are such that many inhabitants are living under conditions that do not measure up to the minimum requirements. Government standards in the mid-1970s classify poor families as those with money incomes below $4,800 (although account must also be taken of family size, age, composition, and place of residence) and poor unattached individuals as those with money incomes below $2,500.

Certain features are salient when the poverty sector of the population is analyzed by the age of the family head, the education of the family head, the sex of the family head, the labor force status of the family head, the color of the family, the number of children under 18 years in the family, the number of wage earners in the family, the regional location of the family, and the type of residence of the family (i.e., rural or urban).

There has been much progress in eliminating poverty since the end of the Second World War. These gains have resulted mainly from rising real national income rather than from any change in the distribution of income. The incidence of poverty is concentrated among nonwhite families, farm families, and families headed by females, the elderly, the poorly educated, and those unable to work. These categories, therefore, constitute the core of the problem and require the greatest attention if poverty is to be eradicated. It should be clear that though it is possible to bring all families to income levels above $4,800, it is impossible to eliminate the situation in which some fraction of the labor force falls into the lowest income group.

Poverty Programs. The New Deal social legislation in the 1930s marked the beginning of federal involvement in the problem of increasing the economic security of individuals and families, and such policies have since been strengthened and expanded. The Social Security Act of 1935 provided programs to reduce economic distress among the aged, the unemployed, and those unable to work. The Employment Act of 1946 laid down the principle of federal responsibility to reduce unemployment. The Area Redevelopment Act of 1961 was intended mainly to assist depressed areas to restore their economies and absorb unemployed labor. The Manpower Development and Training Act of 1962 offered training to those without skills as well as those whose skills had become obsolete as a result of technological change.

The Economic Opportunity Act of 1964 provided ten separate programs intended to assist the poor. These included special training for young persons, aid to localities combating poverty through guidance and training projects, aid to small businesses, and assistance to migrant workers. This law marked a departure in federal policy. For the first time vast government relief projects were set up during a period of prosperity. But these efforts were interwoven with the prevailing philosophy of those heading the government that continued substantial federal injections of purchasing power into the hands of consumers are necessary to prevent cyclical downswings. There has been considerable disagreement in determining the effectiveness of many of these programs in reducing the extent of poverty. During the 1970s the federal government has shown considerably less enthusiasm in pursuing policies to eliminate poverty.

Social Security Programs.   One of the major efforts by the government to provide economic security and to redistribute income occurs through the various social security programs. *Social security* includes government attempts to assure to individuals the financial means to meet misfortunes and emergencies as they arise. Many types of protection have been developed in connection with old age, unemployment, and occupational and nonoccupational injury and sickness, as well as general and special assistance to the needy.

Although several state programs were already in effect at the time, the first comprehensive law dealing with social security was the federal Social Security Act of 1935 (with many subsequent amendments). It provided (1) insurance programs, under which premiums are paid by employers and employees, or both, to cover certain types of benefits and (2) relief programs, under which needy persons are given grants of money appropriated from the general funds of government. The social insurance programs, like relief, are primarily intended to protect the poorer groups, but all who qualify for coverage are eligible for benefits, regardless of need.

The most extensive program under the Social Security Act is a federally administered compulsory insurance program, called old-age, survivors, disability, and health insurance (OASDHI), which provides pensions to insured aged persons and benefits to insured disabled persons and to survivors of those insured. Though the pension is related to the amount paid in, some redistribution occurs because larger contributors get relatively less than do smaller ones and benefits increase to keep pace with rises in the cost of living. A separate federal plan covers railroad workers, and still other pension schemes protect many employees of the federal, state, and local governments.

A major advance in the social security program was enacted in 1965. Under the medicare amendments to the Social Security Act, Congress for the first time approved a limited plan for insured medical care. The benefits apply to the aged, to those under sixty-five years of age who have been entitled to disability checks for at least two consecutive years, and to people who need kidney transplants or dialysis. They are covered by a basic health plan that provides hospital care, posthospital nursing-home care, visits by nurses after discharge from a hospital, and outpatient diagnostic services. The amendments have also set up a supplementary voluntary health insurance plan under which persons over sixty-five years of age are eligible for a variety of health benefits. Medical care insurance for persons not covered by OASDHI or the Railroad Retirement Act is financed through general revenues. Legislation increased the tax base to $15,300 in 1976 and also raised the premium rates. In 1976 the rate paid by employees for OASDHI was 5.85 percent; by 1986 it is scheduled to rise in a series of steps to 6.45 percent.

Unemployment compensation is the other insurance system, also compulsory, set up by the Social Security Act. It is administered by the states within a general framework laid out by the federal government, but the state programs differ considerably. Unemployment compensation provides specified benefits (related to previous earnings) for varying periods to unemployed workers who have attained coverage (those whose former employers have contributed to the insurance fund). An experience rating system to discourage layoffs links the percentage of payroll paid by employers as premiums to the steadiness of employment provided by the firm. A special unemployment compensation program is run by the federal government for railroad workers. As was mentioned previously in connection with fiscal policy, unemployment benefits are classified as one kind of automatic stabilizer.

Each state has enacted workmen's compensation legislation providing social security insurance for workers injured on the job or sustaining an occupational disease. Such compensation is financed through premiums which in almost all cases are paid entirely by the employer. Coverage often excludes agricultural, domestic, and railroad workers and persons holding nonhazardous jobs. A few states provide temporary disability insurance programs for those unable to work because of injury or illness not connected with the job. Special benefit programs for veterans of the U.S. armed forces have also been enacted.

The Social Security Act has also established five relief programs to which the federal government contributes substantially. These plans are intended to help certain selected categories of needy persons and are called special assistance programs. They include (1) old-age assistance, (2) aid to families with dependent children, (3) aid to the blind, (4) aid to the permanently and totally disabled, and (5) medical assistance to the needy (medicaid). Aid to the aged, blind, and disabled is administered by the federal government under a program called supplemental security income (SSI). Aid to needy children and medicaid are administered by state and local governments. Other groups of persons in need may be helped by general public assistance programs that are financed entirely by state and local governments.

All social security insurance and relief programs provide purchasing power to persons who typically have high marginal propensities to consume, since the recipients do not ordinarily have other major sources of income. Although these payments are normally classed as transfers and connote the shifting of income from workers to the idle, it should be borne in mind that in some cases premium payments' for insurance do contribute to production over long periods. For example, premiums paid by employers for workmen's compensation to private insurance companies are readily available as an investment source and hence serve to increase gross national product. Of course, the federal government has the power to use the OASDHI and unemployment insurance funds for investment purposes so that subsequent payment to beneficiaries would be equivalent to factor payments.

Tax Programs. Taxes may be used to redistribute wealth and income. Probably the best examples of levies having this objective are estate, inheritance, and gift taxes. The federal government imposes higher tax rates when estates of decedents are large than when they are small and uses similar tax scales for gifts, thereby reducing the amount of wealth that otherwise would be passed on by one person to another. In addition, states impose taxes on estates and inheritances. Personal income taxes also call for higher rates on larger incomes so that income after taxes is more equally distributed than income before taxes. In practice, because of provisions permitting a variety of deductions, the federal personal income tax does not alter the distribution of income substantially. The percent of total U.S. income that remains to the average family at any level of income after taxes is approximately the same as the percent of total income they had before taxes. Companies declare relatively smaller dividends today than they formerly did because a larger part of the profit must be used to pay higher corporate income taxes, and therefore the share of the largest income receivers is reduced.

A proposal that has widespread support in efforts to provide a minimum guaranteed income is the negative income tax. This system would provide government income transfers to families whose income is below a predetermined minimum. The subsidy would constitute a fraction of the deficit so that incentives to work would remain.

SPECIAL URBAN PROBLEMS

The urbanization and concentration of population that has marked the development of the United States has given rise to a number of serious problems associated with the growth of cities and, to a certain extent, with the poverty common to many of the larger urban communities. The economic questions receiving the most consideration are (1) pollution, (2) housing, and (3) mass transportation.

The pollution of air and water and the defilement of land that have become widespread as a result of increased use of automobiles, production of power for factories, development of new chemicals for industrial and home use, and increased generation of solid wastes requires immediate attention to preserve human health and the environment. Pollution is associated with externalities or external costs, that is, the costs of a production or consumption decision that fall mainly on others rather than on those making the economic decision. Externalities are thus ordinarily ignored by the decision maker unless the government intervenes.

Legislation to reduce the extent of pollution has been enacted at all levels of government. In 1970 the federal government set up the Environmental Protection Agency to develop quality standards for air and water and enforce legal sanctions against violators. Federal and state governments have provided subsidies to discourage pollution. Firms that install pollution-control equipment are allowed to depreciate the investment at a rapid rate. Pollution taxes have been suggested as another method of controlling liquid and gaseous emissions.

Inadequate housing for the poor is a major problem of cities. Private enterprise has not been able to provide low-rent housing profitably in inner cities. Since the 1930s the government has tried, without great success, to develop an effective housing policy and encourage urban renewal. Aspects of this policy have involved making credit available to encourage private housing construction; utilizing zoning regulations, building codes, and rent controls; subsidizing urban renewal programs; and owning and operating public housing. Further efforts by government will be necessary before good housing is generally achieved.

Urban transportation policy concerns the most efficient use and development of transportation facilities. Traffic congestion and growing pollution are the most evident problems created by automobiles. Toll charges, gasoline taxes, and parking fees must be used more effectively to control the short-term problem. In the longer period mass transportation must be improved and expanded to assume a greater share of the burden of moving people in the urban environment. In the past, transportation subsidies for roads and highways have favored automobiles. Mass transit to and from city centers might reduce pollution and increase job opportunities for the poor in suburban areas.

V International Economics

Chapter 18
INTERNATIONAL TRADE

Various benefits and advantages flow from international trade to participating nations, but there are many reasons why some commodities are produced domestically even when foreigners are able to supply them more cheaply. Though some of the many national restrictions imposed on imports and exports are justified, the practice of limiting trade is an undesirable means of improving the economic position of a country. Since the end of the Second World War particularly, the United States has endeavored to minimize the artificial restraints on international trade and has enacted legislation, usually on a reciprocal basis, to reduce restrictions. At the international level efforts have been made by many nations to reach a general agreement that would eliminate some barriers to trade. In recent years the volume of world trade has been rising.

In the last quarter of the twentieth century the interdependence of the countries of the world is particularly evident. The foreign trade policies adopted by the United States influence international relations because they vitally affect the prospects for growth of both underdeveloped and developed nations that depend upon imports and exports to achieve and maintain prosperity.

FACTORS UNDERLYING INTERNATIONAL TRADE

The United States is one of the few countries in the world that does not depend on foreign trade to maintain its standard of living. The diversity of resources and skills and the vast size of the country are such that almost every commodity used by business firms and consumers can be produced domestically. There are a few minerals and metals which are lacking or in short supply, but more costly substitutes are available. Nevertheless, foreign trade is of great importance to the United States for both economic and political reasons.

International trade involves business exchanges between nations. Though national governments that are trying to improve their respective economic positions may engage directly in some transactions, most trade takes place between private enterprises. Profit seeking dominates international trade as it does domestic trade, but there are several unique characteristics which set international economics apart as a separate area of study. Each country has (1) restrictions on trade, (2) a different currency, (3) varied laws and customs, (4) immobility of some resources, and (5) a different degree of economic development and specialization. Although some of these factors may also apply to interregional or intranational trade (for example, mining activity must occur where minerals and ores are located and hence involves immobility), they usually do not give rise to the same problems.

THE PRINCIPLE OF COMPARATIVE ADVANTAGE

Some countries are precluded by climate or geological considerations from producing certain goods. The production of coffee or bananas is limited to tropical areas, and the extraction of nickel or manganese is possible only where such ore is found. Countries that lack such goods must depend upon trade to obtain them. Similarly, when one country has an absolute advantage in production of a good over another country, that is, when it can produce a good by using less labor and fewer raw materials, this good may be traded profitably for goods in which the other country has an absolute advantage. It can be readily shown, however, that even when one country has an absolute advantage over another in the production of all goods, there is nevertheless a mutually profitable basis of trade between them. This basis is clarified by the principle of comparative advantage, which states that total output can be increased if each country specializes in producing those goods in which it has the greatest comparative advantage or the least comparative disadvantage. (Of course, the principle of comparative advantage also applies to trade within a country if there is any immobility of resources.) A simple example of the principle in operation involves two countries, A and B, and two products, shirts and ties. Using labor to represent all resources, assume that the work of one person for one year in country A can produce 1,000 shirts or 4,000 ties and that the same amount of work in country B will yield 800 shirts or 3,000 ties. Country A has an absolute advantage in the production of both commodities, yet there is a basis for trade. Since country A has a relatively greater advantage in the production of ties (a ratio of four to three for ties and only five to four for shirts), country B has a comparative advantage in the production of shirts. Suppose there is no trade and each country employs half of its labor in the production of each commodity. After one year country A will have 500 shirts and 2,000 ties, while country B will have 400 shirts and 1,500 ties. Now let each country specialize. Country A has a greater advantage in ties and can produce 4,000, while country B has a comparative advantage in shirts and can produce 800. Country A may then send 2,000 ties to country B where they are worth two-thirds of a year's work or 533⅓ shirts. Assume that country A receives 525 shirts in return and thus ends the year with 2,000 ties and 525 shirts; this represents more than it can produce through its own efforts. Country B, which ends the year with 2,000 ties and 275 shirts, would require one and one-ninety-sixth of a year to produce this combination of ties and shirts. Both countries have therefore gained from trade even though country A had an absolute advantage in the production of both ties and shirts. Regardless of the final combination of products that each country obtains, both are better off if A buys shirts from B and B buys ties from A at exchange ratios which give them goods at a price below the cost necessary to produce the commodities at home.

Comparative advantage can stem from the immobility of various resources, including restrictions on the movement of labor and capital. Countries where labor is more abundant than capital have lower marginal productivities of labor, lower wage rates, and therefore lower prices for certain goods. This condition may underlie comparative advantage and leads to international trade because the total real income of the trading nation rises. Naturally countries do not specialize only in the one product where they have the greatest absolute or comparative advantage. Aside from the needs of national defense and the desire to create and maintain a particular culture pattern, which depends to some extent on the nature of domestic output and the environment associated with particular types of production, there are also economic considerations. As specialization increases and output rises, marginal returns diminish (i.e., marginal costs rise). As a result there is a point at which the amount of input necessary to secure output increases sufficiently so that the advantage of producing a particular good disappears. This means that the *terms of trade*, or the ratio at which goods are exchanged for each other, change; and when the cost ratios for goods in the trading countries are equal, no basis for trade exists. In the discussion of comparative advantage it is necessary to remember that the production advantage of the exporter must be sufficiently large to allow for the inclusion of the cost of transportation to the importing country.

OTHER BASES OF TRADE

Comparative advantage provides a good reason for international trade, but there are other reasons. Thus, even if the cost of production in two countries is identical, trade between them may be profitable. For example: (1) If each country specializes in manufacturing some of the goods that may be produced under conditions of decreasing costs or increasing returns, sharing of the economies of mass production is possible. (2) If there are different consumer demand schedules in each country (because tastes differ), goods produced in industries subject to increasing costs may be traded advantageously.

Attempts have been made to measure the effect of exports on the volume of employment. It was estimated that in 1972 exports were directly responsible for the employment of 1,527,000 persons in the United States and indirectly (i.e., supporting industries that produce, transport, and market goods used to make products which are exported) for an additional 1,403,000 persons. This total of 2,930,000 persons was about 4.1 percent of the employed civilian labor force that year. On the other hand, the importation of goods tends to reduce domestic production and may therefore be assumed to curtail the opportunities for employment.

THE FOREIGN TRADE MULTIPLIER

Foreign trade affects the multiplier (see chapter 6). Net exports, or the excess of exports over imports, is part of the gross national product. Increasing exports or reducing imports results in the same kind of multiplier effect that more domestic investment or government spending brings about when economic resources are only partially utilized. An increase in exports raises the total output by more than the value of the exports because employment is increased and income is generated and respent. The extent of the multiplier effect is determined by the leakage, which depends upon the marginal propensity to save. But the higher income associated with more exports and output tends to increase the volume of imports. Additional imports that result from each marginal dollar of new income increase the leakage and must be deducted along with savings to determine the foreign trade multiplier.

GOVERNMENT INTERFERENCE IN INTERNATIONAL TRADE

Despite the benefits of international trade, there have been many hindrances to the full implementation of trade between nations. The reasons are partly historical, going back to economic philosophies of former times.

Between the sixteenth and eighteenth centuries the modern centralized European states were developing from medieval towns and building strong domestic economies to protect themselves in time of war and to facilitate territorial expansion and overseas colonization. Self-sufficiency and expansion of manufacturing were encouraged. Gold and silver derived from commerce were used by the government to support strong armies and navies. A favorable balance of trade, that is, an excess of exports over imports, brought in these precious metals to offset the cost of building and expansion programs; and such trade balances were supported vigorously by governments through subsidies for exports and barriers of different kinds against imports. These varied economic objectives came to be systematized as mercantilism.

Adam Smith and the classical economists who followed him criticized the policy of mercantilism for obstructing the international division of labor and lowering productivity and general welfare. The British in particular favored a policy of free trade to enable exports and imports to cross national boundaries without restrictions. Although it was conceded that a few industries might suffer under this arrangement, proponents thought that it was desirable for Great Britain to have access to foreign raw materials and foreign consumer markets under conditions of minimal restraint.

Though the idea of free trade gained wide acceptance among nations as a general principle, protectionism and barriers to free trade had strong support from the public and influenced the policies of many governments. The following arguments have been advanced in favor of restrictions on trade: (1) During war and national emergencies, and for the purposes of defense, countries must be as nearly self-sufficient as possible and therefore domestic industry must be encouraged and protected. This attitude, for example, leads to subsidies for construction and operation of a merchant marine as a potential adjunct to the navy. (2) It is desirable to diversify and balance the domestic market of a country whose production is limited to a few items so that the economy is not overly dependent on selling goods in foreign markets. (3) Infant industries may need some protection against foreign competition until they are capable of standing on their own feet. Eventually domestic production may become more efficient than production in the foreign country. Similarly, protection for an entire economy which is underdeveloped may help it achieve long-run competitive advantages. Although the contention has merit, it frequently happens that protection once given continues after the industry or economy has outgrown the infant stage. (4) A protective duty may improve the terms of trade for the importing country if its demand for a good in the foreign market is high. Thus if a country imposes an import tax on a particular commodity, the domestic price of that good rises relative to the foreign price. But as the quantity demanded by importers falls as a result of the import duty, the foreign price established by the interactions of the world's total demand and supply will tend to decline. The import tax therefore is partly borne by exporters who must sell at lower prices. This argument has some validity. (5) The most usual argument for protection is that the home market must be given support against foreign competition to protect the jobs and the wages of domestic workers. Although it is perfectly true that restriction of specific imports does protect sectors of domestic industry, this occurs only at the cost of higher prices to the consumer and perpetuates the misallocation of resources. If an industry that would have succumbed to foreign competition is kept going only by protection, some workers are not employed where their productivity is highest. International trade, however, need not necessarily eliminate relatively high cost industries because their existence depends on comparative advantage, not absolute advantage. For the economy as a whole, real wages and the standard of living are lowered under a protective policy. There is not much to be said in support of industries unable to compete successfully, except that protection extended for a short period allows workers sufficient time to retain and possibly enables investors to salvage some of their capital outlay through depreciation. The hope of maintaining or increasing employment by imposing protective devices is illusory as it invariably leads to an almost immediate and corresponding retaliation by other countries. Over a longer time span net disadvantages to all parties become evident because protection is not easily removed once it is imposed. It is not ordinarily feasible, therefore, for a country beset by unemployment to create employment by producing and exporting more goods; in effect, the country would be exporting its unemployment. (Higher tariffs, along with exchange devaluation, are sometimes called "beggar-my-neighbor" policies.) (6) Many persons still believe in the desirability of a favorable balance of trade and urge protection to gain this objective. Others maintain that if one industry can gain from protection similar action on behalf of all industries would be advantageous. Some contend that protection must be used to retaliate against countries that restrict imports. It has also been urged that a "scientific" tariff would equalize the costs of production of domestic and foreign producers. Obviously, if duties were imposed to protect the least efficient domestic firms, no basis for international trade linked to comparative advantage would exist. In general these arguments have no real merit.

PROTECTION DEVICES

Various forms of protection have been used by governments. The most important of these devices and the oldest is the tariff.

Tariffs. A tariff is a tax or duty (also known as custom duty) on goods moving across national boundaries. The United States and many other countries limit tariffs to imports, but some countries impose them on exports also. Specific duties are levied directly on articles; ad valorem duties are imposed on the values of articles. Although the main purpose of the tariff today is for protection, it may also serve as a source of revenue. Naturally to the extent that tariffs afford more protection and keep foreign goods out, they yield less revenue. Nevertheless, tariffs may be geared to provide a modicum of revenue and of protection. Tariffs that are most clearly for revenue are those levied on import items not produced in the country; or those in which excise duties of equal amount are imposed on domestic output of the same kind. Some nations maintain a system of preferential tariffs, which set lower rates for some countries than for others, usually on a reciprocal basis. The United States favors an unconditional or unrestricted most-favored-nation clause in all tariff agreements, under which any import duty arrangement with one country is available to all others.

Tariffs are used to limit the import of particular goods. The public often supports tariffs about which it has been misinformed by vested interests seeking protection. Furthermore, Congress may be successfully swayed by the lobbying pressure of small and vocal groups anxious to secure higher duties on specific items. Consumers, who stand to bear the burden of higher prices, are not effectively organized to protest the imposition and maintenance of tariffs.

Some economists believe that a direct subsidy to producers who cannot meet foreign competition is preferable to a tariff. Instead of keeping foreign goods out and forcing up the price of domestic goods, a subsidy out of general tax revenues would enable the high cost producer to meet the lower prices of imports not subject to tariff. This approach shows the cost of such production to the public more clearly and enables it to judge the desirability of the subsidy policy.

Other Restrictions. A number of devices and arrangements other than tariffs have been used as barriers to free trade. These include: (1) Import quotas that impose a quantitative restriction on importers who must secure licenses from the government to bring goods in. The limitations thus imposed may apply generally or only to particular countries and may involve efforts to conserve available foreign purchasing power as well as to protect domestic industry. Export quotas are rarer but are sometimes used to stabilize world prices. (2) Foreign exchange controls that may be imposed by a government on commodities from a particular country under which importers are rationed or cut off from access to the foreign funds or currencies necessary to make purchases abroad. Importers may be able, however, to obtain goods from countries whose currencies are not scarce. (3) Export subsidies, which are grants from the government to domestic producers to enable them to sell abroad at prices below the cost of production. This device is expected to expand foreign markets and to provide additional domestic employment. It essentially involves the technique of dumping goods abroad at a price lower than the price established at home. Dumping is also United States policy for certain agricultural surpluses, which the government attempts to sell abroad at prices below those prevailing in the domestic market. In some cases the goods are given away under a foreign aid program. These efforts are equivalent to export subsidies. (4) International commodity agreements that have been negotiated by governments in control of major sources of particular goods. Output, prices, and markets are thus determined. Wheat, coffee, sugar, rubber, tin, and tea have been subject to such agreements. (5) International cartels which are set up by private businesses in different countries to monopolize domestic sales and divide international markets. Interchange of patents among the firms involved is common. (6) Some less important mechanisms that have been used to restrict trade include bilateral trade agreements between two countries for special kinds of transactions; specific loans by a government to encourage exports; complicated and arbitrary customs regulations to delay the movement of imports, sometimes called "invisible" tariffs; barring of imports because of allegedly unsanitary conditions in their production; and expropriation of foreign holdings and freezing of foreign earnings. In a few nations, such as the Soviet Union, the state conducts all international trade operations through government agencies.

EFFORTS TO INCREASE TRADE

In recent years there has been a trend away from protective tariffs and toward international agreements to facilitate the increase of trade.

U.S. Legislation. For many years, tariffs were a major source of revenue to the government of the United States, and even at the beginning of the twentieth century more than two-fifths of federal revenues were derived from import duties. A tariff for the purpose of raising revenue was the first law enacted by Congress in 1789. After the War of 1812, duties were used to protect the newly established industries that arose during the conflict. The rates were gradually raised, and in the early 1830s some southern states reacted violently to these increases. Congress subsequently reduced the tariffs.

The commercial and industrial states of the Northeast favored protection, while the agricultural South opposed it. After the Civil War, however, the ascendancy of the northern states led to the imposition of high tariffs. This policy continued and achieved its zenith in the Hawley-Smoot Tariff Act of 1930, which imposed the highest tariff rates in U.S. history. Over the years the Republican party generally favored raising duties while the Democratic party was inclined to lower them. Today tariffs are basically a protective device, yielding only a small fraction of federal revenues.

Beginning in 1934, with the Reciprocal Trade Agreements Act that amended the law of 1930, there has been a slow and gradual reduction in tariff rates. Such action has been particularly desirable since the United States has shifted from being a debtor nation to being a creditor nation. This situation made it advisable to allow more foreign goods into this country so that those foreigners owing money could pay their debts. The amendments of 1934 authorized the president to reduce rates on imports up to 50 percent on a reciprocal arrangement. In 1945 Congress authorized a further reduction of 50 percent of the rates then in effect, bringing duties to one-fourth their 1930 levels. Concessions made to one country were to apply to all other countries that do not discriminate against U.S. exports. Additional reductions were authorized in the 1950s by extension of the laws dealing with foreign trade. Policy was based partly on "peril-point" provisions and "escape clauses" under which tariff rates could not be reduced to or kept at a level that would injure domestic industry. In such an instance duties could be increased and trade concessions terminated by the president.

In order to reduce political pressures of special interest groups on Congress for higher tariffs, the president was given power to alter rates in either direction. He depends, however, upon the advice of the U.S. Tariff Commission, which must use as its guide the general rules set forth in the statutes. This agency is in a good position to weigh and to judge the facts of each case impartially and recommend action accordingly.

A major tariff enactment was the Kennedy Trade Expansion Act of 1962. Under this law the president may reduce duties by 50 percent below the levels prevailing in 1962 on many classes of goods and eliminate tariffs completely on other imported goods where the rates had been only 5 percent or less. (A special provision was included for retraining workers displaced from their employment by tariff cuts.) Such legislation is essential so that U.S. export markets may be maintained as tariffs are reduced and eliminated in the trade relations among European nations.

The Common Market. The Common Market (European Economic Community) organized in 1957 included Belgium, France, Italy, Luxembourg, the Netherlands, and West Germany. In 1973 it was joined by Great Britain, Denmark, and Ireland. These countries, which account for a substantial proportion of world exports and imports, have been particularly successful in gradually reducing internal tariff barriers and in working out a common schedule of rates to apply to outside nations. The gross national product of each of the Common Market countries has been increasing at a higher rate than the GNP of most other advanced nations.

Reduction of internal trade barriers and establishment of uniform tariff policies by the Common Market countries have made it more difficult for nonmembers to trade there. These disadvantages, however, have been somewhat offset by the rising living standards in the Market area.

International Agreement. After the Second World War the United States was one of the leaders in efforts to lower world tariffs and to increase free trade. At a conference of many nations held in 1947 a General Agreement on Tariffs and Trade (GATT) was negotiated to encourage lower tariffs and nondiscrimination in the trading policies of the signatories. Since then, additional countries have accepted the agreement. Regular meetings and discussions are held by the participating countries to seek ways of implementing the program. Considerable progress has been made.

The International Trade Organization (ITO), a permanent international body proposed to facilitate the gradual reduction of trade barriers never came into being because Congress refused to approve United States participation. Congress also nullified a 1955 attempt to establish the Organization for Trade Cooperation, designed to carry out the provisions of GATT on a continuing basis.

Soviet Trade. Before the death of Premier Joseph Stalin in 1953 the Soviet Union tried to maintain a self-sufficient economy, though small amounts of some raw materials were exported to obtain certain kinds of capital equipment and raw materials not available at home. Since then, Soviet policy has been modified to permit more trade with noncommunist countries. Soviet trade relations in part involve political considerations and revolve around efforts to create and solidify economic ties. Underdeveloped countries whose friendship the Soviet Union seeks are given economic aid under which they may be supplied with various quantities of armaments and capital equipment. On other occasions special concessions may be offered. Frequently technicians are sent along with the aid to install and maintain equipment, but they also enable the Soviet Union to closely observe the country receiving assistance.

THE VOLUME OF TRADE

The dollar value of the foreign trade of the United States has continued to grow over the years, and the volume of exports of goods and services continues to exceed the volume of imports. Finished manufactures dominate the merchandise trade. In 1920 the value of export merchandise was $8.5 billion while merchandise imports were $5.4 billion. By 1935 such exports had fallen to $2.4 billion and such imports to $2.5 billion. In 1974 total exports of merchandise were valued at $97.1 billion and total imports of goods at $107.1 billion. Table 18-1 shows the percentage distribution of U.S. international trade by categories of commodities.

TABLE 18-1

U.S. TRADE CATEGORIES, 1973

	Percent of Exports	Percent of Imports
Food and beverages	18.4	13.4
Inedible crude materials	11.9	7.2
Mineral fuels and chemicals	10.6	15.2
Machinery and equipment	39.6	30.3
Other manufactured goods	15.8	30.9
Other transactions	3.7	3.0
	100.0	100.0

Source: *Statistical Abstract of the United States,* 1974, pp. 796, 799.

A large fraction of U.S. trade is with Europe, although trade with Asia is growing rapidly. Regional trade is shown in table 18-2.

The volume of world trade in 1974 consisted of $763.9 billion of exports of merchandise and $759.8 billion of imports of merchandise. Although the United States is both the largest buyer and the largest seller in international markets, international trade represents a much smaller fraction of gross national product in the United States than it does in many other countries of the world. Table 18-3 lists the world's leading exporters and importers.

TABLE 18-2

DESTINATION OF EXPORTS (INCLUDING REEXPORTS)
AND ORIGIN OF IMPORTS, 1973

Place	Exports (Billions of Dollars)	Imports (Billions of Dollars)
North America	20.3	22.9
South America	4.9	4.5
Europe	23.4	19.8
Asia	18.5	17.9
Australia and Oceania	1.8	1.6
Africa	2.4	2.4
	71.3	69.1

Source: *Statistical Abstract of the United States*, 1974, p. 792.

TABLE 18-3

LEADING EXPORTERS AND IMPORTERS OF THE WORLD, 1973

Exporter Country	Amount (Billions of Dollars)	Importer Country	Amount (Billions of Dollars)
United States	70.2	United States	68.7
West Germany	68.6	West Germany	55.5
Japan	38.3	Great Britain	38.8
France	35.6	Japan	38.3
Great Britain	30.5	France	37.0
Canada	25.3	Italy	27.8
Netherlands	24.1	Netherlands	23.8
Belgium-Luxembourg	22.4	Canada	23.3
Italy	22.2	Belgium-Luxembourg	21.9
Soviet Union	21.5	Soviet Union	21.1

Source: *United Nations Monthly Bulletin of Statistics*, May 1975, pp. 110–117.

Table 18-4 lists the countries that buy the most goods from and sell the most goods to the United States.

TABLE 18-4

U.S. EXPORTS AND IMPORTS, 1973

Exports		Imports	
Country	Amount (Millions of Dollars)	Country	Amount (Millions of Dollars)
Canada	15,073	Canada	17,443
Japan	8,312	Japan	9,645
West Germany	3,756	West Germany	5,318
Great Britain	3,564	Great Britain	3,642
Mexico	2,937	Mexico	2,287
Netherlands	2,860	Italy	1,988
France	2,263	Taiwan	1,773
Italy	2,119	France	1,715
Brazil	1,916	Venezuela	1,625
Belgium-Luxembourg	1,622	Hong Kong	1,444

Source: *Statistical Abstract of the United States*, 1974, pp. 792–794.

Chapter 19
INTERNATIONAL FINANCE

International trade requires trading nations to pay for imports with some form of negotiable financial instrument. The amount paid by a purchaser of goods generally depends on the rate of exchange or relative value of the currencies of the two countries involved. The growing volume of international transactions, including foreign investments, during the past few decades and the problems associated with trade balances and deficits have led the world community of nations to establish a number of new institutions.

FOREIGN TRANSACTIONS

Since most countries issue their own currencies (paper and coins), persons who import goods, pay foreign debts, invest abroad, or travel beyond their national boundaries may need foreign money. Foreign currency, foreign exchange checks, and letters of credit are available for U.S. dollars from a bank or a dealer in foreign exchange transactions at the prevailing rate of exchange, i.e., the ratio at which currencies exchange for each other. Generally the rate is determined by the interaction of supply and demand for various currencies in the money market, although government regulation may influence the rate. In some countries the government taxes foreign exchange transactions.

Importers generally operate through commercial banks to pay for goods. They obtain letters of credit that are sent to exporters. These letters together with proof of sale, enable the exporter to write and deposit a draft or a bill of exchange to his account at his own bank. His bank then has a claim on the bank that issued the letter of credit; it may collect the sum due from the importer's bank that issued the letter of credit or increase its balance there, as soon as the importer signs the draft. Alternatively, the exporter may begin the payment process by sending a draft to the importer, whose bank provides the foreign currency necessary to complete the transaction by drawing on an account that it keeps at a correspondent bank in the country of the exporter. The exporter is then paid by the correspondent bank. Exports therefore may be financed by increasing the claims on foreigners, as in the first case, or by reducing the claims of foreigners, as in the second case. Banks, of course, receive a commission for each transaction and serve as clearinghouses for foreign trade transactions. Many banks maintain balances in all major foreign commercial centers in order to carry on a variety of international financial dealings.

RATES OF EXCHANGE

In the early twentieth century exchange rates were determined under the gold standard. But this standard was gradually abandoned throughout the world, making currency inconvertible to gold; and paper standards were adopted. A system of exchange rates developed in which the relative value of currencies fluctuated from day to day but subject to government control. Generally, however, the advanced industrial nations soon gave up this form of exchange for a gold-exchange standard. They defined their currency in terms of gold but made gold available only for international payments.

The need to make international payments gives rise to exchange rates. United States sales abroad lead to receipts from foreigners through a process in which foreign currency is offered for dollars. For example, if someone in France buys an automobile from a firm in the United States, there is an increase in the supply of French francs and in the demand for dollars in the international market. Payment of bills or debts which requires funds to be sent from the United States to a foreign country, on the other hand, increases the demand for foreign currency and the supply of dollars.

Free Exchange. Free, flexible, or floating exchange rates exist in the absence of a gold standard and government controls. Under this system the rate of exchange is determined solely by the supply and demand for currency; and the rate may undergo wide fluctuation. For example, assume that the United States and France are operating under a free exchange system. Then if the United States increases imports of French goods (increases obligations) there is an increase in the demand for francs and the exchange rate for francs rise. French francs become relatively more expensive and

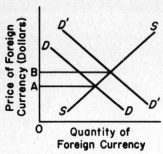

Fig. 19-1. Exchange rate determination

U.S. dollars become relatively cheaper. This is shown graphically in figure 19-1. An increase in the demand for foreign currency (shown by the shift from *DD* to *D'D'*) raises the exchange rate from *OA* to *OB*. The demand for foreign currency may increase because of a decline in foreign prices, higher U.S. incomes, or changes in taste.

The rate of exchange of all currencies remains approximately the same in all markets where foreign exchange takes place, providing there is no government interference. Should the exchange rate of currencies differ at any two points, equilibrium would be restored by traders alert for profit who would buy currency where it is cheap and simultaneously sell it where it is dear. This transaction, called *arbitrage*, tends to eliminate exchange rate differentials.

The Gold Standard. Stable exchange rates were successfully maintained while the gold standard was in effect—prior to 1914 and between 1925 and 1931—because the money unit of each country contained a specified amount of gold. For example, the U.S. dollar contained 23.22 grains of pure gold, and the British pound just over 113 grains. Gold content determined the mint par of exchange; it established that the pound was worth just under $4.87. As currency was converted by the government into gold on demand and the metal could be shipped abroad, parity was maintained. Trading transactions between the two countries could only result in minor fluctuations. If Great Britain were exporting heavily to the United States, so that the demand for pounds to pay for imports increased at United States banks, there was a tendency for the pound to rise above $4.87. But the price could not increase much above $4.89. At that price it would pay the importer to have his bank bring $4.87 to the U.S. Treasury, obtain the quantity of gold equal to a pound, and ship the gold to Great Britain in payment for the imports. The cost of transporting and insuring gold and the loss of interest on funds during the period of transit (which constituted about one-half of 1 percent of the value of the shipment), added to the mint par of exchange, determined the upper gold point or gold export point. Similarly, if the United States were exporting heavily to Great Britain, and if the value of dollars were rising at British banks, it would be cheaper for the merchant needing dollars to have his bank buy gold and send it to the United States for conversion into currency. The lower gold point or gold import point was between $4.84 and $4.85. The flow of gold thus kept the relative value of different currencies within a narrow range.

Despite the fact that countries on the gold standard permitted the metal to be freely exported and imported, the economic system contained a mechanism that prevented any nation from being completely drained of its supply of gold. As the imports of a country exceeded its exports and gold was shipped out, domestic prices tended to fall. Lower prices encouraged a reduction of imports, because foreign goods became relatively dearer, and an increase in exports, because domestic output became more attractive abroad. The flow of gold was reversed, and an equilibrium or balance in gold holdings of all countries was restored. On the domestic scene, a further check on gold drainage occurred because the reduction in gold stocks lowered the reserves of the banking system and hence the availability of credit and currency. Interest rates rose, attracting foreign funds and tending to check the outward movement of gold. Furthermore, the tendency of the domestic price level to decline was conducive to increased unemployment and hence to fewer imports.

During the last third of the nineteenth century, when all the leading trading countries of the world were on the gold standard, there was a downward pressure on prices as the supply of gold failed to keep pace with the rise in output of goods and services. Lower prices were mainly responsible for the widespread support given by farmers and workers to those urging adoption of a bimetallic standard (gold and silver) in the United States. Actually the problem of inadequate gold supply was eased somewhat in the first part of the twentieth century by the discovery of new gold mines and the improvement in gold mining techniques, the use of fractional gold reserves by banks which permitted the output of goods to increase more rapidly than the gold stock without affecting prices, and the adoption by small countries of a monetary standard under which a government holding very little gold nevertheless redeems local currency in gold by having in its possession a supply of currency of a country that operates on a gold standard.

The gold standard and its concomitant fixed, or pegged, exchange rate were generally abandoned during the 1930s as most countries stopped selling gold to the public in unlimited quantities at a fixed price. Fixed rates of exchange require free movement in domestic price levels to permit the volume of exports and imports of a country to be balanced. If prices are relatively high in any country, exports would be discouraged. There was, however, reluctance in many nations to allow prices to decline to the level necessary to balance its exports and imports as such declines tended to increase unemployment and bring on depressed economic conditions. Thus some countries left the gold standard in order to be free to manipulate the domestic price level (for example, the United States in 1933); others did so to avoid rapid loss of gold stocks (for example, Great Britain in 1931).

Problems of Standards Other Than Gold. Under a paper standard the volume of international merchandise and capital transactions and speculative purchases and sales of foreign money determine the supply and demand for foreign currencies and thereby establish the rate of exchange. This rate varies from day to day and may fluctuate over a wide range. Nevertheless, in the absence of both a gold standard and government regulation, an equilibrium of exchange rates in all foreign exchange markets is achieved at ratios which at any time roughly equate the purchasing power of the different currencies in terms of domestic price levels, modified by such factors as tariff barriers, differences in unemployment rates, changing consumer tastes, and available new products.

Widely fluctuating rates of exchange provide an unsatisfactory basis for international trade, as great uncertainty exists regarding the value of the money to be received for exports. Such difficulties were particularly common in the 1920s when paper standards were not controlled by the government. In the 1930s, however, governments that abandoned the gold standard generally undertook regulation of exchange rates to maintain the stability of those rates. A typical technique was to set up an exchange stabilization fund consisting of domestic and foreign currencies and to use the fund for the purchase and the sale of foreign moneys necessary to establish or to maintain a particular exchange rate. Thus if Great Britain wanted to make

U.S. dollars dearer relative to the pound (for example, increase their value from $3.50 for 1 pound to $3.30 for 1 pound) in order to reduce British imports, it would use its stabilization fund to buy dollars. By thus increasing the demand for dollars, the value of dollars would rise. In some cases international agreements combined the financial resources of several governments to help keep exchange rates stable.

During the 1930s and early 1940s some governments maintained more direct controls over exchange. For example, individuals needing foreign exchange to purchase goods or to travel abroad were required to obtain government approval or were allowed to spend only a specified sum of money. Sometimes exchange rates varied for different goods, thus encouraging some imports or exports and discouraging others. In some cases foreign funds were blocked, which means the funds could only be spent locally. On a number of occasions, special bilateral arrangements between countries were negotiated and put into effect in an attempt to maintain balanced volumes of trade.

Table 19-1 shows the relationship of some important world currencies to that of the United States.

TABLE 19-1

FOREIGN EXCHANGE RATES, MARCH 1975

Country	Unit	United States Cents per Unit of Foreign Currency
Australia	dollar	135.85
Belgium	franc	2.903
Canada	dollar	99.954
France	franc	23.804
Germany	deutsche mark	43.120
Great Britain	pound	241.80
Italy	lira	0.15842
Japan	yen	0.34731
Netherlands	guilder	42.124
Soviet Union	ruble	141.84
Sweden	krona	25.481
Switzerland	franc	40.273

Source: *Federal Reserve Bulletin*, April 1975, p. A 75 and *United Nations Monthly Bulletin of Statistics*, May 1975, p. 218.

The value of one currency in terms of another may change as price levels fluctuate. A decline in value of one currency relative to another is called *depreciation*, while an increase in relative value is called *appreciation*. If the value of one currency is deliberately lowered, as for example when a country raises the price of gold, the process is called *devaluation*. Devaluation thus is the equivalent of deliberate depreciation. If two countries devalue proportionately, no relative depreciation of their currencies occurs.

THE INTERNATIONAL BALANCE OF PAYMENTS

The demand for foreign currency and the supply of foreign currency arise from a wide variety of foreign transactions. All these transactions combined determine the balance of international payments of any country. The balance consists of total money receipts from all other countries and total money payments to all other countries resulting from commercial and financial dealings. In the United States each foreign transaction involves dollars and some other currency. Credits, the dollar receipts due for the sale of goods, services, securities, or gold, and debits, the dollar payments due for the purchase of goods, services, securities, or gold balance each other. For convenience seven categories of transactions may be identified. These are (1) export and import of merchandise; (2) transportation, banking, and insurance services connected with international trade; (3) tourist travel; (4) dividends and interest received from and paid to foreigners; (5) international gifts by governments, private individuals, and businesses, called unilateral transfers; (6) foreign capital movements and loans; and (7) government balance actions. The first five items represent the current account.

The difference in quantity between the volume of merchandise exported and merchandise imported is the balance of trade. (Though the idea is misleading, historically an export surplus was called a *favorable* balance of trade.) Merchandise or goods are considered visible items; services, tourist travel, and investment income are invisible items of international trade. The current account of any country does not have to balance since capital movements and government balance actions may be used to make up an imbalance.

The capital account consists of long-term investment abroad by private parties or the government; short-term foreign loans by individuals, business firms, and the government; funds flowing out of the country for political and economic reasons; funds shifted by migrants or others changing their country of residence; and foreign obligations repaid. An investment abroad, a loan to a foreigner, or any other transaction which involves paying out dollars is a debit item in the U.S. international balance of payments. The shipment of gold is similar to the movement of merchandise. The export of gold is a credit, and the import of gold is a debit.

It should be clear that the total credits and debits accumulated by a country over any specified period of time must balance since all international transactions are accounted for by receipts, payments, loans, and government balance actions. Any imbalance in the figures is due to errors and omissions of statistical compilation. A nation with an international balance-of-payments problem makes up the difference by changes in liabilities to foreign official agencies and U.S. official reserve assets. Official reserve assets include SDRs, gold, convertible currencies, and U.S. gold adjustments in the International Monetary Fund. Table 19-2 presents the international balance-of-payments data for the United States.

TABLE 19-2

U.S. INTERNATIONAL BALANCE OF PAYMENTS, 1974

	Amount (Millions of Dollars)
Merchandise	−7,833
Services	3,837
Travel	−2,355
Investment income	9,516
Unilateral transfers	−8,136
Capital movements	−4,894
Changes in liabilities to foreign official agencies	7,177
Changes in U.S. official reserve assets	−2,095
Errors and omissions	4,783
Total	000

Source: *Economic Report of the President,* 1975, pp. 350–351. All figures are net. Negative figures indicate an excess of debits (imports) over credits (exports). Merchandise exports were 97,535 and merchandise imports were 105,368.

INTERNATIONAL FINANCIAL DEVELOPMENTS

The Second World War established the supremacy of the United States in the world economy and made the dollar the most important currency of international exchange. Since then, many countries have held dollars as well as gold in their monetary reserves and exchange rates frequently have been formulated in terms of the dollar. Furthermore, the relatively stable price level in the United States, the convertibility of the dollar to gold at the fixed price of $35 an ounce, and the possibility of investing dollar revenues profitably on a short-term basis in New York City added to the international importance of the dollar.

Dollar Problems. The period immediately after the Second World War was one in which many war-damaged nations needed goods from the United States to rebuild their economies. However, they were faced with a shortage of both dollars and gold and thus were unable to pay for imports from the United States. To help these nations meet their official deficits the U.S. government undertook a European recovery program (Marshall Plan) in 1948. Economic aid was provided either as a gift or as a loan, to be applied toward self-rehabilitation. The program has undergone many revisions, but assistance is now administered to friendly countries by the Agency for International Development. Special attention is given to less developed nations experiencing financial difficulties.

By the end of the 1950s, however, the situation had changed substantially. Most western European countries had made a remarkable recovery and lacked neither gold nor dollars, while the United States was faced with a serious problem. Despite the fact that the annual exports of American merchandise exceeded its imports by a large amount, the nation began to experience a continuing problem of deficits in the balance of payments stemming from extensive private investment activities and heavy government economic and military aid programs.

The international economic policies of the United States caused the foreign balance of short-term funds to rise in the 1960s. An international gold exchange standard, under which foreign currencies held by any government or its citizens may be converted to gold at fixed rates of exchange and withdrawn, was in effect as a result of widespread adherence to free convertibility. This situation (bolstered by fear of dollar devaluation and the relatively low short-term interest rates prevailing in the United States) brought about a balance-of-payments problem, which was manifested by continuing drain and decline of gold stock and simultaneous weakening of the dollar.

The International Monetary Fund. The desirability of maintaining stable exchange rates, of eliminating trade restrictions, and of increasing freedom of movement of goods and capital between countries led to an international conference at Bretton Woods, New Hampshire, in 1944, while the Second World War was still in progress. Out of this conference came the International Monetary Fund. The fund, which began to function in 1947 as a specialized agency of the United Nations, was designed to encourage stability of exchange rates and international monetary cooperation, to reduce government exchange restrictions, and to supervise necessary alterations in exchange rates. There are now more than one hundred countries participating in the fund. Each country contributed to the fund predetermined quotas of gold and domestic currency, based on its national income and its volume of international trade. This money constituted the fund's pool of reserves. Voting strength was based on contributions. Upon joining, each country indicated the value of its currency in terms of gold or U.S. dollars; thus the rate of exchange was fixed.

Members were able to ease temporary difficulties by borrowing from the fund those currencies they needed to avoid altering the rates of exchange or adopting exchange controls. Long-term difficulties involving disequilibriums in the balance of payments were adjusted by allowing fund members to alter rates of exchange. Generally members recognized that they were committed to maintain their economic affairs so as not to violate the rules of the fund, and they agreed to consult with the other members on grave trade problems.

The first major task of the fund involved working out the rates of exchange. The currency of each country was expressed in terms of the U.S. dollar. But many countries undervalued the dollar and their exports to the United States tended to be low. A dollar shortage developed, making devaluation of many currencies necessary. The most publicized of these actions was taken by Great Britain in 1949 when the pound was devalued from $4.03 to $2.80, with the approval of the International Monetary Fund. As a result the British export potential was vastly improved, and it was easier to earn dollars. (Since then, several other changes have occurred in the relation of the pound to the dollar.)

In the 1960s as the status of U.S. dollars began to weaken from the continued American trade deficits, major international monetary changes were introduced to meet world problems concerning balance of payments and reserve shortages. As a result the Bretton Woods Agreement has been completely changed. In 1969 the members of the International Monetary Fund developed a plan to increase reserves by supplementing gold and dollars. The new reserves, called Special Drawing Rights (SDR) and sometimes "paper gold," are created by the fund and are available to countries in relation to their fund quotas. SDRs are backed only by the agreement of nations to accept them as payment and may be used to meet balance deficits. In 1971 the unfavorable balance-of-payments situation of the United States led to a suspension of convertibility of the dollar into gold. Two years later, the official price of gold for payments only between governments was set at $42.22 an ounce. (The free market price of gold not owned by governments is determined by supply and demand. It has recently been as high as $200 an ounce.) The prospects for a larger fund role in future international monetary crises have increased. But the success of the fund will depend on the extent of economic and political stability in the world, the state of unemployment, the reduction of obstacles to trade, and the degree of international confidence that progress will continue.

INTERNATIONAL INVESTMENT

The development of natural resources and industries in a country to improve living standards and increase purchasing power is often carried out with the aid of loans from other countries. International investments may be made on a long-term or a short-term basis. They may involve direct investments, in which case the funds are used to purchase land, factories, and equipment; or they may involve portfolio investments, for which the funds are used to buy securities. They may be made by individuals and private businesses or by governments and their agencies. Foreign investments yield interest and dividend payments to the lender. Any nation whose foreign investments exceed the total investments of foreign nations in its economy is a creditor; if the reverse is true it is a debtor. Sometimes, however, the creditor or debtor status may be determined in terms of whether the returns received on foreign investments are greater or smaller than the payments made to foreign investors.

Although the role of governments and international agencies making foreign investments has expanded in recent years, most investments during the modern era have been undertaken by private

businesses. Entrepreneurs from Great Britain, France, and the Netherlands, in particular, have supplied much of the capital invested abroad
during the past three centuries. Generally the purpose has been to
obtain the raw materials necessary for production at home. But
recent developments have completely altered the situation. Today
the United States supplies a large proportion of investment funds.
With the emergence of colonial regions and backward areas as independent nations the demands for capital to industrialize have
increased. Private foreign investment is often discouraged, however,
by the possibility of seizure or expropriation of property by the
foreign state, by bans on withdrawal of profits from the country,
by high foreign income and foreign property taxes, and by restrictions
on the types of investments permitted.

Evolution of an Economy.   In the process of economic growth a
country usually passes from a debtor to a creditor status. Four stages
may be discerned. (1) The United States was an international
borrower from the founding of the country to about 1873 because
merchandise and invisible imports exceeded exports. (2) The period
between 1873 and 1914 was one in which exports exceeded imports
and the amount of debt repaid was a little larger than the amount of
new capital borrowed. (3) During the First World War and the
period that followed the United States made substantial private and
government loans to European countries and greatly increased its
volume of exports. As a result it became a creditor nation. But the
refusal of the United States to continue lending abroad in the early
1930s made it impossible for foreign nations to meet their debt
obligations. Many U.S. loans were defaulted and had to be written
off as bad debts. The Second World War saw a repetition of extensive
loans by the United States to foreign countries. These obligations
must continue to be met by expansion of United States investments
abroad or an increase in merchandise imports. The United States
is the great creditor nation of the world, and its net creditor position
continues to grow. (4) A mature creditor nation, exemplified by Great
Britain early in the twentieth century, is one that imports more than
it exports and pays for the surplus with the difference between the
returns on former investments and the volume of new loans being
made abroad.

The Role of the United States.   The bulk of private direct foreign
investment of the United States has been placed in developed
economies. Over one-quarter of the total is in Canada and most

of the remainder is in Europe and Latin America. Very little of the capital has gone to Asia and to Africa. Two-fifths of the total funds has been invested in manufacturing and one-quarter in petroleum resources. The balance is scattered over a variety of economic activities. The statistics are included in table 19-3.

TABLE 19-3

U.S. DIRECT FOREIGN INVESTMENTS, 1973

Region	Amount (Millions of Dollars)	Type	Amount (Millions of Dollars)
Canada	28,055	Manufacturing	45,791
Latin America	18,452	Petroleum	29,567
Europe	37,218	Mining and smelting	7,483
Asia	9,318	Other	24,427
Africa	4,070		
Oceania	4,839		
Other	5,316		
Total	107,268	Total	107,268

Source: *Survey of Current Business*, August 1974, part II, pp. 18–19.

Long-term foreign securities in the hands of private persons and businesses are less than two-fifths the amount of direct investments. Short-term assets and claims are about one-seventh the amount of long-term assets. The net creditor status of the United States may be derived from table 19-4. It is computed as the difference between United States assets and investments abroad and foreign assets and investments in the United States, or $50,600,000,000.

U.S. Lending Institutions. In 1934, during a period when conditions were unfavorable for the extension of private foreign credit, Congress established the Export-Import Bank to aid and encourage exporters and importers engaged in international trade. Private loans were guaranteed and loans to foreign governments were made by the bank. Although the projects financed are generally sound, there have been occasions when political considerations and international policies have been involved in decisions whether or not to make loans. In 1961 the United States established the Agency for International Development for the primary purpose of carrying out nonmilitary foreign assistance programs in underdeveloped countries. These

TABLE 19-4

U.S. INTERNATIONAL INVESTMENT POSITION, 1972

	Amount (Billions of Dollars)
U.S. assets and investments abroad	199.3
Private		150.0
Long term		128.4
Direct		94.0
Portfolio		34.3
Short term		16.4
U.S. government credits and claims		49.3
Long term		34.2
Short term		15.2
Foreign assets and investments in the U.S.	148.7
Long term		59.8
Direct		14.4
Portfolio		45.5
Short term		87.0
Government obligations		1.8

Source: *Statistical Abstract of the United States*, 1974, p. 779.

programs have been achieved mainly through development loans, development grants, and investment guarantees.

Table 19-5 shows the foreign direct investment in the United States.

TABLE 19-5

FOREIGN DIRECT INVESTMENT IN THE UNITED STATES, 1973

Region	Amount (Millions of Dollars)	Type	Amount (Millions of Dollars)
Canada	4,003	Manufacturing	8,419
Europe	12,158	Petroleum	4,425
Japan	307	Trade	948
Latin America	424	Insurance and finance	2,712
Other	856	Other	1,244
Total	17,748	Total	17,748

Source: *Survey of Current Business*, August 1974, part II, p. 7.

The International Bank for Reconstruction and Development. During the Second Warld War work was begun to create an international lending institution. The Bretton Woods Conference, which formulated plans to establish the International Monetary Fund, also developed the idea for the International Bank for Reconstruction and Development, more popularly called the World Bank. The World Bank began to function in 1946 as a specialized agency of the United Nations. The members, who number almost as many as belong to the International Monetary Fund, subscribe capital on the basis of a predetermined agreement and receive voting rights approximately proportional to the capital contributed. Under the arrangement the United States is the dominant member. The main purpose of the World Bank has been to promote the flow of loan funds to rehabilitate areas devastated by war and to develop underdeveloped countries, rather than to increase international trade. The World Bank may extend credit by using its own capital for loans, by borrowing private funds to make loans, or by guaranteeing loans privately arranged. Government and private loans are made to permit the execution of projects approved in advance and constructed subject to supervision of the Bank; in all cases repayment is guaranteed, generally in dollars, by the governments involved. Projects normally must meet the profitability standards and expectations of private lenders. The World Bank upon request has also investigated investment opportunities in various countries and proposed profitable undertakings. Since its establishment billions of dollars have been loaned to scores of nations.

Other International Institutions. Two international agencies affiliated with the World Bank have been set up to make loans that entail somewhat greater risk. In 1956 the International Finance Corporation was established to make loans to or buy stocks in private enterprises in underdeveloped countries to assist in industrial development even when the government involved is not able to guarantee repayment. The International Development Association was established in 1960, to finance government projects in less developed areas that are too risky to qualify for loans from the World Bank. Although both agencies have prospects of recovering their loans or outlays over extended periods of time, the risks are relatively great.

RECENT PROBLEMS OF INTERNATIONAL FINANCE

There are several major international financial problems today. The continuous deficits in the balance of payments of the United States began immediately after the Second World War, when the situation was deliberately designed to aid world reconstruction. Although the dollar shortage abroad was gradually reduced, the ultimate effect in the early 1970s was to undermine the strength and stability of the dollar. Differential rates of inflation and unemployment further increased monetary instability. The fixed exchange rates prevalent subsequent to the war were no longer viable and in many cases were replaced by flexible rates in the early 1970s. The United States requires a very careful evaluation of all policies related to military grants to foreign governments and aid to underdeveloped countries. Restrictions on tourist expenditures abroad, taxes on foreign investments, and higher interest rates on short-term obligations to discourage their withdrawal are other matters that need attention.

The whole question of exchange rates should be examined further. The fixed exchange rates are not well-suited to economies experiencing rapid changes in productivity, in comparative advantage, and in world competitive positions. But fluctuating exchange rates serve to disrupt commerce because of their inconvenience and uncertainty. Further international discussion of these various matters is needed.

Selected Bibliography

1. Economic Terminology

Friedman, Milton. *Essays in Positive Economics*. Chicago: University of Chicago Press, 1953.

Robbins, Lionel C. *An Essay on the Nature and Significance of Economic Science*. 2d ed. New York: St. Martin, 1935.

Robertson, Dennis H. *Lectures on Economic Principles*. 3 vols. London: Staples Press, 1957, 1958, 1959.

Robinson, Marshall A.; Morton, Herbert C.; and Calderwood, James D. *An Introduction to Economic Reasoning*. 4th ed. Washington, D.C.: The Brookings Institution, 1967.

2. The Economic System

Friedman, Milton. *Capitalism and Freedom*. Chicago: University of Chicago Press, 1962.

Galbraith, John K. *Economics and the Public Purpose*. Boston: Houghton Mifflin, 1973.

Hayek, Friedrich A. *The Road to Serfdom*. Chicago: University of Chicago Press, 1944.

3. Measuring National Income

Abraham, William I. *National Income and Economic Accounting*. Englewood Cliffs, N.J.: Prentice-Hall, 1969.

Collery, Arnold. *National Income and Employment Analysis*. 2d ed. New York: Wiley, 1970.

Heilbroner, Robert L. *Understanding Macroeconomics*. 5th ed. Englewood Cliffs, N.J.: Prentice-Hall, 1975.

Kuznets, Simon S. *Toward a Theory of Economic Growth*. New York: Norton, 1968.

U.S. Department of Commerce. *Do You Know Your Economic ABC's?* Rev. ed. Washington, D.C.: U.S. Government Printing Office, 1966.

4. Money and Prices

Bernstein, Peter L. *A Primer on Money, Banking, and Gold.* 2d ed. New York: Random House, 1968.

Einzig, Paul. *A Textbook on Monetary Policy.* 3d ed. London: Macmillan, 1972.

Lerner, Abba P. *Flation.* Baltimore: Penguin, 1973.

Meigs, A. James. *Money Matters: Economics, Markets, Politics.* New York: Harper & Row, 1972.

5. The Banking System

The Story of American Banking. New York: American Bankers Association, Banking Education Committee, 1963.

The Federal Reserve System: Purposes and Functions. 5th ed. Washington, D.C.: Board of Governors of the Federal Reserve System, 1963.

Maisel, Sherman J. *Managing the Dollar.* New York: Norton, 1973.

Nadler, Paul S. *Commercial Banking in the Economy.* Rev. ed. New York: Random House, 1973.

6. Income and Output

Chandler, Lester V. *America's Greatest Depression, 1929–1941.* New York: Harper & Row, 1970.

Friedman, Milton, and Heller, Walter H. *Monetary Versus Fiscal Policy.* New York: Norton, 1969.

Gordon, Robert A. *Economic Instability and Growth.* New York: Harper & Row, 1974.

Pechman, Joseph. *Federal Tax Policy.* Rev. ed. New York: Norton, 1971.

Schultze, Charles L. *National Income Analysis.* 3d ed. Englewood Cliffs, N.J.: Prentice-Hall, 1971.

7. Economic Growth

Denison, Edward F. *The Sources of Economic Growth in the United States and the Alternatives Before Us.* New York: Committee for Economic Development, 1962.

Fabricant, Solomon. *A Primer on Productivity.* New York: Random House, 1969.

Mazur, Paul M. *The Dynamics of Economic Growth.* Englewood Cliffs, N.J.: Prentice-Hall, 1965.

Passell, Peter, and Ross, Leonard. *The Retreat from Riches: Affluence and Its Enemies.* New York: Viking, 1973.

Phelps, Edmund S., ed. *The Goal of Economic Growth*. Rev. ed. New York: Norton, 1969.

Rostow, Walt W. *The Stages of Economic Growth: A Non-Communist Manifesto*. 2d ed. Cambridge: Cambridge University Press, 1971.

Ward, Barbara. *The Rich Nations and the Poor Nations*. New York: Norton, 1962.

8. Alternative Economic Systems

Dow, John C. R. *The Management of the British Economy 1945–1960*. Cambridge: Cambridge University Press, 1964.

Heilbroner, Robert L. *The Worldly Philosophers: The Lives, Times, and Ideas of the Great Economic Thinkers*. Rev. ed. New York: Simon & Schuster, 1972.

Maddison, Angus. *Economic Progress and Policy in Developing Countries*. New York: Norton, 1971.

Nove, Alec. *The Soviet Economy*. 2d ed. New York: Praeger, 1969.

Polanyi, Karl. *The Great Transformation*. New York: Octagon, 1973.

Schumpeter, Joseph A. *Capitalism, Socialism, and Democracy*. 3d ed. New York: Harper & Row, 1950.

Wu, Yuan-Li. *The Economy of Communist China: An Introduction*. New York: Praeger, 1965.

9. The Organization of Business

Adams, Walter, ed. *The Structure of American Industry: Some Case Studies*. 4th ed. New York: Macmillan, 1971.

Mueller, Willard. *A Primer on Monopoly and Competition*. New York: Random House, 1970.

Prather, Charles L., and Wert, James E. *Financing Business Firms*. 5th ed. Homewood, Ill.: Irwin, 1975.

Smith, Adam. *Supermoney*. New York: Random House, 1972.

Weiss, Leonard W. *Case Studies in American Industry*. 2d ed. New York: Wiley, 1971.

10. Demand and Supply

Henderson, Hubert D. *Supply and Demand*. New York: Cambridge University Press, 1958.

Marshall, Alfred. *Principles of Economics*. 8th ed. 2 vols. New York: Macmillan, 1961.

Shackle, George L. S. *Economics for Pleasure*. 2d ed. Cambridge: Cambridge University Press, 1968.

11. Consumer Satisfaction and Cost

Cohen, Kalman J., and Cyert, Richard M. *Theory of the Firm: Resource Allocation in a Market Economy.* Englewood Cliffs, N.J.: Prentice-Hall, 1965.

Murray, Barbara B., ed. *Consumerism: The Eternal Triangle: Business, Government, and Consumers.* Pacific Palisades, Calif.: Goodyear Publishing, 1973.

Packard, Vance O. *The Hidden Persuaders.* New York: McKay, 1957.

12. Competitive and Monopoly Markets

Andrews, Philip W. S. *On Competition in Economic Theory.* New York: St. Martin, 1964.

Haveman, Robert H., and Knopf, Kenyon A. *The Market System.* 2d ed. New York: Wiley, 1970.

McKenna, Joseph P. *The Logic of Price.* New York: Holt, Rinehart & Winston, 1973.

Mansfield, Edwin, ed. *Monopoly Power and Economic Performance.* 3d ed. New York: Norton, 1974.

Robinson, Edward A. G. *The Structure of Competitive Industry.* Rev. ed. Chicago: University of Chicago Press, 1958.

13. Government Regulation and Control of Business

Caves, Richard E. *American Industry: Structure, Conduct, Performance.* 3d ed. Englewood Cliffs, N. J.: Prentice-Hall, 1972.

Massel, Mark S. *Competition and Monopoly: Legal and Economic Issues.* Washington, D.C.: The Brookings Institution, 1962.

Scherer, Frederic M. *Industrial Market Structure and Economic Performance.* Chicago: Rand McNally, 1970.

14. Public Finance

Buchanan, James M. *The Public Finances.* 4th ed. Homewood, Ill.: Irwin, 1975.

Duc, John F., and Friedlaender, Ann F. *Government Finance: Economics of the Public Sector.* 5th ed. Homewood, Ill.: Irwin, 1973.

Ferguson, James M., ed. *Public Debt and Future Generations.* Chapel Hill: University of North Carolina Press, 1964.

Haveman, Robert H. *The Economics of the Public Sector.* New York: Wiley, 1973.

Phelps, Edmund S., ed. *Private Wants and Public Needs*. Rev. ed. New York: Norton, 1965.

15. Rent, Interest, and Profit

Clawson, Marion. *America's Land and Its Uses*. Baltimore: Johns Hopkins Press, 1972.

Homer, Sidney. *A History of Interest Rates*. New Brunswick, N.J.: Rutgers University Press, 1963.

Lamberton, Donald M. *The Theory of Profit*. Oxford: Blackwell, 1965.

16. Labor and Wages

Galenson, Walter. *A Primer on Employment and Wages*. 2d. ed. New York: Random House, 1970.

Okun, Arthur M., ed. *The Battle Against Unemployment*. Rev. ed. New York: Norton, 1972.

Rees, Albert. *The Economics of Trade Unionism*. Chicago: University of Chicago Press, 1962.

Slichter, Sumner H.; Healy, James J.; and Livernash, Edward R. *The Impact of Collective Bargaining on Management*. Washington, D.C.: The Brookings Institution, 1960.

17. Inequality of Income

Batchelder, Alan B. *The Economics of Poverty*. 2d. ed. New York: Wiley, 1971.

Freeman, A. Myrick; Haveman, Robert H.; and Kneese, A. V. *The Economics of Environmental Policy*. New York: Wiley, 1973.

Galbraith, John K. *The Affluent Society*. 2d ed. Boston: Houghton Mifflin, 1969.

Harrington, Michael. *The Other America: Poverty in the United States*. Rev. ed. New York: Macmillan, 1970.

Miller, Herman P. *Rich Man, Poor Man*. New York: Crowell, 1971.

Mills, Edwin S. *Urban Economics*. Glenview, Ill.: Scott, Foresman, 1972.

Netzer, Dick. *Economics and Urban Problems: Diagnoses and Prescriptions*. 2d ed. New York: Basic Books, 1974.

18. International Trade

Balassa, Bela. *Trade Prospects for Developing Countries*. Homewood, Ill.: Irwin, 1964.

Ingram, James C. *International Economic Problems*. 2d ed. New York: Wiley, 1970.

Kenen, Peter, and Lubitz, Raymond. *International Economics*. 3d ed. Englewood Cliffs, N.J.: Prentice-Hall, 1971.

Pen, Jan. *A Primer on International Trade*. New York: Random House, 1967.

19. International Finance

Aliber, Robert Z. *The International Money Game*. 2d ed. New York: Basic Books, 1975.

Cohen, Benjamin J. *Balance of Payments Policy*. Harmondsworth, Middlesex: Penguin, 1969.

Haberler, Gottfried. *Money in the International Economy*. 2d ed. Cambridge: Harvard University Press, 1969.

Rolfe, Sidney E., and Burtle, James L. *The Great Wheel: The World Monetary System*. New York: Quadrangle, 1974.

Stevens, Robert W. *A Primer on the Dollar in the World Economy*. New York: Random House, 1972.

Wasserman, Max J., and Ware, Ray M. *The Balance of Payments: History, Methodology, Theory*. Cambridge: Schenkman Publishing Co., 1965.

Index